Participatory
Community
Research

Participatory Community Research

Theories and Methods in Action

Edited by

Leonard A. Jason
Christopher B. Keys
Yolanda Suarez-Balcazar
Renée R. Taylor
Margaret I. Davis

with

Joseph A. Durlak
Daryl Holtz Isenberg

DECADE
of BEHAVIOR
2000-2010

AMERICAN PSYCHOLOGICAL ASSOCIATION
Washington, DC

Second Printing, January 2006

Published by
American Psychological Association
750 First Street, NE
Washington, DC 20002
www.apa.org

To order
APA Order Department
P.O. Box 92984
Washington, DC 20090-2984
Tel: (800) 374-2721; Direct: (202) 336-5510
Fax: (202) 336-5502; TDD/TTY: (202) 336-6123
Online: www.apa.org/books/
E-mail: order@apa.org

In the U.K., Europe, Africa,
and the Middle East,
copies may be ordered from
American Psychological Association
3 Henrietta Street
Covent Garden, London
WC2E 8LU England

Typeset in Century Schoolbook by World Composition Services, Inc., Sterling, VA

Printer: Edwards Brothers, Inc., Ann Arbor, MI
Cover Designer: Naylor Design, Washington, DC
Project Manager: Debbie Hardin, Carlsbad, CA

The opinions and statements published are the responsibility of the authors, and such opinions and statements do not necessarily represent the policies of the American Psychological Association.

Library of Congress Cataloging-in-Publication Data

Chicago Conference on Community Research (2nd : 2002 :
  Loyola University of Chicago
  Participatory community research : theories and methods
in action / edited by Leonard A. Jason ... [et al.]. — 1st ed.
    p. cm. — (APA decade of behavior volumes)
  Based on presentations and discussions at the Second
Chicago Conference on Community Research, held June
2002 at Loyola University.
  Includes bibliographical references and index.
  ISBN 1-59147-069-2 (alk. paper)
    1. Social problems—Research—Citizen participation—Congresses.
  2. Community psychology—Research—Citizen participation—Congresses.
  3. Community development—Research—Citizen participation—Congresses.
  4. Human services—Research—Citizen participation—Congresses.   5. Public
health—Research—Citizen participation—Congresses.   6. Action research—
Citizen participation—Congresses.   7. Evaluation research (Social action
programs)—Citizen participation—Congresses.   I. Jason, Leonard.   II. Title.
  III. Series: Decade of behavior.

  HN29.C5317 2002
  361.1′07′2—dc22   2003014265

British Library Cataloguing-in-Publication Data
A CIP record is available from the British Library.

Printed in the United States of America
First Edition

APA Science Volumes

Sleep and Cognition

Sleep Onset: Normal and Abnormal Processes

Stereotype Accuracy: Toward Appreciating Group Differences

Stereotyped Movements: Brain and Behavior Relationships

Studying Lives Through Time: Personality and Development

The Suggestibility of Children's Recollections: Implications for Eyewitness Testimony

Taste, Experience, and Feeding: Development and Learning

Temperament: Individual Differences at the Interface of Biology and Behavior

Through the Looking Glass: Issues of Psychological Well-Being in Captive Nonhuman Primates

Uniting Psychology and Biology: Integrative Perspectives on Human Development

Viewing Psychology as a Whole: The Integrative Science of William N. Dember

APA Decade of Behavior Volumes

Acculturation: Advances in Theory, Measurement, and Applied Research

Animal Research and Human Health: Advancing Human Welfare Through Behavioral Science

Computational Modeling of Behavior in Organizations: The Third Scientific Discipline

Family Psychology: Science-Based Interventions

Memory Consolidation: Essays in Honor of James L. McGaugh

Models of Intelligence: International Perspectives

The Nature of Remembering: Essays in Honor of Robert G. Crowder

New Methods for the Analysis of Change

On the Consequences of Meaning Selection: Perspectives on Resolving Lexical Ambiguity

Participatory Community Research: Theories and Methods in Action

Personality Psychology in the Workplace

Principles of Experimental Psychopathology: Essays in Honor of Brendan A. Maher

Psychosocial Interventions for Cancer

Unraveling the Complexities of Social Life: A Festschrift in Honor of Robert B. Zajonc

Visual Perception: The Influence of H. W. Leibowitz

Contents

Contributors

Jaleel Abdul-Adil, University of Illinois at Chicago
Josefina Alvarez, DePaul University, Chicago, IL
Fabricio E. Balcazar, University of Illinois at Chicago
Audrey K. Bangi, DePaul University, Chicago, IL
Donna R. Baptiste, University of Illinois at Chicago
Thomas Behrens, Night Ministry, Chicago, IL
Tom Benziger, Access Living of Metropolitan Chicago, Chicago, IL
Michelle Bloodworth, University of Illinois at Chicago
Barbara Bolson, Night Ministry, Chicago, IL
Renée I. Boothroyd, University of Kansas, Lawrence
Mary Buntin, University of Illinois at Chicago
Nancy Carlin, Access Living of Metropolitan Chicago, Chicago, IL
Cary Cherniss, Rutgers, The State University of New Jersey, Piscataway
Richard Contreras, DePaul University, Chicago, IL
Margaret I. Davis, DePaul University, Chicago, IL
Dorenda Dixon, Cook County Sheriff's Department, Chicago, IL
Lura Duncan, Head Start: Parents Care & Share, Chicago, IL
Joseph A. Durlak, Loyola University Chicago, Chicago, IL
Steven Everett, Men Overcoming Violence, Chicago, IL
Stephen B. Fawcett, University of Kansas, Lawrence
Joseph Ferrari, DePaul University, Chicago, IL
Paul Flaspohler, University of South Carolina, Columbia
Pennie G. Foster-Fishman, Michigan State University, East Lansing
Angela Glass, Head Start: Parents Care & Share, Chicago, IL
Gary W. Harper, DePaul University, Chicago, IL
Richard Herrell, National Institute of Mental Health, Bethesda, MD
Jean L. Hill, New Mexico Highlands University, Las Vegas, NM
Barton J. Hirsch, Northwestern University, Chicago, IL
Carole Howard, Chicago Chronic Fatigue Syndrome Association,
    Chicago, IL
Keith Humphreys, Veterans Affairs and Stanford University Medical
    Centers, Palo Alto, CA
Daryl Holtz Isenberg, Illinois Self-Help Coalition, Chicago
Leonard A. Jason, DePaul University, Chicago, IL
Peter Ji, DePaul University, Chicago, IL
Sabrina Johnson, Access Living of Metropolitan Chicago, Chicago, IL
Chisina Kapungu, Loyola University Chicago, Chicago, IL
Lorraine Keck, Grow in America, Champaign, IL
Dana C. Keener, University of South Carolina, Columbia
James G. Kelly, University of Illinois at Chicago
Christopher B. Keys, DePaul University, Chicago, IL
Gary W. Kielhofner, University of Illinois at Chicago

Cécile Lardon, University of Alaska, Fairbanks
Linda Lesondak, Chicago Department of Public Health, Chicago, IL
Melanie Livet-Dye, University of South Carolina, Columbia
Lorna London, Rush-Copley Medical Center, Chicago, IL
Colleen Loomis, Wilfrid Laurier University, Waterloo, Ontario, Canada
Sybil Madison-Boyd, University of Illinois at Chicago
John Majer, DePaul University, Chicago, IL
Kenneth I. Maton, University of Maryland Baltimore County,
    Baltimore
Katherine McDonald, University of Illinois at Chicago
Susan McMahon, DePaul University, Chicago, IL
Julia Mendez, University of South Carolina, Columbia
Robin Lin Miller, University of Illinois at Chicago
Ricardo Millett, Woods Fund of Chicago, Chicago, IL
Lynne Mock, University of Illinois at Chicago
Paul Molloy, Oxford House, Chicago, IL
Maritza Montero, Universidad Central de Venezuela, Caracas
J. R. Newbrough, Vanderbilt University, Nashville, TN
Philip Nyden, Loyola University Chicago, Chicago, IL
Bradley Olson, DePaul University, Chicago, IL
Roberta L. Paikoff, University of Illinois at Chicago
Nancy Peddle, Prevent Child Abuse America, Chicago, IL
Ana Pedraza, Project VIDA, Chicago, IL
Francisco Perez, Chicago Project for Violence Prevention, Chicago, IL
Steven B. Pokorny, DePaul University, Chicago, IL
Elena Quintana, University of Illinois at Chicago
Julian Rappaport, University of Illinois at Urbana–Champaign
Lisa Razzano, University of Illinois at Chicago
Olga Reyes, University of Illinois at Chicago
Stephanie Riger, University of Illinois at Chicago
LaVome Robinson, DePaul University, Chicago, IL
Doreen D. Salina, Northwestern University, Chicago, IL
Bernadette Sánchez, DePaul University, Chicago, IL
Aparna Sharma, Loyola University Chicago, Chicago, IL
Marybeth Shinn, New York University, New York
Jessica Snell-Johns, University of South Carolina, Columbia
Andrea L. Solarz, Independent Consultant, Arlington, VA
Yolanda Suarez-Balcazar, University of Illinois at Chicago
Bruce Talbot, Woodridge Police Department, Chicago, IL
Karen Tamley, Access Living of Metropolitan Chicago, Chicago, IL
Renée R. Taylor, University of Illinois at Chicago
Patrick Tolan, University of Illinois at Chicago
Paul Toro, Wayne State University, Detroit, MI
Susan R. Torres-Harding, DePaul University, Chicago, IL
Edison Trickett, University of Illinois at Chicago
Constance W. Van der Eb, Chicago Chronic Fatigue Syndrome
    Association, Chicago, IL

Judah Viola, DePaul University, Chicago, IL
Abraham Wandersman, University of South Carolina, Columbia
Roderick W. Watts, Georgia State University, Atlanta
Roger P. Weissberg, University of Illinois at Chicago
Bianca Wilson, University of Illinois at Chicago

Foreword

In early 1988, the American Psychological Association (APA) Science Director-ate began its sponsorship of what would become an exceptionally successful activity in support of psychological science—the APA Scientific Conferences program. This program has showcased some of the most important topics in psychological science and has provided a forum for collaboration among many leading figures in the field.

The program has inspired a series of books that have presented cutting-edge work in all areas of psychology. At the turn of the millennium, the series was renamed the Decade of Behavior Series to help advance the goals of this important initiative. The Decade of Behavior is a major interdisciplinary campaign designed to promote the contributions of the behavioral and social sciences to our most important societal challenges in the decade leading up to 2010. Although a key goal has been to inform the public about these scientific contributions, other activities have been designed to encourage and further collaboration among scientists. Hence, the series that was the "APA Science Series" has continued as the "Decade of Behavior Series." This represents one element in APA's efforts to promote the Decade of Behavior initiative as one of its endorsing organizations. For additional information about the Decade of Behavior, please visit http://www.decadeofbehavior.org.

Over the course of the past years, the Science Conference and Decade of Behavior Series has allowed psychological scientists to share and explore cutting-edge findings in psychology. The APA Science Directorate looks forward to continuing this successful program and to sponsoring other conferences and books in the years ahead. This series has been so successful that we have chosen to extend it to include books that, although they do not arise from conferences, report with the same high quality of scholarship on the latest research.

We are pleased that this important contribution to the literature was supported in part by the Decade of Behavior program. Congratulations to the editors and contributors of this volume on their sterling effort.

Kurt Salzinger, PhD
Executive Director for Science

Virginia E. Holt
Assistant Executive Director for Science

Preface

The chapters in this book deal with many issues in participatory community research, ranging from methodology and power sharing to how to ensure the work is appropriately sensitive to and respectful of cultural differences and issues. It contains multiple methodological perspectives and insights well worth pondering, and it will set the stage for participatory community research in the future. The collection stems from a conference held in Chicago in June of 2002. The conference itself was a major undertaking, with sponsorship and support from local foundations and universities as well as from the American Psychological Association.

This book provides examples of coordinated, collaborative, and longitudinal community-related research and action projects that are based on participatory methods and practices. Unlike more traditional approaches to research in which professionals–academics generate the ideas for the research project, define the methods, and interpret the outcomes, participatory approaches empower participants to shape the research and service agenda. There are many excellent reasons to value participatory community research. Participation raises the likelihood that research questions and designs will be more responsive to community needs; that research executions will be more accurate in capturing community nuances; and that community members, having been brought into the research enterprise, will be more likely to pay attention to, agree with, and implement the recommendations of the research findings.

Little attention has been given to the analyses of participatory research methodologies and outcomes in books or journals. One of the unique contributions of this volume is that it sets to rest many ill-informed assumptions that participatory methodologies are somehow less rigorous in their approaches. This is accomplished not only by theoretical discussions of methods but also by providing exemplary case examples of how participatory approaches have led to high-quality collaborations, interventions, and prevention projects. Concrete examples bring theoretical issues to life and provide vivid illustrations of the difficulties that arise when working in real-world settings. At the same time, they serve to inspire both those who are already undertaking similar ventures in the field and those who strive to be.

This volume contains a series of chapters by distinguished theorists and practitioners in the field, each from a different methodological vantage point and each dealing with different content areas. The roster of authors includes many of the leading community psychologists in the country, individuals well qualified to raise and answer questions about participatory research in the community. The chapters demonstrate extensive conceptual and practical engagement with participatory community research. Many recommendations for approaching and conducting such research are put forth in the chapters, which are both experience-based and useful for those wanting to learn more about this research approach. We believe that this book will be useful for its natural audience of advanced graduate students and community psychology researchers, and it also will be attractive for community practitioners outside psychology in such fields as social work and public health. This book is a source of cutting-edge knowledge and reflection that will be useful to interdisciplinary audiences, including readers who are not necessarily university-based or urban.

In each of the chapters, the authors answer several key questions pertaining to the effects of participatory research on communities and research quality, collaborative obstacles and challenges, most appropriate research designs and methodologies, research-based best practices, and the implications for training in and development of community psychology. We believe that this book will advance the field by demonstrating what is already known and what is yet to be learned.

Participatory
Community
Research

Introduction: Capturing Theory and Methodology in Participatory Research

Renée R. Taylor, Leonard A. Jason,
Christopher B. Keys, Yolanda Suarez-Balcazar,
Margaret I. Davis, Joseph A. Durlak,
and Daryl Holtz Isenberg

The field of community psychology studies and addresses significant social problems and their psychological sequelae within larger ecological and multi-systemic contexts (Duffy & Wong, 2000). Such problems include (but are not limited to): violence and abuse; juvenile delinquency; gang warfare; teenage pregnancy; academic underachievement; school dropout; drug, alcohol, and tobacco abuse; homelessness; poverty; and the oppression of disenfranchised groups, including ethnic minorities and individuals with disabilities (Dalton, Elias, & Wandersman, 2001). Participatory approaches to research, character-ized by the active participation of community members in the planning, imple-mentation, or evaluation of research, is an understudied topic in psychology. Yet knowledge of this approach is essential if psychologists want to collaborate with community members to define and intervene with the numerous social problems facing contemporary communities.

Community psychologists have taken an active role in developing and refining a number of theoretical constructs that are now commonly used by other social scientists and a wide range of disciplines (Jason, 1997). Some of these emergent concepts and research developments include empowerment-based research (Rappaport, 1994; Zimmerman 2000); self-help and social sup-port research (Barrera, 2000); developing and evaluating primary prevention programs (Cowen & Durlak, 2000; Durlak, 1998); ecological validity and the measurement of person-in-environment fit (Kelly, 1986; Kelly, Ryan, Altman, & Stelzner, 2000); organizational, school, and advocacy-based intervention re-search (Keys & Wener, 1980); defining and measuring psychological sense of community (Jason, 1997; Sarason, 1974); developing culturally sensitive prevention and intervention programs (Marin, 1994; Rogler, Cortes, & Malgady, 1991); and measuring concepts pertinent to human diversity, such as institutionalized racism and oppression (Harrell, 2000; Ruiz, 1995; Trickett, Watts, & Birman, 1994). These contributions have served to enrich the field with the language and tools necessary for more than four decades of community-based action research and reflection, but there remains an imminent need for continued advancement, particularly in the refinement of theories and methodologies that guide participatory research. To address this need, the second Chicago Conference on Community Research was hosted at Loyola University in Chicago in June of 2002. This book was inspired by information and dialogue generated by that conference.

Participatory Research

Participatory research is a broad term for a wide range of approaches to empowering community members to engage in research that increases citizen power and voice in communities. Participatory approaches encompass a number of activities that are both directly and peripherally related to the research itself. These include engaging citizens to participate as active partners in the creation, delivery, and refinement of services, program evaluation, education, data collection, interpretation of findings, and dissemination of products and research findings. One of the fundamental aspects of participatory research is that it aims to involve community groups and/or community members in an egalitarian partnership with researchers. In essence, it seeks to provide a means of enabling people to re-establish power and control in their own lives (Balcazar, Keys, Kaplan, & Suarez-Balcazar, 1998) and to realize their power as a member of a collective community (Charlton, 1998; Freire, 1993; Minkler, 1985). Formal boundaries between traditional roles (e.g., researcher, consumer, service provider) are reduced or eliminated, and anyone who participates in participatory work may assume a variety of roles and responsibilities in the research and action process.

Participatory action research is one subdomain within the broader area of participatory approaches to research. In this book, the terms *participatory research* and *participatory action research* are used interchangeably. However, a more precise definition of participatory action research may be necessary in justifying the need for the use of the two distinct terms. Participatory research focuses more broadly on increasing citizen voice and power in a wide range of research and programmatic contexts (Prilletensky & Nelson, 2002). Participatory action research can be distinguished in that it incorporates Lewin's (1946) concept of action research (Prilleltensky & Nelson, 2002). It adds an element of social action that involves building sociopolitical awareness and facilitating social action, policy reform, and other types of social or systemic change (Nelson, Ochocka, Griffin, & Lord, 1998). Chapter 1 in this volume is specifically dedicated to reviewing one example of a participatory action research project in detail.

In contrast to the traditional models of research in which professionals generate their own ideas of what research questions to ask or what services clients need, participatory approaches charge the participants themselves with the task of shaping the research questions and developing the services. Participants can also be active determinants in identifying the criteria or standards against which effective service should be judged. This results not only in collective, egalitarian relationships but also in a common language in which key information is shared and expanded. As a result, all participants in the process broaden and enrich their understanding and knowledge of the social issue. This type of reflexivity is a key component of the researcher–participant relationship in any participatory approach (Bradbury & Reason, 2001). Thus, knowledge acquisition by both participants and the researchers is another central goal of participatory action research.

Traditionally, participatory research emphasizes the achievement of local, consumer-driven goals over the traditional aims of positivist science (Bradbury & Reason, 2001). The idea of what is knowledge is broadened to not only include traditional forms of knowledge that arise from rational–deductivist approaches to science but also alternative epistemologies that can involve experiential, aesthetic, presentational, and representational forms of knowledge (Bradbury & Reason, 2001). This conceptualization of different kinds of knowing and capturing of different kinds of knowledge can provide important evidence about the effectiveness of interventions, programs, and other community-based services (Bradbury & Reason, 2001).

Characteristically, participatory approaches assume a strengths-based approach in which participants are encouraged to recognize, use, and build on their own strengths and existing resources to accomplish their goals, as well as the strengths and power of their collective communities. These characteristics are consistent with principles embraced by community psychology. Contrary to traditional approaches to practice, which involve diagnosis of pathology and attempts to facilitate change through the modification of thoughts or behavior, a strengths-based, or empowerment-oriented approach deemphasizes limitations and capitalizes on internal and external strengths, supports, and resources (Rappaport, 1994). Participatory approaches also focus on constructing individual and collective identities, allowing citizens to assume power and control over life decisions, occupations, and roles (Taylor, Braveman, & Hammel, in press).

Kelly (1986) has used principles of participatory research to urge professionals to join in long-term collaborative relationships with persons and settings. By being actively involved in the planning of intervention programs, the recipients receive support, learn to identify resources, and become better problem solvers who are more likely to manage future challenges and issues. Kelly has suggested that interventions that have been generated from collaboratively defined, produced, and implemented change efforts are more apt to endure because such an approach analyzes community traditions for responding to community problems. This approach also helps evaluate or create settings that provide individuals with opportunities to continue receiving support after the termination of formal programs, and it encourages close collaboration with community leaders in all aspects of health care intervention. Finally, it can be used to evaluate positive and negative second-order ripple effects of interventions.

Despite its creditable reputation as an empowerment-generating intervention tool, a focal point for consciousness raising and social change, and a means by which researchers can achieve a more accurate and authentic picture of the social realities of citizens (Balcazar et al., 1998), comparative analyses of participatory research methodologies and outcomes are not given adequate attention at conferences and in journals. As a result, researchers and students of participatory research are left with few informational resources to answer practical questions and resolve natural tensions, such as those involving researcher–consumer power differentials and those arising from the competing demands of scientific rigor and the interests of multiple community stakeholders.

The Five Questions

Five questions will be introduced in this chapter and addressed to varying degrees in each of the subsequent chapters in this book. They were written to provide a framework for advancing and refining the methodologies that make up participatory research, and each of the chapter authors was asked to evaluate his or her own research project in light of the five questions. The first issue that inspired this book was a felt need for more evidence to support the efficacy of participatory collaborations between researchers and community members in addressing social problems and in improving the quality of research. Therefore, the first question is, *"How have collaborations between community members and researchers affected both communities and research quality?"* The field also faces the need for an honest and public examination of the unique challenges and obstacles that community members and researchers confront in participatory research and the lessons learned from such interactions.

The second question is, *"What are the challenges that community members and researchers face in their collaborations?"* There is a need to identify specific research designs, methodologies, and strategies most suited to participatory research, provide a rationale for why these approaches work, and describe any modifications to these approaches that maximize their relevance to this kind of research. Thus, the third and fourth questions are, *"What particular research designs, methodologies, and strategies facilitate participatory work?"* And, *"What are the best practices that have emerged regarding community participation in research?"* Finally, there is a need for increased dialogue between researchers, community agency representatives, students, and community members about participatory methodologies, and there is a need for the dissemination of these innovative approaches. Thus, the fifth question is, *"What implications do these best practices in participatory work have for the training and continued development of all community psychologists?"*

To address these questions, this book was intended to promote the advancement of paradigms and methods of participatory research through a planned discussion about recent theoretical advances in the area and the showcasing of prevention and intervention programs that incorporate such methodologies. These questions were designed to advance the understanding of participatory methods in community psychology by prompting a critical analysis of current methodological approaches and their real-world significance and impact on various stakeholder groups, including community members, students, and researchers in the field of community psychology. The reader is encouraged to search for answers to one or more of these questions in each of the chapters in this volume.

Developments Leading to a Focus on Participatory Research

Before this book, there were no known books within the field of community psychology specifically dedicated to advancing paradigms and exploring methodologies associated with participatory research. The primary predecessor was a book written by Tolan, Keys, Chertok, and Jason (1990), which responded to a multitude of issues facing the field of community psychology more than 10 years ago. These involved tensions between achieving scientific rigor through the use of traditional reductionistic research designs and accurately capturing processes involved in real-world interventions with persons in the context of community settings (adventuresome community research). The book introduced a dialogue regarding how to negotiate the influence of researcher and stakeholder value systems, criteria necessary to define research of merit, issues involving dissemination and feedback to host settings, methodological considerations in implementing ecologically driven research, and unique ethical standards for community researchers.

The idea for this book was born from a desire to generate collaborative research and dissemination activity through the Chicago site of the network of Community Research and Action Centers (CA–RC). The CA–RC was organized by Dr. John Robert Newbrough to address political and social changes occurring within communities and use research to increase collaborative social and community structures. In total, a central hub at Vanderbilt University and three CA–RC sites were created: (a) the University of Puerto Rico site: Centro Universitario de Servicios y Estudios Psicológicos; (b) the University of Kansas, Lawrence, site: Work Group on Health Promotion and Community Development; and (c) the Chicago site: University of Illinois at Chicago, DePaul University, and Loyola University. In part, this book was intended to serve as an interface for intellectual activity, community building, and exchange between the Chicago site, community-based organizations, consumers, and the other CA–RC research sites.

The book is organized according to five thematic areas. In terms of structure, the first four areas are made up of integrative chapters, each of which covers a different topical aspect of participatory research. Each of the integrative chapters includes comment on the theoretical underpinnings of the particular methodological approach to participatory research, description of a Chicago-based action exemplar of the approach, and concluding remarks. To varying degrees, each chapter addresses the five questions raised earlier in this chapter regarding the value, relevance, challenges, and procedures of participatory research. Each of the research strategies and projects showcased is presented from multiple perspectives, including those of psychologists, students, community agency representatives, and consumer groups. The final thematic area of the book presents the perspectives and reactions of stakeholder groups commonly involved in this type of research, including the voices of community members, psychology students, and faculty.

Part I: Principles and Practices

The chapters in the first part of the book describe both traditional as well as new and unique approaches to conducting participatory research. In chapter 1, participatory action research is defined and the scope and limits of the term are explored according to a continuum of control, collaboration, and commitment in the research process. Some researchers are deeply committed to what appears to be a purist ideological paradigm of participatory action research that wholly locates control in the hands of participants and produces higher order social action and change (Selener, 1997). Such researchers label the work of people who more loosely apply participatory methodologies in fields such as management and education as "pseudoparticipatory work" and see clear boundaries in defining what constitutes participatory work (Selener, 1997). Others appear to endorse a more inclusive vision of participatory research that can be defined by any number of approaches to involving community members in research (Reason & Bradbury, 2001). Acknowledging these differences, this chapter attempts to represent a diverse range of projects and theoretical approaches to participatory work. Other aspects of participatory action research are explained, including researcher reflexivity and redefining the researcher's role as a catalyst for social change, empowerment, learning how to learn, social change and transforming social realities, and approaching data collection and interpretation using multiple epistemologies (including experiential knowledge). The authors discuss the relevance of participatory action research to community psychology, they cover general principles for implementing participatory action research in community research, and they share their experiences using this research approach with people with chronic illness and disabilities. A participatory action research project designed to empower individuals with chronic fatigue syndrome and build capacity to address this syndrome in larger social contexts, such as centers for independent living, is presented.

Chapter 2 also reflects the theme of principles and practices in participatory research. In this chapter, the authors define community development as practices focused on increasing the strength and effectiveness of community life, improving local conditions, and enabling people to participate in decision making for the improvement of communities. They summarize the literature on community development and its contributions to community improvement and raise issues involving a lack of consensus about the methods, goals, and criteria for positive outcomes of community development efforts. The chapter summarizes the issues, target populations, setting, intervention, design, measurement, major findings, and conclusions from 42 community development studies, classified in terms of distant outcomes, intermediate outcomes, and process outcomes. The authors conclude that findings were variable in terms of the degree of evidence of an association between community development interventions and positive outcomes, and they attributed such variability to methodological weaknesses or differences between studies. The authors then propose a number of recommendations for practice, research, and communication in community development studies according to a framework of emerging knowledge.

In chapter 3, the authors present a unique approach to participatory research that expands its traditional definition to include application of principles of participation and shared ownership to epidemiological science. The authors observe that most epidemiological studies involve multiple stakeholders with diverse and, at times, divergent agendas. They acknowledge that, although it may not be realistic to fully include the voices and perspectives of all stakeholders involved (e.g., the research population, those charged with the health of that population, government, health insurers, and pharmaceutical companies), a more attainable goal may involve addressing how the voices of community members can be incorporated into the scientific and ethical requirements of good research. An example of such an endeavor is provided in which community participation is used in a large-scale epidemiological study of chronic fatigue syndrome. In this study, consultants with the syndrome were present at all research meetings to aid in the development of the approach to research, the selection of measures, and the training of staff interviewers. Individuals with the syndrome also assisted with problem solving to address barriers that arose during the research process, such as transportation difficulties and other issues of particular concern to the participants under study.

Part II: Creation and Structure of Partnerships

The second part of this book focuses on the processes and outcomes of building partnerships between various stakeholders in participatory research, including university researchers, school officials, law enforcement, clergy, media officials, neighborhood community members, and research participants.

Chapter 4 describes the partnerships involved in participatory approaches to primary prevention through competence promotion. The authors argue that, when implementing preventive interventions, the participation of community members may be best secured through interventions that adapt a competence–enhancement rather than a problem–prevention perspective. Moreover, they argue that prevention programs that emphasize competence promotion and specify different emphases according to group membership, circumstances, and developmental stage lead to the optimal development of competencies and are more likely to produce enduring benefits to systems and community members. In this chapter, an example of a program that used this approach is provided. The case example, the Chicago Project for Violence Prevention, combines an effort to change behavioral norms with a program involving youth outreach, collaboration with law enforcement, clergy outreach and collaboration, public education messaging, and community mobilization.

The authors of chapter 5 explain the importance of careful partnership building that facilitates a delicate balance between the internal validity wrought by scientific rigor and control and external and ecological validity in prevention programs. They define and discuss different approaches to academic–community collaborative relationships, which vary in nature, power distribution, and intensity of community participation, depending on the scientific tasks involved. An example from prevention science of an intervention to reduce youth access to retail sources of tobacco is then provided. This example describes a community–university collaboration in which community representatives documented an effective strategy for reducing tobacco use, and academic researchers then tested this strategy with eight communities in a random community trial.

Chapter 6 reviews the literature on university–community partnerships and presents a framework of 10 characteristics that characterize successful partnership endeavors. Examples include building relationships based on trust and mutual respect, maximizing and exchanging resources, establishing open lines of communication, learning about the culture of the organization, and respecting diversity. A case example describes the Oxford House Project as a successful exemplar of a 10-year university–community collaboration between a university research team and a community-based, self-governed, residential substance abuse program. Opportunities and constraints in adopting a participatory approach to inquiry and action within this project are presented. Broader implications of such partnerships and the challenges that arise in attaining these partnerships are discussed.

Part III: Power Sharing in Participatory Research

Shared power between researchers and community participants is an essential element of participatory research. This section reviews the benefits and challenges involved in research endeavors that empower community stakeholders to assume almost total control over the research or evaluation process.

The authors of chapter 7 highlight an important paradox. Although there is an apparent ideological similarity between participatory research and research conducted with self-help groups, there is a relative paucity of participatory research on self-help groups in the literature. A preliminary theoretical framework for self-help group participatory action research is described. This framework acknowledges a number of ideals shared by self-help and participatory research. They include the importance of experiential knowledge of a shared situation, peer-governed groups, a democratic process, empowerment, supportive relationships, social change, learning as an ongoing process, consciousness raising, member involvement in research design and activities, local and grassroots orientation, and freedom from professional control. They also challenge a number of underlying assumptions about power sharing that are not always facilitative in participatory research. An example is provided that summarizes perceptions of research relationships by 26 representatives of 17 self-help organizations involved in participatory research. Perceptions of seven self-help group researchers are also shared.

In chapter 8, the authors describe empowerment evaluation as a means of enhancing the quality of programs and achieving results by building the capacity of program stakeholders to plan, implement, and evaluate their own programs. The chapter provides an overview of the definition of empowerment evaluation, the purposes of empowerment evaluation, the guiding principles of empowerment evaluation, and a perspective about the relationships between empowerment evaluation and citizen participation in which citizen participation is viewed as a means to enhance program effectiveness, acceptability, and responsiveness to community needs. They point out that evaluation methodologies differ with respect to the degree of citizen participation and power and describe benefits of involving stakeholders in the evaluation process. They conclude with a cost–benefit analysis of stakeholder participation in evaluation, and they acknowledge that participatory approaches are not unilaterally appropriate or relevant to evaluation. A case study in empowerment evaluation is provided using a program that provides mental health, health, and spiritual services to Chicago's nighttime street communities. This program used empowerment evaluation to build and recognize competencies, inform organizational change, to push the program in new directions, to increase inclusiveness, and to prevent the program from becoming an agent of the status quo. Reflections on the strengths of this approach and the challenges encountered in the process are provided.

Part IV: Culture and Gender

The fourth section of the book focuses on the complexities of participatory research as contextualized within inequalities imposed by aspects of human diversity. It is argued that power inequities in participatory research are unavoidable, and in such cases the essential responsibility of the researcher is to acknowledge, reflect on, and work to counteract power differentials through alternative, socially constructed forms of knowledge. The authors of the various chapters discuss direct efforts to prevent oppression through consciousness raising, assertion of voice, and creative approaches to reflexive learning, including the use of narrative to facilitate personal and social change.

In chapter 9, the authors raise fundamental questions about the unavoidable power differentials between researchers and community members engaging in collaborative projects. They propose that intellectual rejection of the positivistic approach to science is not sufficient in facilitating social equity when engaging in participatory work. They describe how feminist theory can help flesh out important emotional realities of power relationships and areas of potential conflict that require acknowledgment when engaging in participatory work. They point out the necessity of researchers to recognize their biases, values, privilege, power, and resulting areas of conflict with community members, and they argue for the adoption of alternative, socially constructed forms of knowledge and for use of feminist critique and feminist trust, or the assertion of voices of the oppressed, as bases for social change. An example of collaboration, action, and reflexivity in participatory feminist research is provided. The authors describe the process of partnering with incarcerated women, the Chicago Department of Public Health, and the Chicago Department of Corrections to develop and implement an effective STD/HIV prevention program. This partnership required the establishment of a long-standing, trusting, intimate relationship with the women, so that accurate, first-hand knowledge of the issues leading to risk-related behaviors could be built into the program of services.

In chapter 10, the authors present a framework for contextualizing research within the culture of members of oppressed groups. Three concepts relevant to participatory research are presented: societal oppression, being in controlling relationships, and coming to terms with one's identity. The chapter describes how each of these issues affect marginalized groups; the implications that the issues present for community researchers; and the values, constructs, and perspectives offered by community psychology in thinking critically about the issues. The paper also provides guidelines for research with marginalized groups derived from community psychology principles, along with numerous examples to illustrate the use of these principles to contextualize the research in the culture of members of marginalized groups. One example is of an attempt to establish an egalitarian relationship with research participants. A second example of a process of preparation for research with African American youth is provided in which the researcher took several steps to build cross-cultural competency, including partnering with an African American male who had a great deal of experience with the population under study, spending many hours talking with people at all levels from the target population and school settings, reflecting on how her own background influenced her identity development and how it differed from the population she intended to work with, and conducting pilot study research that included observation, focus groups, and assessment of measures. A third example describes methods and outcomes of a community-based multicultural program to prevent prejudice or bias motivated aggression among 10- to 13-year-olds. The program, which aimed to decrease children's prejudices by providing an atmosphere where positive cross-cultural interactions could take place, was described as effective in raising self-esteem and decreasing multigroup prejudice.

The authors of chapter 11 describe a theoretical framework of personal and social change initiated through the use of community narratives. Narrative theory and its components, including description and critical analysis of community and setting narratives, dominant cultural narratives, and personal stories are defined, and the art of storytelling in research is described. The idea of promoting personal and social change through the sharing and shaping of personal and community narratives is described, and it is argued that change cannot be accomplished alone but that it must be accomplished in collaboration between researchers and the people of concern. An example is provided in which community narratives were used to improve the sexual health of Mexican American adolescent girls at risk for HIV, pregnancy, and sexually transmitted diseases.

Part V: Stakeholder Perspectives

Three consensus groups reflecting the perspectives of community members (i.e., grassroots leaders and advocates, members of self-help groups, and staff of community-based organizations), psychology students, and psychology faculty were formed to summarize and critically review the contents of this book. Members of each of the three consensus groups were asked to respond to the five questions posed at the beginning of this chapter. The three consensus groups felt that that the five consensus questions were too confining and they preferred to use them as a guide. The editors acknowledged their request and endorsed the reframing of their task. This final section of the book presents commentary on the various theoretical and methodological approaches to participatory research covered in this book.

Appendixes

The appendixes include critical commentary on the state of the science regarding participatory research as well as a description of the Community Action Research Project. This project provided the impetus for this book.

Conclusion

This book illustrates the application of the theory and methodology of community participation to a wide range of established research traditions. Although not exhaustive of the numerous other possible areas of application, this book provides a thorough exploration of each area and offers readers a beginning framework for understanding the varying potentials for the application of participatory research within the field of psychology.

We hope that this volume will serve as a textbook source of cutting-edge knowledge and reflection for scientific professionals and students using participatory research methodologies in psychology. We believe that this textbook will fill a gap in the scientific knowledge and practice of community-based research methodologies emphasizing consumer participation (participatory research). In addition, we hope this volume will facilitate a structured intellectual discussion of methodological issues in participatory research among psychology professionals, students, community agency representatives, and consumer groups. We believe that this book will benefit researchers and community members who use consumer participation in research to mobilize participants, enhance relevance, and thereby prevent and intervene with major social problems facing communities around the world.

References

Balcazar, F. E., Keys, C. B., Kaplan, D. L., & Suarez-Balcazar, Y. (1998). Participatory action research and people with disabilities: Principles and challenges. *Canadian Journal of Rehabilitation, 12,* 105–112.

Barrera, M. (2000). Social support research in community psychology. In J. Rappaport & E. Seidman (Eds.), *Handbook of community psychology* (pp. 215–245). New York: Kluwer Academic/Plenum.

Bradbury, H., & Reason, P. (2001). Conclusion: Broadening the bandwidth of validity: Issues and choice-points for improving the quality of action research. In P. Reason & H. Bradbury (Eds.), *Handbook of action research: Participative inquiry and practice.* London: Sage.

Charlton, J. I. (1998). *Nothing about us without us.* Los Angeles: University of California Press.

Cowen, E. L., & Durlak, J. A. (2000). Social policy and prevention in mental health. *Development and Psychopathology, 12,* 815–834.

Dalton, J. H., Elias, M. J., & Wandersman, A. (2001). *Community psychology: Linking individuals and communities*. Belmont, CA: Wadsworth.

Duffy, K. G., & Wong, F. Y. (2000). *Community psychology* (2nd ed.). Boston: Allyn & Bacon.

Durlak, J. A. (1998). Primary prevention mental health programs for children and adolescents are effective. *Journal of Mental Health, 7,* 463–469.

Freire, P. (1993). *Pedagogy of the oppressed*. New York: Herder & Herder.

Harrell, S. P. (2000). A multidimensional conceptualization of racism-related stress: Implications for the well-being of people of color. *American Journal of Orthopsychiatry, 70,* 42–7.

Jason, L. A. (1997). *Community building: Values for a sustainable future*. Westport, CT: Praeger.

Kelly, J. G. (1986). Context and process: An ecological view of the interdependence of practice and research. *American Journal of Community Psychology, 14,* 581–589.

Kelly, J. G., Ryan, A. M., Altman, E., & Stelzner, S. P. (2000). Understanding and changing social systems: An ecological view. In J. Rappaport & E. Seidman (Eds.), *Handbook of community psychology* (pp. 133–159). New York: Kluwer Academic/Plenum Press.

Keys, C., & Wener, R. (1980). Organizational intervention issues: A four-phase approach to post-occupancy evaluation. *Environment and Behavior, 12,* 533–540.

Lewin, K. (1946). Action research and minority problems. *Journal of Social Issues, 2,* 34–46.

Minkler, M. (1985). Building supportive ties and sense of community among the inner-city elderly: The Tenderloin senior outreach project. *Health Education Quarterly, 12,* 303–314.

Nelson, G., Ochocka, J., Griffin, K., & Lord, J. (1998). "Nothing about me without me," Participatory action research with self-help/mutual aid groups for psychiatric consumers/survivors. *American Journal of Community Psychology, 26,* 881–912.

Prilleltensky, I., & Nelson, G. (2002). *Doing psychology critically: Making a difference in diverse settings*. Basingstroke, UK: Palgrave, MacMillan.

Rappaport, J. (1994). Empowerment as a guide to doing research: Diversity as a positive value. In E. J. Trickett, R. J. Watts, & D. Birman (Eds.), *Human diversity: Perspectives on people in context*. San Francisco: Jossey-Bass.

Reason, P., & Bradbury, H. (Eds.). (2001). *Handbook of action research: Participative inquiry and practice*. London: Sage.

Rogler, L. H., Cortes, D. E., & Malgady, R. G. (1991). Acculturation and mental health status among Hispanics: Convergence and new directions for research. *American Psychologist, 46,* 585–597.

Ruiz, P. (1995). Assessing, diagnosing, and treating culturally diverse individuals: A Hispanic perspective. *Psychiatric Quarterly, 66,* 329–341.

Sarason, S. B. (1974). *The psychological sense of community: Prospects for a community psychology*. San Francisco: Jossey-Bass.

Selener, D. (1997). *Participatory action research and social change* (2nd ed.). Ithaca, NY: Cornell Participatory Action Research Network, Cornell University.

Taylor, R. R., Braveman, B., & Hammel, J. (in press). Developing and evaluating community-based services through participatory action research: Two case examples. *American Journal of Occupational Therapy*.

Tolan, P., Keys, C., Chertok, F., & Jason, L. (1990). *Researching community psychology: Issues of theory and methods*. Washington DC: American Psychological Association.

Trickett, E. J., Watts, R. J., & Birman, D. (1994). *Human diversity: Perspectives on people in context*. San Francisco: Jossey-Bass.

Zimmerman, M. (2000). Empowerment theory: Psychological, organizational, and community levels of analysis. In J. Rappaport & E. Seidman, *Handbook of community psychology* (pp. 43–63). New York: Kluwer Academic/Plenum Press.

Part I

Principles and Practices

1

Participatory Action Research: General Principles and a Study With a Chronic Health Condition

*Fabricio E. Balcazar, Renée R. Taylor,
Gary W. Kielhofner, Karen Tamley, Tom Benziger,
Nancy Carlin, and Sabrina Johnson*

The construct of participatory action research (PAR) has been gradually gaining recognition in the social sciences as a promising strategy for actively involving research participants in the development and implementation of the research process while attempting to pursue socially relevant research issues. A central characteristic of PAR is that it not only aims to empower individuals, but more important, it aims to facilitate higher order social, organizational, or political change (Reason & Bradbury, 2001). The authors of this chapter have used this research approach with people with disabilities in the context of promoting businesses' accessibility compliance with the Americans With Disabilities Act in minority communities (Kaplan, Hernandez, Balcazar, Keys, & McCullough, 2001); developing and implementing a peer-mentoring model for individuals with violence acquired spinal cord injuries (VASCI; Hernandez, Hayes, Balcazar, & Keys, 2001); and developing and implementing a model to empower individuals with chronic fatigue syndrome (CFS; Taylor & Jason, 2002).

PAR combines social investigation, education, and social action to define and address social problems, particularly among disenfranchised and oppressed groups (Brown & Tandon, 1983). It is both a research ideology and a strategy for conducting research. As an ideology, PAR represents a set of beliefs regarding the role of social science research in alleviating social injustice and promoting community involvement in social change efforts. PAR offers specific guidelines for planning and implementing research projects (Tandon, 1998). The approaches involving participatory research emerged from the need

Funding for this project was provided in part by the U.S. Department of Education National Institute on Disability and Rehabilitation Research Grant #H133G000097. The authors thank Dr. Leonard A. Jason of DePaul University in Chicago and Dr. Christopher Keys of the University of Illinois at Chicago for their thoughtful contributions to the manuscript.

of oppressed populations to empower themselves by participating as partners, and in some cases, key directors of various aspects of the research process, thereby generating sociopolitical awareness and mobilizing to effect larger social and systemic change. Participatory action research provides a framework by which people with disabilities can take an active role in designing programs, conducting research, and reestablishing power and control over their own lives (Balcazar, Keys, Kaplan, & Suarez-Balcazar, 1998). Most individuals with disabilities have faced tremendous oppression through social stigmatization, discrimination, and the loss of political and economic resources (Block-Lourie, Balcazar, & Keys, 2001; Charlton, 1998). This chapter provides an overview of key conceptual issues associated with PAR, a brief review of the principles for PAR implementation, and a field research example with individuals with CFS. Readers interested in more extensive reviews of PAR are encouraged to read Selener (1997), Reason and Bradbury (2001), and Whyte (1991).

Definitions of Participatory Action Research

The particular form that the PAR process actually takes depends on the context of the research. The defining factor is the degree of power (control) that the constituents of the study have over the process. Danley and Langer-Ellison (1999) suggested that we can think of a continuum of power held by researchers and research participants that goes from little power to full power or control. At the low end of the spectrum are advisory committees, which are sometimes called PAR because research participants have some involvement but ultimately very little power or authority over the project. On the other end, participants have full control over the research process, including hiring and firing authority over the professional researchers. Midpoints on the continuum may include hybrid projects in which research participants have a high degree of control over the research process but professionals are responsible to outside funding agencies and thus retain decision-making authority over some areas. Table 1.1 provides an overview of the research participants' roles in the PAR implementation process provided by Phillips-Tewey (1997). The participants' roles are classified on the basis of three criteria: the degree of control that participants have over the research process (Litvak, Frieden, Dresden, & Doe, 1997), the extent of collaborative decision making between participants and professional researchers (Turnbull & Friesen, 1997), and the levels of input from and commitment of participants with the research process (Gordon, 1995).

There are also variations of PAR based on *its purpose,* which can influence the conceptualization and direction of the study. The first was represented by Whyte (1991) and reflects an organizational perspective influenced by the sociotechnical systems approach to organizational behavior and by social research methodology. Whyte (1991) defined PAR as a "powerful strategy to involve practitioners in the research process from the initial design of the project through data gathering and analysis, to the final conclusions and actions arising out of the research" (p. 7). From this perspective, members of the organization become actively involved in the quest for information and ideas

Table 1.1   The Continuum of Participant Involvement in PAR Implementation

Level of PAR	Degree of control	Amount of collaboration	Degree of commitment
No PAR	Research participants with no control	Minimal	None
Low	One consumer adviser Group of consumer advisers	Advisory board members	Minimal
Medium	Responsibility for oversight and representation in research meetings	On-going advisers Reviewers Consultants Possible contractual agreement	Multiple commitments Increased ownership of the research process
High	Equal partners Leading partners with capacity to hire the researchers	Active researchers Research leaders	Full commitment Full ownership of the research process

to guide their future actions. The purpose can be to *improve efficiency or effectiveness* in a particular operation, to *improve quality,* or to *develop new products.*

The second approach was presented by Selener (1997) and reflects the view of the methodology as *an instrument for social change in the struggle against oppression,* influenced by Paulo Freire, Orlando Fals Borda, and other developing-world social researchers. Selener (1997) defined PAR as "a process through which members of an oppressed group or community identify a problem, collect and analyze information, and act upon the problem in order to find solutions and to promote social and political transformation" (p. 17). A form of compromise between these two positions is the definition offered by Elden and Levin (1991), who defined PAR as "a way of learning how to explain a particular social world by working with the people who live in it to construct, test, and improve theories about it, so they can better control it" (p. 131). The authors are interested in generating theories that help people learn how to better control the circumstances of their lives, through a process they characterize as "learning for empowerment and democratization." This definition suggests a focus on empowerment as a way to increase people's control over relevant aspects of their work or living environments. They also imply a belief in the people's capacity to participate in the research process. This is the perspective that seems closer to community psychology and will be the one guiding our analysis.

Epistemological Assumptions in PAR

An important and innovative component of PAR is its capacity to empower participants with learning. Elden and Levin (1991) argued that PAR as learning can empower in three ways: First, because of the specific insights, new understandings, and new possibilities that participants discover in the process of creating better explanations about their social reality, they become empowered. Such awareness changes the way people see themselves and their human potential.

Second, by engaging in PAR, participants learn how to learn. People who have a history of marginalization or have simply been ignored often feel insecure about themselves and their own knowledge. To complicate matters, typical schooling experiences are rarely conducive to instilling a passion for learning and self-discovery of new understandings. Students are primarily asked to regurgitate content out of context with the intention of meeting some arbitrary test standards. So often people do not know how to learn and PAR offers them an opportunity to learn from each other and to enhance the understanding of their own social reality by engaging in intense dialogue with each other.

Third, PAR can empower when participants learn how to transform their own social reality. In this case, knowledge becomes social praxis. This learning is in effect what Freire (1970) characterized as the necessary step to comprehend one's potential to act to transform the world. Therefore, the process of learning becomes a process of taking control conducive to transformative action.

Selener (1997) suggested that thinking, feeling, and acting are ways of knowing. He argued that traditional scientific methods rely exclusively on cognitive activities as a source of knowledge. Earlier, Lewin (1948) had identified feeling and acting as ways of knowing. He acknowledged that when the feeling and acting dimensions of learning are ignored, we are left with a limited view of human beings and their capacity to learn. Participatory action researchers argue that thinking, feeling, and acting are three integrated aspects in the process of creating knowledge. The subjective (captured through qualitative research) becomes a necessary part of the process of understanding social reality. Elden and Levin (1991) argued that those who spend their work lives in a particular organization or those who live in a particular community get to know more about it and have more ways of making sense of their world than would be possible for any outsider to appreciate. It follows that the best way to access such knowledge is through dialogue, allowing individuals to share their views in a free and supportive context.

Practice Should Inform Theory and Vice Versa

Theory without links to empirical data is likely to be sterile, and similarly, methodology without any guidance from theory is bound to be unproductive. It is recognized that some hard-nosed scientists reject qualitative data and field observations as being simply "storytelling." On the other hand, it is hardly scientific to accept measures of behavior simply based on what people say about what they do. No matter how many sophisticated quantifications are made with most survey results, the source is still subjective.

PAR proposes to measure interactions and actions that are indeed much more difficult to assess than attitudes or opinions. Most PAR projects are interested in measuring outcomes: What are the specific changes resulting from the research process? What changes in the degree of control (empowerment) participants experienced as a result of the research? Theory in the context of PAR is built on the accumulation of knowledge based on repeated field experiences (Park, 1993). It is experiential knowledge that accumulates and combines to improve our understanding of the way a particular organization or community functions. Such theory reflects the nature of the interactions and activities under study, considering the contextual and personal factors that intervene in the process. The theories may help explain interactions and in some cases even predict certain outcomes based on past experiences. In our opinion, this is a rich approximation to the phenomenon under study.

Redefining the Researcher's Role as a Catalyst for Social or Organizational Change Carried Out by the Research Participants

Elden and Levin (1991) proposed that empowering participation occurs between insiders and outsiders in what they call cogenerative learning. This implies that both groups operate out of their initial frames of reference but communicate at a level where old frames can be changed and new frames generated. The insiders are not simply sources of data but they actively help create new meanings for the information generated in the research process; they become cocreators of knowledge (Elden & Levin, 1991). This process improves as the research process advances and participants gain experience. On the other hand, it is important to remember that the insiders carry out the actual change, and the outsiders only play a supportive role. Montero (in press) repeatedly reminded us that the role of the outsiders in the social transformation process is not to lead but to support. The professionals are not the liberators; they are merely the facilitators in a struggle in which people seek to liberate themselves.

Relevance of PAR to Community Psychologists

PAR is taking a central role in the field of community psychology. This is an approach that is not only consistent with our values and philosophy but our methods too. Some of the reasons follow.

CITIZEN PARTICIPATION IS CENTRAL TO COMMUNITY PSYCHOLOGY. Wandersman, Chavis, and Stucky (1983) advocated that involving citizens as partners in the research process is fundamental to ensuring that the research is responsive to their needs and values. In addition, they suggested that such a collaborative effort can improve the quality and applicability of the research, encourage public support for its findings, enhance the potential for use of research results, and serve to empower citizens by increasing their sense of control over their lives. Kelly et al. (1988) explained how citizen participation is essential for the research activity to be ecologically relevant, understood, and valued by the community members.

SOCIAL CHANGE IS A DESIRABLE GOAL TO COMMUNITY PSYCHOLOGY. Heller, Price, Reinharz, Riger, and Wandersman (1984) argued that social change is a pervasive condition in the world and multiple factors, such as diverse populations with diverse and multiple needs, declining resources, growing demands for service accountability, expanding knowledge and changing technologies, economic changes, community conflict, and dissatisfaction with traditional approaches to deal with social problems could lead the list of reasons for change. Community psychologists deal with these issues, and PAR is one strategy to pursue such change.

PAR OFFERS COMMUNITY PSYCHOLOGY A METHOD OF RESEARCH AND ACTION. Selener (1997) offered methodological guidelines for conducting PAR. These include the initial stages of organizing the research project and gathering knowledge of the community or organization, the process of defining and critically analyzing the problem, and defining a plan of action. Balcazar, Seekins, and Fawcett (1985) developed an action guide to help individuals engage in community change, which was later adapted to guide community health change efforts (Altman, Balcazar, Fawcett, Seekins, & Young, 1994). Balcazar, Keys, and Suarez-Balcazar (2001) also developed a guide to community capacity building that incorporates the Community Concerns Report Methodology (Fawcett, Seekins, Whang-Ramos, Muiu, & Suarez-Balcazar, 1987) and specific strategies for community organizing and leadership development.

PAR INCREASES COMMUNITY PSYCHOLOGISTS' OWN CRITICAL AWARENESS AND COULD LEAD TO RADICALIZATION. In the case of PAR applications toward community change, the researcher often finds him- or herself in conflict with his or her own class interests. This conflict can lead the researcher to raise some basic questions about his or her position of privilege and his or her role in society (Fals Borda, 1994). Prilleltensky (1994) argued that if psychologists are going to become a vehicle for conscientization for other people, we should be the first ones to subject ourselves to this very process. In PAR, the researcher becomes involved in developing community members' capacities for collective identification and analysis of problems and the implementation of solutions. This may place the researcher in conflict with people who may not be willing to relinquish their power. Although conflict can sometimes be avoided through compromise, it is often an integral part of the process of power redistribution.

General Principles for Implementing PAR in Community Research

Consider participants as social actors, with a voice, ability to decide, reflect, and capacity to participate fully in the research process. This principle recognizes the central role that participants play in the research process and to their capacity to do so. It implies minimal biases from the external agent toward the people's capacity to become successfully involved. It also implies the need to change the way we train researchers on how to conduct community and organizational research. Kelly et al. (1988) pointed out how the extent of citizen participation is the fundamental criteria to determine whether community research will be implemented and have an impact. Brydon-Miller (1993) illustrated how a small group of individuals with physical disabilities working with the researcher organized to improve the accessibility at a local shopping mall. They obtained the appropriate regulations under the Americans With Disabilities Act and used them to press their case successfully.

The ultimate goal of PAR is the transformation of the social reality of the participants by increasing the degree of control they have over relevant aspects of their community or organization. The principle implies that empowerment is the ultimate objective of the PAR process and therefore its attainment has to become an explicit part of the purpose of any action. Hernandez, Hayes, Balcazar, and Keys (2001) described a PAR approach designed to use peer mentors to help recent victims of gun violence who become paralyzed set and pursue goals in their rehabilitation process. The peer mentors became role models to their mentees and showed them the life options and opportunities available to them after the injury. Mentees were encouraged by their mentors to take control of their rehabilitation process and become independent. Preliminary results suggest that peer mentors can help their mentees attain personal goals by providing information and direct assistance in the process.

The problem originates in the community/organization itself and is defined, analyzed, and solved by the participants. The external agent's role in this case is that of facilitating the dialogue among community members to develop consensus over the specific target of the study. Helping people realize that they are the ones who can solve their own problems is not easy. Most people are skeptical and insecure about their capacity to change their social reality (Freire, 1970). Balcazar, Seekins, Fawcett, and Hopkins (1990) implemented an advocacy training program to help a small group of people with physical disabilities identify issues and implement actions to address those issues. Participants were successful with approximately 60% of the issues identified, improving the accessibility and the quality and types of services available to people with disabilities in the community.

Active participation leads to a better understanding of the history and culture of the community/organization and a more authentic analysis of the social reality. This process allows for a more accurate appreciation of the issues and challenges experienced by the participants. External agents can never achieve a full understanding of the nature of the organization or community without an authentic dialogue with community members. Bartuneck, Foster-Fishman, and Keys (1996) conducted a series of qualitative interviews with several individuals with developmental disabilities, family members, service providers, and professionals with the purpose of documenting the development of a support and advocacy group for individuals with developmental disabilities. Participants offered their perspectives about the history of the process, including the individual and organizational support, as well as the cultural shift that led to the creation of the organization.

Engaging in a dialogical approach also leads to critical awareness. The dialogue with community or organizational members can give researchers not only a more accurate understanding and appreciation of the reality of the community or the organization but a more critical understanding of the social reality to participants. Dialogue can lead participants to reflect on their history and the factors that maintain their condition of oppression or exploitation. This reflection can in turn lead people to move away from a passive perception of victimization to a perception of actors responsible for forging their own future. Balcazar et al. (2001) described their work with a group of immigrant Latino parents of children who are deaf. The parents were associated with a local agency that was not responding to all of their needs. Their involvement in the research process led them to become critically aware of their situation and especially of their own capacity to act. They left the agency and started their own organization, providing services and supports with volunteers to approximately 60 families.

Recognizing people's strengths also increases their awareness about their existing resources and mobilizes them to help themselves. This principle is also commonly used in community research. Building from strengths reinforces people's capacity to act. Very often community members and employees do not have an awareness of the latent resources available among them. Balcazar, Mathews, Francisco, and Fawcett (1994) documented the actions and outcomes of four advocacy organizations of people with disabilities. The advocacy training process helped the groups identify and build strengths and resources, which were later used to promote their agenda. Perceptions of people with disabilities often focus on their shortcomings, and such negative perceptions are often internalized. Taking actions to transform their community and succeeding led in turn to a revaluation of their abilities and potential.

The research process also promotes personal change both for participants and researchers. PAR is a transformative experience in the sense that the dialogue and the process of analysis of the social reality lead participants to question their own roles and responsibilities toward social change. Engaging in true dialogue is a transforming experience. It is a process of mutual discovery that leads one to rediscover who we are and why. PAR often leads participants to question their motives and to overcome their fears and perceived limitations. It is a liberating process both for the insiders as well as the outsiders. Balcazar et al. (1990) reported how several of the participants in the advocacy organization changed their perceptions about their own abilities and their personal effectiveness. For the researchers, the experience led them to a sustained effort to replicate and disseminate the advocacy training materials and procedures among several groups of people with disabilities from around the country. For example, in the state of Idaho, a statewide coalition of individuals with chronic mental illnesses and family members from the Alliance for the Mentally Ill (AMI) was organized using the advocacy-training model. The process was replicated using a train-the-trainer approach, resulting in more than 150 individuals being trained over a period of four years, transforming the parent and consumer involvement in issues related to mental health in the state.

To conclude, PAR allows people with disabilities to shape the research process to meet their needs and to direct the research process toward the generation of desired outcomes. The research endeavor becomes a process of social renovation or transformation. Issues associated with physical accessibility, quality and availability of services, community attitudes or discrimination against people with disabilities are attended to. Consumers move from a passive victim stance to a proactive citizen-with-rights stance. Once they have made this transformation, they can no longer be victimized without a fight.

The following section presents a community-based action project that applies PAR as a paradigm for empowering individuals with chronic fatigue syndrome, an emergent disability that is new to the independent living movement.

Case Study: PAR Applied to Chronic Fatigue Syndrome

Chronic fatigue syndrome (CFS) is a highly debilitating condition characterized by six or more months of medically and psychiatrically unexplained, persistent fatigue and four or more of the following symptoms for at least six months: impaired short-term memory or concentration, sore throat, tender lymph nodes, muscle pain, multijoint pain without swelling or redness, new-type headaches, unrefreshing sleep, and postexertional malaise for ≥ 24 hours (Fukuda et al., 1994; Holmes et al., 1988).

CFS has been recognized as a disability under the Americans With Disabilities Act (ADA; Banks, 1993) and legitimated as a medically determinable condition by the Social Security Administration (Social Security Ruling 99-2p, 1999). Despite these developments, individuals with CFS continue to report negative experiences with service providers characterized by outright disbelief, lack of knowledge or understanding of CFS, overemphasis on psychological or psychosocial explanations, and a general lack of responsiveness or treatment planning (Anderson & Ferrans, 1997; Banks & Prior, 2001; Green, Romei, & Natelson, 1999). Perhaps as a result of this tension, people with CFS report a lack of social and public support and tend to underuse rehabilitative services and community-based resources traditionally available to individuals with other disabling conditions (Jason, Ferrari, Taylor, Slavich, & Stenzel, 1996).

Traditional medical and psychological treatment approaches for individuals with CFS have demonstrated contradictory outcomes and remain in an experimental phase of development (Taylor, Friedberg, & Jason, 2001). It is possible that empowerment-oriented support efforts emphasizing the integration of public and private community-based service systems, peer counseling, advocacy, civil rights, and education may offer effective means of supplemental support for individuals with this syndrome. For these reasons, Centers for Independent Living offer a most appropriate avenue for resource acquisition and coordination for individuals with CFS.

Centers for Independent Living epitomize the concept of community participation. They are community-based, empowerment-oriented organizations that are operated by and for individuals with disabilities, endorsing the concepts of freedom, choice, and control. The independent living philosophy locates many of the problems for people with disabilities within society and in its environmental barriers, discriminatory acts, and socially stigmatizing attitudes. According to this externalizing orientation, the main objective is to break down societal barriers, allowing people to integrate themselves fully into the community in an effort to be treated equally.

The CFS Empowerment Project, funded by the National Institute on Disability and Rehabilitation Research, was designed to provide individuals with CFS entry into Centers for Independent Living, and an opportunity to struggle with and incorporate relevant aspects of the independent living philosophy, such as learning self-advocacy and empowerment. Until this project began, few people with CFS were aware that Centers for Independent Living existed, and even fewer felt entitled to seek support from these centers. This project was initiated through one such center, Access Living of Metropolitan Chicago, a cross-disabilities organization that outreaches to underserved populations and individuals with emergent disabilities.

Additional aims of the project include improving quality of life; symptom management skills; and resource acquisition by offering peer counseling groups, one-on-one mentoring in self-advocacy, and ongoing consultation and economic support for resource acquisition while following a PAR approach. Participant-centered goal setting serves as the linchpin of the program. It is woven into both the group phase and the one-on-one phase of the project to contribute to participants' empowerment and facilitate relevance of the program for participants on a more individualized basis. A collaborative process allowed for the researchers, the peer counselors with CFS, and the staff of Access Living to iron out disagreements involved in integrating the agenda of the participants and peer counselors with CFS with the ideology and practices of the independent living movement. The CFS community has not historically seen themselves as members of the disability community but rather from a medical model perspective as sick. Through this project we worked to change the paradigm about how individuals with CFS view themselves.

Step 1: Planning the Project

An extensive amount of participation was elicited from the CFS community as well as from the staff of Access Living, the Center for Independent Living, during the initial steps of project planning. A number of professionals and community members who have CFS or are closely connected with an individual with CFS contributed to the design and development of the project and grant proposal by providing the principal investigator with consultation regarding a number of pragmatic aspects of the project, including the structure of the program (e.g., the need for both group and one-on-one contact), the pacing of the program (e.g., biweekly groups rather than weekly groups), the location of the program (e.g., need for a chemically and environmentally safe setting), the need for personalized transportation to and from the program site to maximize the opportunity that even the most disabled individuals with CFS would attend, and the need to provide reasonable access to key resources, such as personal assistance with activities of daily living, housekeeping, low-cost accessible transportation, subsidized housing, affordable legal assistance, energy assistance, and vocational rehabilitation services. Staff of the Center for Independent Living provided suggestions and advice about how to position the program within the center to best facilitate the transfer of knowledge and expertise about CFS from the peer counselors and program participants to the other staff members at the center for independent living. The goal of having the program offered through the Center for Independent Living was to provide a natural structure within which to sustain the program over time in the absence of support from the research staff.

Step 2: Implementing the Program

Part 1 of the program involved peer counseling groups. In accord with the empowerment-oriented model of PAR, the peer counselors with CFS conducted one 2-hour focus group with participants as the first of eight peer counseling sessions that occurred biweekly over a period of 16 weeks. During this focus group, members introduced themselves and provided background information about their experiences with CFS and about what they hoped to accomplish as a result of participating. This process enabled members to establish rapport, select goals, and construct an individualized goal plan with assistance from the peer counselors (as needed). This individualized goal plan allowed participants to delineate goals they then addressed during the program period. In addition to the goal plan, peer counselors provided an overview during this focus group of major themes relevant to resource acquisition, advocacy, and CFS management that could be covered in the seven group sessions to follow. Participants then selected seven of these topics from a list of educational themes previously identified as a result of the needs assessment (Jason et al., 1996) and recommended by other consultants with CFS as most pertinent to the resource needs and quality of life of individuals with CFS.

The themes (potential group topics) included (a) developmental stages of living with CFS (Fennell, 1995); (b) activity pacing using the Envelope Theory (Jason et al., 1999); (c) skills to manage physical and cognitive symptoms of CFS independently (Friedberg & Jason, 1998); (d) economic self-sufficiency (e.g., obtaining public assistance with electricity needs, transportation needs, and personal assistant needs and obtaining social security and disability income); (e) employment issues (e.g., issues related to the ADA and workplace accommodations, vocational rehabilitation, and modifying employment); (f) personal relationships (partner, family, friends, coworkers, employers, etc.); (g) relating to medical providers; (h) medical approaches and current medical research on CFS; (i) alternative medical approaches; (j) relaxation and meditation; (k) journal writing; and (l) nutritional approaches. After voting and selecting seven of these topics, members were then encouraged to select areas of more specialized focus within each of these major themes according to their individualized needs and goals for the program.

Once members decided which areas to focus on within each of the seven themes, members shared and discussed their experience and knowledge in each of these areas. Members with particular experience or expertise in one of these areas were encouraged to prepare a presentation on that area for the group session dedicated to that theme, again consistent with the ideology of PAR fueling this project.

Following the initial focus group, a series of seven peer-facilitated group sessions occurred biweekly over a 14-week period. The emphasis of the first

60 minutes of group focused on goal setting, with each member revising and reporting on attainable objectives and goals using her or his own individualized goal plan and receiving feedback from peers in overcoming any obstacles they faced. The second 60 minutes of group involved an educational presentation on one of the seven topics, and reflections and feedback were gathered at the end of each group. In many cases, the peer counselors or participants served as the lecturers. This process promoted maximal participation in the research process on the part of participants, a key point when implementing PAR (Bradbury & Reason, 2001). The end-of-group reflections form was administered at the end of each group. This form was designed to allow participants to provide direct feedback to the peer counselors regarding their opinions of the quality and practical relevance of each group. Suggestions and feedback were then incorporated into the continued implementation of the project, increasing the ecological relevance of the program and allowing participants additional control over the process of program development and research. In addition, the form was designed to assess the relevance of each group to the concepts of empowerment, sense of community, advocacy, and the independent living philosophy. This allowed for an indication of whether participants would be willing to act on what they learned in the process of the research, a reflexive concern for practical outcomes that is essential to the PAR process (Bradbury & Reason, 2001).

SELF-ADVOCACY TRAINING/ONE-ON-ONE PHASE (PART 2 OF THE PROGRAM). Part 2 of the program, the one-on-one phase, involved peer counseling and self-advocacy training. To manage CFS, many individuals require supportive services (e.g., peer mentoring, social services, professional counseling to facilitate adjustment to disability, assistance in developing activity management strategies, vocational counseling, occupational and physical therapy, and personal assistance/housekeeping services). Through self-advocacy training and case coordination services available through Access Living, participants were provided with the training, skills, knowledge, and financial support to create their own linkages to supportive services during this period. Each participant also engaged in self-advocacy training and role playing according to a help-recruiting model previously used by Balcazar, Keys, and Garate-Serafini (1995). This training program was designed to assist adjudicated youth with disabilities to attain their personal and rehabilitation goals, and it corresponds with goal-setting methods typically used in action plans to facilitate goal attainment during community-based programs (Balcazar et al., 1995).

RESOURCE FUNDS (USED THROUGHOUT PARTS 1 AND 2 OF PROGRAM PERIOD). Resource funds were provided to each participant in an amount of $300 during the entire program period to support services and resources needed by participants to accomplish the objectives listed on their goal plans. Participants were empowered to use these funds for a variety of purposes, provided that the use of the funds enabled them to accomplish one or more of their set goals. Actual use of the funds ranged from covering the cost of a job seminar for a participant seeking to become re-employed, to covering the cost for ergonomically designed furniture and other adaptive devices to reduce pain while performing common

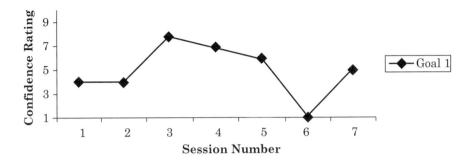

Figure 1.1.   Goal 1: Obtain disability insurance benefits.

activities of daily living. The funds were also to be used to allow participants to sample certain services to maximize independence, such as hiring a personal assistant to help a participant to accomplish activities of daily living (e.g., doing dishes, paying bills, grocery shopping, preparing food, keeping up with housework).

Participant's Perspective

The following section presents time-series data regarding specific goals selected by one of the participants during the group phase. For each goal, confidence ratings ranging from 1 (low) to 10 (high) were charted over a seven-session (14-week) period to reflect the level of certainty the participant felt about each session with respect to meeting the objectives required to accomplish her goal by the end of the group phase. In addition to data related to goals, the participant's reflections regarding empowerment, the independent living philosophy, CFS advocacy, and sense of community are presented and discussed. Identifying details about the participant have been altered to protect her confidentiality.

This participant was a woman newly diagnosed with CFS following an episode of infectious mononucleosis who had been forced to take a four-month leave of absence from her work before the program. During the program, she had managed to work full-time for five months. Her goals for the program revolved around ensuring her own economic self-sufficiency, managing CFS symptoms, and locating and accessing various health care professionals. During the group phase, the participant rated her confidence regarding the ability to accomplish each goal on a scale of 1–10, where 1 indicated expected failure and 10 indicated expected achievement. Figures 1.1 through 1.3 summarize the participant's confidence ratings of goal attainment reported during the group sessions.

Based on her confidence ratings, which corresponded to qualitative data reported during the groups and written on her goal plan, it is clear that this participant made significant progress toward two of her three goals. With respect to her first goal, the participant was neither as confident nor as success-ful with respect to obtaining disability insurance benefits. In part, this was due to the fact that she became re-employed during the program and was

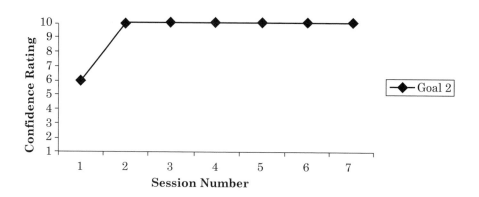

Figure 1.2. Goal 2: Improve management of CFS symptoms.

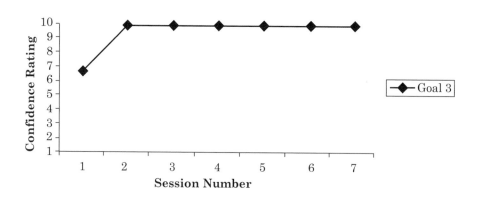

Figure 1.3. Goal 3: Locate and consult with health care professionals to assist in managing CFS.

attempting to apply retroactively for coverage to which she had been entitled but never received. Although she was able to obtain the necessary information from her long-term disability insurance company regarding reasons for denial of coverage and was able to obtain information regarding resources to assist her with the appeals process, she became overwhelmed by the inaccuracies cited by the insurance company as reasons for her denial of coverage. In addition, because she began to feel significantly better during the program period, she reported feeling more financially secure and stated she was unsure as to whether she would appeal the decision of the insurance company regarding the period in which she took the leave of absence. However, she felt the appeal might be worth pursuing as a matter of principle. The participant experienced the most difficulty and the least confidence in obtaining this goal because she felt that the external barriers imposed by the insurance company would outweigh her own efforts to appeal the decision. Thus, the outcome regarding this goal was not solely within her control.

In terms of the second goal of managing CFS symptoms, the participant's confidence ratings reached the highest possible rating in Session 2, and she was able to maintain that confidence and work toward her objectives throughout the group phase. Specifically, she incorporated many aspects of the educational components covered during group training into her symptom management regime, including principles of activity pacing and energy conservation, empowerment and self-advocacy in her employment setting, learning how to reframe negative self-statements and manage perceived criticism from others, sleep hygiene techniques that included establishing a regular sleep–wake routine, and relaxation–meditation skills.

Regarding her third goal of locating and consulting with health care professionals, the participant consulted with a number of health care professionals to supplement her use of the information she learned during group training. She consulted with a primary care physician, a nutritionist, a psychotherapist, a massage therapist, and an allergist. She also attempted to obtain legal assistance. Her confidence ratings reached the highest possible rating in Session 2, and she was able to maintain confidence and tenaciously work toward her objectives throughout the group phase.

Based on her responses to the end-of-group reflections form, explained on the previous pages, the participant appears to have enacted what she learned during the group meetings according to the concepts of empowerment, the independent living philosophy, and sense of community. In terms of the independent living philosophy, the participant reported that she became aware of the ADA and learned more about sources for free legal advice and specialized transportation options. With respect to empowerment, the participant reported feeling optimistic and empowered regarding the possibility that she may still be able to pursue the private disability income. She also felt empowered in learning activity pacing (the envelope theory) to help her manage symptoms and in knowing that she could obtain books on tape free from the library to listen to when she felt too tired to read. With respect to sense of community, the participant reported: "It's good to have a sense of community—to be able to vent what's going on with myself and my health to others who have been there and understand—and can make suggestions from experience."

The perspectives presented indicate that participants can initiate and direct their own goals and plan care effectively with peer support, despite the fact that CFS is a highly complex and difficult illness to manage. As a whole, the CFS Empowerment Project applied the methods of PAR to its design, implementation, evaluation, and dissemination. For instance, individuals with CFS highly familiar with the needs of the CFS population shaped the design and development of the research proposal and made useful suggestions regarding the structure, pacing, and resources that would be required to retain and support participants in the program. In addition, results of a national survey of service needs of people with CFS conducted by our research team (Jason et al., 1996) were incorporated into program planning and selection of topics for the peer counseling groups and one-on-one self-advocacy training period. In terms of the program, the principal investigator collaborated with Center for

Independent Living staff to employ two high-functioning individuals with CFS to serve as peer counselors. The peer counselors absorbed primary responsibility for implementing the entire program in collaboration with the participants themselves. Moreover, participants shaped the contents of the peer counseling groups during a focus group in which they selected and refined 7 of 12 potential educational topics to be presented during the group phase. Participants also assumed control of the program by setting, working toward, and evaluating their own goals. Participants also exerted an impact on the program by providing written feedback and suggestions, many of which were incorporated into the continued implementation of the project. Finally, participants have been involved in the outcome dissemination process by discussing their experiences in the program and sharing personal outcomes resulting from the project. These outcomes will eventually be used to shape the types of support provided by centers for independent living and other community-based organizations.

Conclusion

In this chapter, PAR has been described in terms of its definition, epistemology, and relevance for theory and practice in community-based research. We have suggested that there are three epistemological assumptions in PAR that involve empowerment through the generation and acquisition of knowledge, and we have provided a case example that illustrates how individuals with CFS can empower themselves through varied forms of knowledge generated by a participatory action research program. We have described a program that involved ongoing reciprocal feedback and communication between the participants, the community-based organization, and the researchers such that the program could be developed and refined in an ecologically relevant way, leading to its sustainability within the community-based organization over time. In the case study, participants assumed a moderate degree of control over the research process, high collaboration in the process, and a high degree of commitment to the process.

In sum, the program illustrated the seven general principles of PAR reviewed in this chapter. First, both the community-based organization and the community of interest—people with CFS—were active participants in the planning, implementation, and dissemination of the research. Second, the participants were successfully able to transform their own social reality by increasing their control over their own health. They also succeeded in transforming the social reality of access to community-based resources for other individuals with CFS living in the area by increasing their presence and degree of power within the community-based organization, the Center for Independent Living, such that the program could be sustained over time. Third, the problem of lack of knowledge about ways to manage CFS and a lack of knowledge about the availability of and entitlement to community-based resources that have been traditionally available to individuals with other types of disabilities was defined by individuals with CFS that planned the program and was addressed by the participants during the program, through educational presentations, self-advocacy training regarding rights and entitlements for persons with disabilities, and through the exchange of information about available resources. As a result, both the participants and the community-based organization achieved a more authentic picture of the social reality of individuals with CFS as persons with disabilities willing and able to empower themselves through knowledge and by learning their rights to access the resources and services to which they are entitled. Participants in the program also engaged in an ongoing dialogue about the program and about their service needs in general, not only with the researchers but also with staff from the community-based organization. As a result, both the researchers and the community-based organization acquired new knowledge about the advocacy and service needs of individuals with CFS, and participants became more aware of what it meant to become a part of the independent living movement.

The project assumed a strengths-based approach in which participants were encouraged to recognize, use, and build on their own strengths and existing resources to accomplish their goals. Finally, the project led to personal change in both the participants and the researchers. As a result of the project, participants began to see new roles and possibilities for themselves as activists within their communities, such as within their families, social networks, and places of employment. In turn, the researchers have been influenced to replicate the program for individuals with other conditions and disabilities involving severe fatigue.

References

Altman, D. G., Balcazar, F. E., Fawcett, S. B., Seekins, T., & Young, J. Q (1994). *Public health advocacy: Creating community change to improve health.* Palo Alto, CA: Stanford Center for Research in Disease Prevention.

Anderson, J. S., & Ferrans, C. E. (1997). The quality of life of persons with chronic fatigue syndrome. *Journal of Nervous and Mental Disease, 185,* 359–367.

Balcazar, F. E., Keys, C. B., & Garate-Serafini, J. (1995). Learning to recruit assistance to attain transition goals: A program for adjudicated youth with disabilities. *Remedial and Special Education, 16,* 237–246.

Balcazar, F. E., Keys, C. B., Kaplan, D. L., Suarez-Balcazar, Y. (1998). Participatory action research and people with disabilities: Principles and challenges. *Canadian Journal of Rehabilitation, 12,* 105–112.

Balcazar, F. E., Keys, C. B., & Suarez-Balcazar, Y. (2001). Empowering Latinos with disabilities to address issues of independent living and disability rights: A capacity-building approach. *Journal of Prevention and Intervention in the Community, 21*(2) 53–70.

Balcazar, F. E., Mathews, R. M., Francisco, V. T., & Fawcett, S. B. (1994). The empowerment process in four advocacy organizations of people with disabilities. *Rehabilitation Psychology, 39*(3), 191–206.

Balcazar, F. E., Seekins, T., & Fawcett, S. B. (1985). *Teaching consumers how to conduct action-oriented meetings.* Lawrence: Research and Training Center on Independent Living, University of Kansas.

Balcazar, F. E., Seekins, T., Fawcett, S. B., & Hopkins, B. L. (1990). Empowering people with physical disabilities through advocacy skills training. *American Journal of Community Psychology. 18*(2), 281–295.

Banks, J., & Prior, L. (2001). Doing things with illness. The micro politics of the CFS clinic. *Social Sciences and Medicine, 52,* 11–23.

Banks, M. L. (1993, Summer). The Americans With Disabilities Act: CFS and employment. *Heart of America News.* Retrieved Aug. 26, 2003, from http://www.sunflower.org/cfsdays/ADA-CFS.htm

Bartuneck, J., Foster-Fishman, P., & Keys, C. (1996). Using collaborative advocacy to foster intergroup cooperation: A joint insider–outsider investigation. *Human Relations, 49,* 701–733.

Block-Lourie, P., Balcazar, F. E., & Keys, C. B. (2001). From pathology to power rethinking race, poverty, and disability. *Journal of Disability Policy Studies, 12*(1), 18–27, 39.

Brown, D. L., & Tandon, R. (1983). Ideology and political economy in inquiry: Action research and participatory research. *Journal of Applied Behavioral Science, 19,* 277–294.

Brydon-Miller, M. (1993). Breaking down barriers: Accessibility self-advocacy in the disabled community. In P. Park, M. Brydon-Miller, B. Hall, & T. Jackson (Eds.), *Voices of change: Participatory research in the United States and Canada* (pp. 125–144). Westport, CT: Bergin & Garvey.

Charlton, J. I. (1998). *Nothing about us without us.* Los Angeles: University of California Press.

Danley, K., & Langer-Ellison, M. (1999). *A handbook for participatory action researchers.* Boston: Center for Psychiatric Rehabilitation, Boston University.

Elden, M., & Levin, M. (1991). Cogenerative learning: Bringing participation into action research. In W. F. Whyte (Ed.), *Participatory action research* (pp. 127–142). Newbury Park, CA: Sage.

Fals Borda, O. (1994). *El problema de como investigar la realidad para transformarla por la praxis.* [The problem of how to investigate reality in order to transform it by praxis]. Bogotá, Colombia: Tercer Mundo Editores.

Fawcett, S. B., Seekins, T., Whang-Ramos, P., Muiu, C. & Suarez-Balcazar, Y. (1987). Involving consumers in decision-making. *Social Policy, 13*(6), 36–41.

Fennell, P. A. (1995). The four progressive stages of the CFS experience: A coping tool for patients. *Journal of Chronic Fatigue Syndrome, 1,* 69–79.

Freire, P. (1970). *Pedagogy of the oppressed.* New York: Continuum.

Friedberg, F., & Jason, L. A. (1998). *Understanding chronic fatigue syndrome: An empirical guide to assessment and treatment.* Washington, DC: American Psychological Association.

Fukuda, K., Straus, S. E., Hickie, I., Sharpe, M. C., Dobbins, J. G., et al. (1994). The Chronic Fatigue Syndrome: A comprehensive approach to its definition and study. *Annals of Internal Medicine, 121,* 953–959.

Gordon, W. A. (1995). *PAR: A realistic strategy for medical rehabilitation research?* Paper presented at the 1995 NIDRR conference on participatory action research, Washington, DC.

Green, J., Romei, J., & Natelson, B. J. (1999). Stigma and chronic fatigue syndrome. *Journal of Chronic Fatigue Syndrome, 5,* 63–75.

Heller, K., Price, R. H., Reinharz, S., Riger, S., & Wandersman, A. (1984). *Psychology and community change.* Homewood, IL: Dorsey.

Hernandez, B., Hayes, E., Balcazar, F. E., & Keys, C. B. (2001). Responding to the needs of the underserved: A peer-mentor approach. *Spinal Cord Injury Psychosocial Process, 14*(3), 142–149.

Holmes, G. P., Kaplan, J. E., Gantz, N. M., Komaroff, A. L., Schonberger, L. B., et al. (1988). Chronic fatigue syndrome: A working case definition. *Annals of Internal Medicine, 108,* 387–389.

Jason, L. A., Ferrari, J. R., Taylor, R. R., Slavich, S. P., & Stenzel, C. L. (1996). A national assessment of the service, support, and housing preferences by persons with Chronic Fatigue Syndrome: Toward a comprehensive rehabilitation program. *Evaluation and the Health Professions, 19,* 194–207.

Jason, L. A., Tryon, W. W., Taylor, R. R., King, C., Frankenberry, E., et al. (1999). Monitoring and assessing symptoms of chronic fatigue syndrome: Use of time series regression. *Psychological Reports, 85,* 121–130.

Kaplan, D., Hernandez, B., Balcazar, F. E., Keys, C. B., & McCullough, S. (2001). Assessing and improving accessibility of public accommodations in an urban Latino community. *Journal of Disability Policy Studies, 12*(1), 55–62.

Kelly, J. G., Dassoff, N., Levin, I., Schreckeugost, J., Stelzer, S., et al. (1988). *A guide to conducting prevention research in the community: First steps.* New York: Haworth.

Lewin, K. (1948). *Resolving social conflicts.* New York: Harper.

Litvak, S., Frieden, L., Dresden, C., & Doe, T. (1997). Empowerment, independent living research and participatory action research. In B. Phillips-Tewey (Ed.), *Building participatory action research partnerships in disability and rehabilitation research.* Washington, DC: U.S. Department of Education, National Institute on Disability and Rehabilitation Research.

Montero, M. (in press). Consciencia e ideología: Reflexiones para la psicología social comunitaria [Conscience and ideology: Reflections for community–social psychology]. In I. Serrano-García, M. Figueróa, & D. Pérez Jiménez (Eds.), *Contribuciones Puertoriqueñas a la psicología Social-Comunitaria II*. San Juan, Puerto Rico: Editorial Universitaria.

Park, P. (1993). What is participatory research? A theoretical and methodological perspective. In P. Park, M. Brydon-Miller, B. Hall, & T. Jackson (Eds.), *Voices of change: Participatory research in the United States and Canada* (pp. 1–19). Wesport: CT: Bergin & Garvey.

Phillips-Tewey, B. (1997). *Building participatory action research partnerships in disability and rehabilitation research*. Washington, DC: U.S. Department of Education, National Institute on Disability and Rehabilitation Research.

Prilleltensky, I. (1994). *The morals and politics of psychology: Psychological discourse and the status quo*. Albany: State University of New York Press.

Reason, P., & Bradbury, H. (2001). *Handbook of action research: Participative inquiry and practice*. London: Sage.

Selener, D. (1997). *Participatory action research and social change*. Ithaca, NY: Cornell Participatory Action Research Network, Cornell University.

Social Security Ruling 99-2p. (1999). Titles II and XVI: Evaluating cases involving chronic fatigue syndrome (CFS). Social Security Administration. Notice of Social Security ruling. *Federal Register, 64,* 23380–23384.

Tandon, S. D. (1998). *Participatory action research: A viable methodology for social science research*. Unpublished manuscript, University of Illinois at Chicago.

Tandon, S. D., Kelly, J. G., & Mock, L. D. (2001). Participatory action research as a resource for developing African American community leadership. In D. L. Tolman & M. Brydon-Miller (Eds.), *From subjects to subjectivities: A handbook of interpretive and participatory methods* (pp. 200–217). New York: New York University Press.

Taylor, R. R., Friedberg, F., & Jason, L. A. (2001). *A clinician's guide to controversial illnesses: Chronic fatigue syndrome, fibromyalgia, and multiple chemical sensitivities*. Sarasota, FL: Professional Resource Press.

Taylor, R. R., & Jason, L. A. (2002). Group intervention involving a client with chronic fatigue syndrome. *Clinical Case Studies, 1,* 183–210.

Turnbull, A. P., & Friesen, B. J. (1995, April). *Forging collaborative partnerships with families in the study of disability*. Paper presented at the 1995 NIDRR conference on participatory action research, Washington, DC.

Wandersman, A., Chavis, D., & Stucky, P. (1983). Involving citizens in research. In R. Kidd & M. Saks (Eds.), *Advances in applied social psychology: Volume 2* (pp. 189–212). Hillsdale, NJ: Erlbaum.

Whyte, W. F. (1991). *Participatory action research*. Newbury Park, CA: Sage.

2

Community Development: Enhancing the Knowledge Base Through Participatory Action Research

Renée I. Boothroyd, Stephen B. Fawcett, and Pennie G. Foster-Fishman

Community development involves people who share a common place or experience working together to bring about community improvements that matter to them (Fawcett, 1999). Local people have been engaged in efforts to address a variety of concerns such as health (e.g., Duan, Fox, Derose, & Carson, 2000), the environment (e.g., McCauley, Beltran, Phillips, Lasarev, & Sticker, 2001), education (e.g., Dewees & Velazquez, 2000), economic self-sufficiency (e.g., Walsh, 1997), and power (e.g., Mandell, 2001). As both a process and an outcome (e.g., Foster-Fishman, Berkowitz, Lounsbury, Jacobson, & Allen, 2001; Roussos & Fawcett, 2000), community development approaches are widely acknowledged as a strategy for addressing complex dilemmas that matter to local communities (e.g., Dixon & Sindall, 1994; Ploeg et al., 1996; Sorensen, Emmons, Hunt, & Johnston, 1998).

In this age of accountability in science, community development (e.g., Hausman, 2002) joins other fields such as health promotion (e.g., Rimer, Glanz, & Rasband, 2001; Tones, 1997) and medicine (e.g., Sackett, 1989) in the debate on the importance and role of evidence to improve research and practice. Information supporting conclusions, especially scientific evidence, suggests a basis in causality and proof (McQueen & Anderson, 2001). Traditionally, evidence-based assessments are formal inquiries that use experimental arrangements to determine causality, often considering the randomized controlled trial as

The authors wish to thank Yolanda Suarez-Balcazar, who graciously facilitated our involvement in the Second Chicago Conference on Community Research. This chapter is based on Ms. Boothroyd's review paper, written in partial fulfillment of her PhD in Child and Developmental Psychology at the University of Kansas. We are grateful to others who helped us consider these issues, including Kathleen Stratton and David Butler with the Institute of Medicine at the National Academy of Sciences, Adrienne Paine-Andrews with the School-Community Sexual Risk Reduction Initiative funded by the Kansas Health Foundation, and our colleagues at the Work Group on Health Promotion and Community Development at the University of Kansas.

the most suitable design for supporting conclusions. Community development uses a mix of approaches to assess evidence of effectiveness and appropriateness along a continuum of the work—from community-building processes that engage local people, to intermediate outcomes such as changes in the environment facilitated by community efforts, to more distant population-level outcomes. Recognizing differences in context, evidence in community development may come from highly controlled community trials (e.g., Perry et al., 2002), time series analyses (e.g., Holder et al., 2000), and empirical case studies (e.g., Lane & Henry, 2001). Similarly, the social significance or urgency of community concerns such as poverty, violence, or child well-being, as well as local experience in addressing these and other critical issues, adds to what supports conclusions about what works in community development. Given the complexity and variety of community development efforts, a functional evidence base must optimize the potentially conflicting goals of contributing to understanding through rigorous scientific methods and improving practice that is responsive to the complex and dynamic contexts of communities (e.g., Biglan, Ary, & Wagenaar, 2000; Judd, Frankish, & Moulton, 2001; Tones, 1997).

What do we count as evidence in community development? How can we amass and organize a knowledge base for colearning and improvements in research and practice? Community-determined efforts and their contexts do not lend themselves easily to experimenter-determined trials of efficacy. Accordingly, the traditional science-based approach cannot be the sole source of evidence for advancing community development. This chapter outlines a framework for a knowledge base that attempts to account for both scientific and significance assessments of evidence. A knowledge base for community development should attend to the needs of community members, funders, researchers, and practitioners who seek support for conclusions about how to take action, allocate funds, solve problems, and make informed decisions for understanding and improvement. It should rest on evidence that is based on contextually appropriate science *and* experience, suggesting a balance between rigor and relevance (e.g., Fawcett, 1991b). As such, this chapter draws on community development literature to describe conclusions and recommendations for research and practice across the continuum of community development work, and suggests approaches to enhance the knowledge base using multiple sources and ways of knowing.

A Framework for Enhancing the Knowledge Base in Community Development

As Figure 2.1 suggests, community development work occurs along a continuum of community engagement in planning and action for change, where local people create environments to improve outcomes that matter to them (e.g., Christenson & Robinson, 1989; Fawcett, Paine, Francisco, & Vliet, 1993; Rothman, 1999). Accordingly, a search for evidence in community development may be better served by an inclusive review of studies that explore a range of questions and sources of knowledge related to (a) process, such as how community members are involved in problem setting and taking action; (b) intermedi-

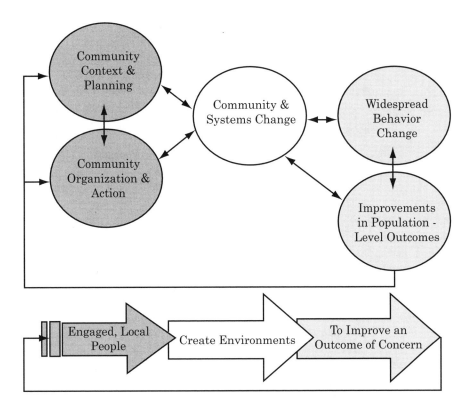

Figure 2.1. A framework of community engagement to create environments to improve an outcome of concern.

ate outcome, such as whether the group facilitates changes in the environment (i.e., programs, policies, and practices related to its goals), and how important these changes are to address their shared mission; and (c) more distant outcomes, such as whether the effort made a difference in widespread behavior change or improvements in population-level outcomes. To address the breadth of the field's interests, from community involvement and participation to community change and improvement, a knowledge base must draw on evidence from both research and practice.

A comprehensive assessment of evidence in community development may need to expand beyond sole reliance on a positivistic paradigm that focuses exclusively on scientific control and causality. For some questions, such as the mechanisms of brain functioning, controlled laboratory conditions may provide a suitable context for discovery. However, the complex, dynamic contexts of community development efforts do not present conditions in which it is either possible or appropriate to maximize experimental control arranged by outside professionals. The nature of community development, where local people are actively engaged in the effort rather than passive subjects, calls for more participatory approaches to research and action (e.g., Fawcett et al., in press; Fawcett, Schultz, Carson, Renault, & Francisco, 2003). This involves extending the "proof game," with its requirements for more levels of experimental control, to include a "plausibility game" that recognizes the value of knowledge derived from experience in less controlled but more ecologically valid contexts (Baer, 1985; Fawcett, 1991b). In this expanded view, both research and experiential knowledge aid in the illumination of community development (Biglan et al., 2000), helping to shed light on how, and perhaps why, desirable changes happen in communities. By recognizing the limitations of a strict focus on proof in community development research to identify and strengthen what is working, we can be open to a more judicial review of evidence (Tones, 1997).

Figure 2.2 presents a framework for advancing the knowledge base in community development that reflects (a) a broader view of evidence based on both scientific and significance assessments, (b) conclusions about what works and conditions required for it to work, and (c) recommendations for improvements in both research and practices. This framework is adapted from a similar approach used in other contexts by the Institute of Medicine of the National Academy of Sciences (Stratton, Wilson, & McCormick, 2002). Two primary sources contribute to the evidence base for community development: research knowledge and experiential knowledge. In dialogue among community scientists and practitioners, we draw conclusions about causal relationships between inputs and outputs (scientific assessment) and the significance of community-determined issues, actions, and accomplishments (significance assessment). Considering the continuum of community development work along aspects of process, intermediate outcome, and more distant outcomes, as well as the field's emphases on community involvement and participation, an integrated and more inclusive assessment of evidence about community development work can contribute to recommendations for improvement in research and practice. Thus, a more complete and evolving knowledge base for community development can help give voice to community concerns and promote adoption of promising approaches for sustainable change and improvement (Judd, Frankish, & Moulton, 2001; Sorensen et al., 1998).

A View of Evidence in Community Development

A first step toward developing an integrated knowledge base in community development is to review the scientific and significance assessments of work in community development. Community development research examines a range of concerns such as health promotion and disease prevention, child and youth development, and urban and rural development. Most interventions include community mobilization as one of several components for change and involve local people to varying degrees in program planning, implementation, and evaluation. Typically, community development interventions use one or more of the following strategies for widespread behavior change: (a) providing information and enhancing skills (i.e., telephone counseling sessions, mass media campaigns); (b) enhancing services and support (i.e., expanded health screening services); (c) modifying access, barriers, and opportunities (e.g., reducing the effort to vote); (d) changing consequences for behavior (i.e., increasing social recognition for community involvement); (e) and modifying policies (i.e., passing local ordinances to restrict selling alcohol). In addition, the purpose

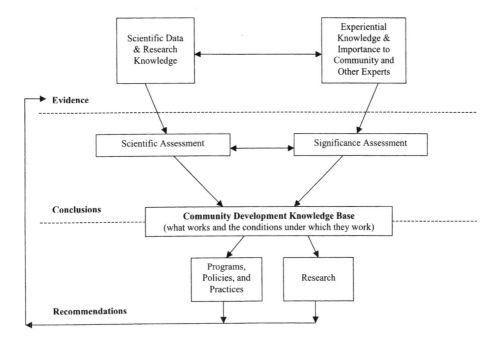

Figure 2.2. A framework for enhancing the knowledge base in community development. From *Immunization Safety Review: Multiple Immunizations and Immune Dysfunction* (p. 26), by K. Stratton, C. B. Wilson, and M. C. McCormick (Eds.), 2002, Washington, DC: Immunization Safety Review Committee, Board on Health Promotion and Disease Prevention, National Academies Press. Adapted with permission.

of and support for community development efforts vary, including those originating as community-based projects, formal research programs, or indigenous grassroots efforts.

Scientific Assessment

The primary goal of a scientific assessment is to determine evidence of causality or the strength of an association between an intervention and outcome of interest. A variety of factors such as study design, measurement issues, and duration and intensity of the intervention can influence a determination of causality or association. Although several evidence frameworks (e.g., McQueen & Anderson, 2001; Rimer et al., 2001) stress the primacy of the randomized trial design to assess cause and effect, few community development studies meet experimental control conditions necessary for determining causal evidence (e.g., Hancock et al., 1997). Many outcome studies use some type of experimental or quasi-experimental design to evaluate the effects of community development approaches on indicators of change and improvement. The pressing needs of communities, complexity of community development efforts, and dynamic conditions of communities often challenge a study's ability to determine causality. Yet, with a broader view of sources of evidence, there can be ample opportunity for determining the strength of an association between a range of community development interventions and related outcomes. As such, use of a more composite framework of evidence that goes beyond sole reliance on the randomized trial (e.g., Biglan et al., 2000; Dixon & Sindall, 1994; Judd et al., 2001; Tones, 1997; *Veterans and Agent Orange,* 1994) can enhance opportunities for colearning from a greater diversity of community development work.

Following scientific assessment standards from the National Academy of Sciences (e.g., *Veterans and Agent Orange,* 1994), evidence of causality can be classified along a continuum: strong, limited, insufficient to determine an association, and suggestive of no association. For example, some research provides strong evidence of a positive association between exposure to a community development intervention and related outcome in studies where chance, bias, and confounding can be ruled out with reasonable confidence (e.g., Biglan et al., 1996; Forster et al., 1998; Holder et al., 2000; Perry et al., 2002; Wagenaar et al., 2000). Many of these studies used randomization, matched communities, repeated measures, extensive study periods, and triangulation of measures to address threats to internal validity and enhance believability of findings. Yet, outcome evaluations with strong evidence of associations were often characterized by researcher (not community) control of the design and implementation of the intervention. Although such research arrangements served to strengthen the integrity of the independent variable, they are more community-based than community-controlled, thereby a less valid test of true community development approaches. In other cases, especially research with multiple communities and a mixture of contexts such as local leadership and political climates, it was often difficult to explicate the exact components of the independent variable as well as the relevant contextual features that may affect an association. Accordingly, drawing conclusions based on grouping communities that experienced a range of heterogeneous interventions into one set of analyses may result in misleading recommendations for practice.

Some other studies found limited evidence (e.g., Earp et al., 2002; Fawcett et al., 1997; Grossman, Walker, Kotloff, & Pepper, 2001) of an association through quasi-experimental designs that partially, but not fully, ruled out chance, bias, and confounding. Some studies used strong designs such as randomized trials and interrupted time series designs to evaluate evidence, yet confounds could not be ruled out because of limited comparisons and inconsistent measurements. In some cases, studies relied predominantly on self-reported behaviors, and failed to strengthen the validity of behavior changes by triangulating these results with other forms of measurement (i.e., assessing rates of breast cancer screening using interviews as well as medical records). Others found insufficient evidence (e.g., Duan et al., 2000; Higginbotham, Heading, McElduff, Dobson, & Heller, 1999; Lane & Henry, 2001) of an association when community studies were of insufficient quantity, quality, consistency, or depth to permit a conclusion regarding the presence or absence of an association. In such cases, detection of an effect were compromised because of short study periods, lack of intensity of the independent variable, the use of indicators that were not sensitive or representative of the changes sought by the intervention, or contamination of the independent variable into comparison communities.

Some studies with limited or insufficient evidence of an association may have had adequate measures of the process of community involvement and action, or even intermediate outcomes such as environmental change, but lacked evidence of improvement in behaviors or population-level outcomes. Yet, they may extend our understanding of context or community competence or capacity as potential early markers of a community's ability to come together to create environments supportive of improvement (e.g., Eng & Parker, 1994). Some of these studies used case study designs to identify and take inventory of conditions such as facilitating and impeding factors related to success in environmental change and outcome. Other studies used stakeholder interviews and community surveys to provide preliminary information regarding the level of the problem, extent of community involvement and leadership, and even culturally relevant and appropriate features necessary for developing interventions for optimal reach, effectiveness, and intensity; for instance, one preliminary study explored preventing pesticide exposure for non–English-speaking children of migrant farm workers (McCauley, Beltran, Phillips, Lasarev, & Sticker, 2001). Although findings from these studies do not clearly identify causality, they suggest elements that may be critical in the community action chain of events that contribute to subsequent community change and improvement.

In some cases, despite attempts to incorporate strong research designs, conclusions drawn from community development studies suggested evidence of *no* association (e.g., Cheadle et al., 2001; Hancock et al., 2001; Wagner et al., 2000). Evidence from several adequate studies showed mutually consistent findings of no positive association between exposure to a specific intervention and an outcome. Note that a conclusion of no association is inevitably limited to the specific conditions, levels of intensity of the intervention, and levels of exposure to it. Despite the use of strong experimental designs, failure to demonstrate an association was perhaps related to insufficient study periods required to produce and observe results, lack of statistical power, measurement and detection problems, limited strength and intensity of the intervention, and exposure to this and other interventions in comparison communities. In some cases, evidence of no association was perhaps the direct result of a selection confound. For example, nonawarded grant applicants can become "control" communities. The control communities' interest and commitment to change might have led to the implementation of various activities designed to address the problem, making detection of a true effect in the "experimental" communities impossible.

Scientific assessments focus on evidence of an independent variable and improvements in behavioral and population-level outcomes. Yet, as Figure 2.1 suggests, a range of evaluation questions are required to be representative of the various phases of community development efforts. Because community development includes the process of engagement of local people in community-determined efforts, there is often a tension in a search for evidence between demands for internal validity, evidence that the intervention and not something else caused the results, and external validity, a likelihood that the effects would generalize to typical contexts for community development. As such, scientific assessments may tell us "what works" in experimentally contrived situations, but say little about the efficacy of an intervention in the natural context of local people working together to change environments and improve outcomes.

Significance Assessment

The issue of significance—the social validity of goals, procedures, and outcomes—is a critical and necessary dimension for determining effectiveness and the value of community development efforts (Fawcett, 1991a). The perspective of community residents and other experts is critical for a knowledge base in community development that builds on community culture and strengths to develop and test locally determined interventions that are responsive to community concerns. Some community development efforts, such as an advocacy effort to enhance access to decent jobs and housing, spring from community passions that are often less prescribed or systematic than those externally designed and often categorical programs such as for increasing immunizations or reducing risks for cardiovascular disease. In these and other cases, the experience of community members and practitioners are a significant source of knowledge for understanding, planning, implementing, and learning from community development interventions.

Using methods of a social validity assessment (Fawcett, 1991a), we can assess—from the perspective of community members and other experts—the relative importance of community goals, the social acceptability of community interventions, and the social significance of effects produced by such efforts. This information may be reported in process evaluations of community development efforts; for instance, some community development studies assess community satisfaction with leadership and the importance of accomplishments facilitated by the community development effort (e.g., Lane & Henry, 2001; Paine-Andrews et al., 2002). Others may document the lack of community interest in and support for the problem and proposed solution, even to the point of actively resisting the intervention (e.g., Higginbotham et al., 1999). In these examples of participatory action research (PAR), community members were involved in defining the problem, determining and implementing strategies to address it, and evaluating results. Efforts to assess the value of community planning and action and the changes it facilitates can strengthen the bridge forward for making inferences that "community development"—its process *and* outcomes—actually occurred.

Community residents are the primary stakeholders in changing community behavior, and their experiential knowledge can contribute to conclusions and recommendations to advance a knowledge base for colearning and improvements. When community development interventions recognize the community as a vehicle for change, not just the site for an intervention (e.g., Wagenaar et al., 2000), they test the effects of community activation, not just that of a single externally controlled intervention strategy or activity. For example, community members are often involved in developing asset and needs maps to prioritize issues and concerns and participate in opportunities to name and frame the shared goals as well as design and implement strategies for intervention (i.e., Perry et al., 2000). Through community engagement and influence, interventions are adapted to fit the local context, analysis of the problem, and shared indicators of success (e.g., Dewees & Velazquez, 2000; Eng & Parker, 1994). In these cases, effects are not merely the result of an externally controlled intervention, but rather the unfolding of environmental change and related outcomes appropriate to the community context.

An important question of a community development intervention relates to how and under what conditions it worked, rather than simply a summative judgment about whether it worked. Community development takes place in diverse, dynamic, and complex community contexts, and these layers of influence and sometimes-competing expectations can affect the strength and stability of change efforts. Maintenance of procedures and effects, as well as prospects for generalization and replication, are often difficult to discern based on scientific assessments alone, and assessments of significance by community and outside experts can contribute to building the knowledge base.

In many community development studies, the inclusion of homogeneous communities with similar geography and ethnicity limited conclusions about the external validity and generalizability of positive findings (e.g., Higginbotham et al., 1999). Other studies examined the stability of any positive effects, reporting loss of effects on completion of projects or maintenance of certain program components on securing additional funding (Wagenaar et al., 2000). A few studies examined the costs and benefits related to addressing local concerns and building capacities through community development interventions (Biglan et al., 1996; Fawcett et al., 1997), many stressing the impracticality, inefficiency, and inadequacy of the randomized trial design as a vehicle for identifying principles about variables that influence community practices. A significance assessment—of contextual issues, social validation from community members and other experts, and aspects of sustainability such as practicality, feasibility, and adaptability—can provide valuable information to support conclusions about what works and the conditions under which they work.

Taken together, significance assessments, when coupled with scientific evidence, can aid in conclusions about the overall "value added" by a community development effort. Such information can help guide efforts to bring about change that matters to real communities with real problems and goals. Informed by both science and community experience, a knowledge base can help advance research and practice in community development.

Case Study: Knowledge From Community Mobilization to Prevent Teenage Pregnancy

Consider the knowledge contributed from a case study, a school–community effort to reduce risks for adolescent pregnancy. Based on earlier work in South Carolina (Koo, Dunteman, George, Green, & Vincent, 1994; Vincent, Clearie, & Schluchter, 1987), three communities in Kansas participated in a three-year effort to mobilize a community response to create environments supportive of healthy youth behaviors to reduce risks for adolescent pregnancy. Community coalitions and task forces made up of diverse sets of community partners worked to bring about environmental changes such as new peer education and support programs, enhanced mass media and prevention awareness campaigns, improved access to health services and contraceptives for youth, and modified policies such as adopting a revised human growth and development curricula for grades kindergarten through 12 (Paine-Andrews et al., 1999).

Scientific Assessment

A scientific assessment revealed limited evidence of an association between a multicomponent community mobilization effort to reduce risk for adolescent pregnancy and resulting changes in birth rates for teenage girls in selected areas (Paine-Andrews et al., 2002). A multiple time series design was used with three intervention and three matched comparison communities, and improvements in reported sexual behaviors and estimated pregnancy rates for ages 14 to 17 were observed with slight increases noted in comparison counties. Additional analyses enhanced the believability of results by analyzing the contribution of environmental changes to changes in birth rates. When the distribution of community changes (i.e., new programs, policies, and practices) were examined by zip code for an urban community, lower birth rates were found in a target neighborhood with enhanced exposure to and intensity of the intervention compared to higher birth rates in an adjacent neighborhood with limited exposure (Paine-Andrews et al., 2002). This analysis shed light on aspects of the dose–response relationship and strengthened inferences about an association between the community-developed intervention and changes in behavior and population-health outcomes related to the mission. In this dynamic context of a gradually unfolding intervention, this analysis suggested the value and appropriateness of understanding the contribution (rather than attribution) of locally determined environmental change to population-level improvements.

Significance Assessment

An example of PAR, the School–Community initiative is also a case study of community leadership and involvement to build capacity and create and maintain environments to support lasting change in local communities. Efforts to understand what was significant and appropriate included focus groups, surveys, and dialogue among local action teams and community leaders. Community members and agents learned and contributed to understanding about the project's planning, implementation, and evaluation: (a) lack of peer support and access to contraceptives are critical aspects of the problem of adolescent pregnancy; (b) school curricula enhancements and teacher training in sexuality education methods are critical elements of the intervention; and (c) enhanced health department clinic hours and the provision of incentives such as graduate credit hours for teachers to participate in sexuality education workshops are highly relevant and significant environmental changes for addressing the project mission. Through participation and leadership in local evaluation efforts, project staff and community partners (a) identified schools as an important place to begin intervening, (b) clarified staff and the project's capacity-building roles in relationship to other community-based partners who were predominantly service providers, (c) regularly revised local action plans to attend to making contraceptives available confidentially in rural areas, and (d) addressed competing interests and shrinking county budgets to garner public support and local funding to sustain project efforts past the initial period of grant funding (Paine-Andrews et al., 1999). Community constituents concluded that involvement from a variety of community sectors is required across phases of the project to create an effective and lasting community response to teenage pregnancy prevention.

Emerging Knowledge Base and Recommendations

In this case study of PAR, community members were actively involved in both scientific and significance assessments of evidence. They were engaged in the planning, implementation, and evaluation of this community development intervention to reduce adolescent pregnancy, drawing on their knowledge of the local context. Outside researchers led efforts to draw scientific conclusions about the strength of association between the community development effort and observed changes in behaviors and population-health outcomes. Significance assessments were obtained from community members about the importance of the broad goals and specific changes to be sought, satisfaction with leadership and other aspects of the intervention, and the importance of the environmental changes actually brought about (intermediate outcomes) to the mission of reducing risk for teenage pregnancy. In addition, structured dialogues with community members and outside researchers about the results and their meaning were used to help integrate scientific and significance assessments regarding conclusions to be drawn about this work. Taken together, the information that emerged helps shed light on the "value added" of this intervention and suggests an emerging knowledge base and recommendations for improving research and practice.

First, in dynamic and complex community contexts, rigorous evaluations of process and intermediate outcomes can help document the unfolding of the intervention and examine its possible associations with more distant population-health outcomes. Community members such as leaders of the School–Community initiative can play a vital role in documenting the development of a community development intervention in its particular social and political contexts. Second, in studies with multiple communities, threats to the consistent implementation of the independent variable can be minimized by specifying intervention components such as sexuality education and access to contraceptives that are shared across communities. Although maintaining consistent components, intervention elements, such as the type of sexuality education or ways to enhance access, can be adapted to become situationally specific to particular community needs, assets, and values. Maintaining core components and minimal levels of implementation can help ensure the relatively consistent implementation or integrity of the independent variable across study communities. Third, community development efforts may benefit from longer study periods to examine the sustainability of environmental changes and related effects. Additional research is also needed to better understand the conditions under which community-determined environmental changes are associated with improvements in more distant population-health outcomes (Paine-Andrews et al., 2002; Roussos & Fawcett, 2000).

Community members, through their experience with the planning, implementation, and evaluation of this School–Community initiative, contributed several recommendations for improving practice in community development (Paine-Andrews, Fisher, Campuzano, Fawcett, & Berkley-Patton, 2000; Paine-Andrews et al., 1999). First, because the political and social contexts of communities vary, it may be critical to consider the readiness or supportive characteristics of a lead agency when selecting a community administrator for a research study or grant award. For example, although a school district may be better able to negotiate adoption of a sexuality education curriculum in public schools, a county health department may be better positioned to enhance preventive health services and access to contraceptives. Second, community leaders often play multiple roles in community development initiatives such as grant administrator, supervisor, trainer, and documenter of the community change effort. To make evaluation easier and more rewarding, a documentation system needs to be flexible to busy schedules and responsive to real-time needs of community members for accessible and useable data reports. Ongoing efforts to improve documentation and sense making in community development initiatives need to focus on making participatory research easier and more rewarding (e.g., Fawcettet al., 2003).

Third, community members contributed several recommendations for addressing implementation barriers and promoting sustainability of promising practices for preventing adolescent pregnancy (Paine-Andrews, Fisher, Campuzano, et al., 2000; Paine-Andrews, Fisher, Harris, et al., 2000). In particular, through a series of interviews and focus groups, they suggested that (a) local initiatives address a broader mission, such as that of adolescent health and development, to overcome some of the political and moral debates surrounding the issue of teenage pregnancy prevention; (b) community members be actively involved in gathering information and providing feedback to promote progress toward objectives and inform local decision making; and (c) community initiatives should be careful not to become too staff-driven and should take time to nurture community members as "champions of community change" to help foster broad ownership of the initiative for lasting environmental change and improvement.

Conclusion

Community development efforts offer tremendous opportunities for integrating multiple sources of evidence to generate a knowledge base that helps to advance the field. Through collaboration in fact-finding, action, and reflection, local people and outside researchers can contribute to and strengthen the coproduction of information for a knowledge base for community development. By giving voice to the experience of community members and researchers, an inclusive assessment of evidence in community development can help develop a more complete and evolving knowledge base about community-determined change efforts.

Considering the continuum of community development, from the process of local engagement and community-building to environmental change to improvements in population-level outcomes, a knowledge base for community development efforts should attend to a range of evaluation questions. Appreciation for the rigors of science and sensitivity to community context do not have to be framed as a dichotomy of expert knowledge versus community experience. By integrating scientific and significance assessments of evidence, we can build a bridge between traditional scientific and experiential knowledge. The resulting knowledge base for community development will help select for what works while giving voice to community partners in determining what matters.

The inclusive review of evidence in this chapter draws on and is limited to work in community development that has been published. Because many professional journals often use only scientific assessments to judge value, the literature offers a biased and inadequate sample of the value-added by community development efforts. To help advance the knowledge base in community development, we should clarify and disseminate criteria for significance assessments for use by community members, practitioners, researchers, grant makers, and journal editors. These criteria can be used to extend available information about evidence in community development efforts. As data on significance assessments becomes more available and systematic, we can examine how they can best be integrated with scientific assessments to bring together a more complete basis for guiding research and practice.

Development of a contextually appropriate knowledge base also requires continued dialogue and colearning among outside researchers, community members, and practitioners. First, we should make it easier for community members to collaborate with outside researchers in selecting research questions and methods, developing frameworks for intervention, and producing, interpreting, and applying findings. Longer term engagements with communities can build local capacity for using a wide range of research methods, including epidemiological, experimental, survey research, focus group, and qualitative interviews. These can be used by and with local collaborators to generate knowledge, assess evidence, and determine conclusions.

Second, no hierarchy of methods exists. Rather, the choice of methods depends on the questions to be addressed, the knowledge being sought, and the feasibility of particular methods in local circumstances. Third, given the importance of understanding the process of community-determined efforts a knowledge base would benefit from clearer guidelines about how to systematically gather, interpret, and integrate information for use in drawing conclusions and making recommendations for research and practice. Fourth, the practice of community development and PAR should make community involvement in the coproduction of knowledge more rewarding. For example, community collaborators should be involved more consistently as paid documenters and as coauthors of manuscripts and other reports that describe research findings. Fifth, as the knowledge base for community development emerges, additional efforts are needed to enhance its refinement and use by researchers and practitioners working with a variety of locally determined issues in diverse communities.

Knowledge building involves recognizing the important attributes of something, such as the work of community-determined change and improvement. We acknowledge its important features through both systematic investigation (science) and actual acquaintance (experience). By integrating evidence from both science and community experience, we can advance our understanding of what matters, what works, and the conditions under which they work. Through colearning and action, as outside researchers and local experts, we can better recognize and improve how people work together to affect conditions and outcomes that matter.

References

Baer, D. M. (1985). Comment on Denkowski and Denkowski: Community-based residential treatment of the mentally retarded adolescent offender. *Journal of Community Psychology, 13,* 306–307.

Biglan, A., Ary, D., Koehn, V., Levings, D., Smith, S., et al. (1996). Mobilizing positive reinforcement in communities to reduce youth access to tobacco. *American Journal of Community Psychology, 24,* 625–639.

Biglan, A., Ary, D., & Wagenaar, A. C. (2000). The value of interrupted time-series experiments for community intervention research. *Prevention Science, 1,* 31–49.

Cheadle, A., Wagner, E., Walls, M., Diehr, P., Bell, M., et al. (2001). The effect of neighborhood-based community organizing: Results from the Seattle Minority Youth Health Project. *Health Services Research, 36,* 671–689.

Christenson, J. A., & Robinson, J. W. (1989). *Community development in perspective.* Ames: Iowa State University Press.

Dewees, S., & Velazquez, J. A. (2000). Community development in rural Texas: A case study of Balmorhea public schools. *Journal of Community Development Society, 31,* 216–231.

Dixon, J., & Sindall, C. (1994). Applying logics of change to the evaluation of community development in health promotion. *Health Promotion International, 9,* 297–309.

Duan, N., Fox, S. A., Derose, K. P., & Carson, S. (2000). Maintaining mammography adherence through telephone counseling. *American Journal of Public Health, 90,* 1468–1471.

Earp, J. A., Eng, E., O'Malley, M. S., Altpeter, M., Rauscher, G., et al. (2002). Increasing use of mammography among older, rural African American women: Results from a community trial. *American Journal of Public Health, 92,* 646–654.

Eng, E., & Parker, E. (1994). Measuring community competence in Mississippi Delta: Interface between program evaluation, empowerment. *Health Education Quarterly, 21,* 199–220.

Fawcett, S. B. (1991a). Social validity: A note on methodology. *Journal of Applied Behavior Analysis, 24,* 235–239.

Fawcett, S. B. (1991b). Some values guiding community research and action. *Journal of Applied Behavior Analysis, 24,* 621–636.

Fawcett, S. B. (1999). Some lessons on community organization and change. In J. Rothman (Ed.), *Reflections on community organization: Enduring themes and critical issues* (pp. 314–334). Itasca, IL: F.E. Peacock.

Fawcett, S. B., Boothroyd, R. I., Schultz, J. A., Francisco, V. T., Carson, V., et al. (in press). Building capacity for participatory evaluation within community initiatives. *Journal of Prevention and Intervention in the Community.*

Fawcett, S. B., Lewis, R. K., Paine-Andrews, A., Francisco, V. T., Richter, K. P., et al. (1997). Evaluating community coalitions for prevention of substance abuse: The case of Project Freedom. *Health Education and Behavior, 24,* 812–828.

Fawcett, S. B., Paine, A. L., Francisco, V. T., & Vliet, M. (1993). Promoting health through community development. In D. S. Glenwick & L. A. Jason (Eds.), *Promoting health and mental health in children, youth, and families* (pp. 233–255). New York: Springer.

Fawcett, S. B., Schultz, J. A., Carson, V. L., Renault, V. A., & Francisco, V. T. (2003). Using Internet-based tools to build capacity for community-based participatory research and other efforts to promote community health and development. In M. Minkler & N. Wallerstein (Eds.), *Community-based participatory research for health* (pp. 155–178). San Francisco: Jossey-Bass.

Forster, J. L., Murray, D. M., Wolfson, M., Blaine, T. M., Wagenaar, A. C., et al. (1998). The effects of community policies to reduce youth access to tobacco. *American Journal of Public Health, 88,* 1193–1198.

Foster-Fishman, P. G., Berkowitz, S. L., Lounsbury, D. W., Jacobson, S., & Allen, N. A. (2001). Building collaborative capacity in community coalitions: A review and integrative framework. *American Journal of Community Psychology, 29,* 241–261.

Grossman, J. B., Walker, K. E., Kotloff, L. J., & Pepper, S. (2001). *Adult communication and teen sex: Changing a community.* Philadelphia: Public/Private Ventures.

Hancock, L., Sanson-Fisher, R., Perkins, J., Girgis, A., Howley, P., et al. (2001). The effect of a community action intervention on adolescent smoking rates in rural Australian towns: The CART Project. *Preventive Medicine, 32,* 332–340.

Hancock, L., Sanson-Fisher, R. W., Redman, S., Burton, R., Butler, L., et al. (1997). Community action for health promotion: A review of methods and outcomes, 1990–1995. *American Journal of Preventive Medicine, 13,* 229–239.

Hausman, A. (2002). Implications of evidence-based practice for community health. *American Journal of Community Psychology, 30,* 453–467.

Higginbotham, N., Heading, G., McElduff, P., Dobson, A., & Heller, R. (1999). Reducing coronary heart disease in the Australian coalfields: Evaluation of a 10-year community intervention. *Social Science & Medicine, 48,* 683–692.

Holder, H. D., Gruenewald, P. J., Ponicki, W. R., Treno, A. J., Grube, J. W., et al. (2000). Effect of community-based interventions on high-risk drinking and alcohol-related injuries. *Journal of the American Medical Association, 284,* 2341–2347.

Judd, J., Frankish, C. J., & Moulton, G. (2001). Setting standards in the evaluation of community-based health promotion programmes—A unifying approach. *Health Promotion International, 16,* 367–380.

Koo, H. P., Dunteman, G. H., George, C., Green, Y., & Vincent, M. (1994). Reducing adolescent pregnancy through a school- and community-based intervention: Denmark, South Carolina, revisited. *Family Planning Perspectives, 26,* 206–211 & 217.

Lane, M., & Henry, K. (2001). Community development, crime and violence: A case study. *Community Development Journal, 36,* 212–222.

Mandell, M. P. (2001). Collaboration through network structures for community building efforts. *National Civic Review, 90,* 279–288.

McCauley, L. A., Beltran, M., Phillips, J., Lasarev, M., & Sticker, D. (2001). The Oregon migrant farm worker community: An evolving model for participatory research. *Environmental Health Perspectives, 109,* 449–455.

McQueen, D. V., & Anderson, L. M. (2001). What counts as evidence: Issues and debates. In I. Rootman (Ed.), *Evaluation in health promotion: Principles and perspectives* (pp. 63–81). Copenhagen, Denmark: World Health Organization.

Paine-Andrews, A., Fisher, J. L., Berkley-Patton, J., Fawcett, S. B., Williams, E. L., et al. (2002). Analyzing the contribution of community change to population health outcomes in an adolescent pregnancy prevention initiative. *Health Education and Behavior, 29,* 183–193.

Paine-Andrews, A., Fisher, J. L., Campuzano, M. K., Fawcett, S. B., & Berkley-Patton, J. (2000). Promoting sustainability of community health initiatives: An empirical case study. *Health Promotion Practice, 1,* 248–258.

Paine-Andrews, A., Fisher, J. L., Harris, K. J., Lewis, R. K., Williams, E. L., et al. (2000). Some experiential lessons in supporting and evaluating community-based initiatives for preventing adolescent pregnancy. *Health Promotion Practice, 1,* 66–76.

Paine-Andrews, A., Harris, K. J., Fisher, J. L., Lewis, R. K., Williams, E. L., et al. (1999). Effects of a replication of a school/community model for preventing adolescent pregnancy in three Kansas communities. *Family Planning Perspectives, 31,* 182–189.

Perry, C. L., Williams, C. L., Komro, K. A., Veblen-Mortenson, S., Forster, J., et al. (2000). Project Northland high school interventions: Community action to reduce adolescent alcohol use. *Health Education and Behavior, 27,* 29–49.

Perry, C. L., Williams, C. L., Komro, K. A., Veblen-Mortenson, S., Stigler, M. H., et al. (2002). Project Northland: Long-term outcomes of community action to reduce adolescent alcohol use. *Health Education and Research, 17,* 117–132.

Ploeg, J., Dobbins, M., Hayward, S., Ciliska, D., Thomas, H., et al. (1996). *Effectiveness of community development projects.* Retrieved May 16, 2002 from http://web.cche.net/ohcen/groups/hthu/95-5abs.htm

Rimer, B. K., Glanz, K., & Rasband, G. (2001). Searching for evidence about health education and health behavior interventions. *Health Education & Behavior, 28,* 231–248.

Rothman, J. (1999). *Reflections on community organization: Enduring themes and critical issues.* Itasca, IL: F.E. Peacock.

Roussos, S. T., & Fawcett, S. B. (2000). A review of collaborative partnerships as a strategy for improving community health. *Annual Review of Public Health, 21,* 369–402.

Sackett, D. L. (1989). Rules of evidence and clinical recommendations on the use of antithrombotic agents. *Chest, 95,* 2S–4S.

Sorensen, G., Emmons, K., Hunt, M. K., & Johnston, D. (1998). Implications of the results of community intervention trials. *Annual Review of Public Health, 19,* 379–416.

Stratton, K., Wilson, C. B., & McCormick, M. C. (Eds.). (2002). *Immunization safety review: Multiple immunizations and immune dysfunction.* Washington, DC: Immunization Safety Review Committee, Board on Health Promotion and Disease Prevention, National Academies Press.

Tones, K. (1997). Beyond the randomized controlled trial: A case for "judicial review." *Health Education Research, 12,* 1–4.

Veterans and agent orange: Committee review of the health effects on Vietnam veterans of exposure to herbicides. (1994). Washington, DC: Institutes of Medicine, National Academy of Sciences.

Vincent, M. L., Clearie, A. F., & Schluchter, M. D. (1987). Reducing adolescent pregnancy through school and community based education. *Journal of the American Medical Association, 257,* 3382–3386.

Wagenaar, A. C., Murray, D. M., Gehan, J. P., Wolfson, M., Forster, J. L., et al. (2000). Communities mobilizing for change on alcohol: Outcomes from a randomized community trial. *Journal of Studies on Alcohol, 61,* 85–94.

Wagner, E. H., Wickizer, T. M., Cheadle, A., Psaty, B. M., Koepsell, T. D., et al. (2000). The Kaiser Foundation Community Health Promotion Grants Program: Findings from an outcome evaluation. *Health Services Research, 35,* 561–581.

Walsh, J. (1997). Community building in theory and practice: Three case studies. *National Civic Review, 86,* 291–314.

3

Epidemiological Research: Science and Community Participation

Susan R. Torres-Harding, Richard Herrell, and Carole Howard

Community participatory research holds much promise in strengthening the validity of epidemiological research, and has recently emerged as an innovative strategy to address the limitations of traditional survey research methods. The involvement of community members has been crucial in the design and implementation of research investigating illnesses that are highly stigmatized and when investigating at-risk populations that cannot be reached using traditional recruitment methods. Community participatory research also has the potential to promote collaboration between researchers and community members, and to address the agendas, political motivations, and goals of each group. This chapter provides a discussion of the issues of community involvement and participation in epidemiological research. These concepts are illustrated in a case study describing a research study investigating the prevalence of a controversial illness, chronic fatigue syndrome.

Definitions, Goals, and Controversies in Epidemiology

The conventional definition of epidemiology is the study of the distribution and determinants of disease or injury in populations (Gordis, 2000; MacMahon & Trichopoulos, 1996). Textbooks typically distinguish clinical research on individual health and epidemiological research on population health. Most critical for understanding the purpose of epidemiological studies is the emphasis on using the *distribution* of diseases across categories of persons to make inferences about their *cause,* whether environmental or individual or some interaction between the two. A classic statement of the goal of an analytic epidemiological study comes from the text of Breslow and Day on case-control studies of cancer: The purpose of a study is to "provide a valid, and reasonably

The authors thank Leonard Jason for his important contributions to the CFS epidemiology research described in this chapter and his supportive encouragement in the development of this chapter. We also thank Stevan Hobfall for his insightful observations as a discussant at the community conference presentation. Financial support for the CFS epidemiology study described in this chapter was from NIAID grant number AI36295, for which Leonard Jason was the principal investigator.

precise, estimate of the strength of at least one hypothesized cause–effect relationship" (Breslow & Day, 1980). This statement can be easily generalized to include randomized control trials in which the *cause*—also typically called a *risk factor,* which in epidemiology is *any* characteristic that effects a change in the probability of developing disease—is an intervention such as a drug therapy or program of behavioral change. Similarly, descriptive epidemiology, which presents the distribution of disease by rates specific for demographic and social characteristics such as sex, age, and race, implicitly assumes that these characteristics are the imprecise beginnings of causal investigations.

Kenneth Rothman is prominent among those who emphasize that epidemiology is not an exercise in statistical hypothesis testing; rather it aims to measure the effect of exposures on diseases (Rothman, 2002). Typically this takes the form of relative measures (risks, rates, odds, hazards). In practice, these measures have two components: the best guess of the *magnitude* of the effect (the point estimate) and the *precision* of the estimate (usually given as the 95% confidence interval of the estimate). Epidemiology aims to quantify the occurrence of illness and to relate disease occurrence to characteristics of people and their environment.

Many questions arise as attempts are made to judge how well epidemiology fulfills this ideal. How do we judge the results of an epidemiological study? Is the association likely to be due to chance? Is the association likely to be due to bias? Is the association likely to be due to confounding? Many questions go to the heart of the goals of epidemiology: Was the right sample drawn? Can the results be generalized to the population of interest? Do the measures introduce systematic misclassification that will bias results? Did researchers fail to measure factors related to exposures and outcomes of interest that confound the association of primary interest?

The points in the chains of disease causation where epidemiology introduces measurement are at the center of lively, even contentious, debate between those advocating study of social factors in disease causation and those who focus primarily on genetic or molecular factors. Many argue that epidemiology is the science of proximate causes of diseases and that we should concern ourselves with infectious agents and industrial contaminants as they damage cells and organs or with alleles that cause or predispose to disease. Others draw attention to the health effects of poverty, racial discrimination, or access to local services as key components in the web of disease causation. Yet others advocate the study of all such effects, from cell to society, making opportunities for intervention to prevent disease the central priority (Susser & Susser, 1996a, 1996b). Indeed, although the single most important contribution of public health has been separating drinking water from sewerage, John Snow and his mid-19th-century contemporaries knew nothing about the bacterium that causes cholera when they demonstrated that contaminated water must cause the disease.

Social epidemiology has become a subdiscipline devoted to measuring and assessing the effects of contextual social variables, such as the role of family, neighborhood, community, and other social groups (Berkman & Kawachi 2000). New statistical methods (such as random effects models) can now estimate not only individual effects (e.g., hypertension and hyperlipidemia on heart disease) but also the effect of contextual variables, such as average neighborhood income or access to stores, on mortality rates.

Studying the role of the community presents certain ethical and practical challenges. However, community participation holds much promise in strengthening research designs by more accurately describing the population at risk for developing an illness and by identifying the actual community practices, prevention strategies, and resources around a particular disease. Using participation from the community being studied can assist researchers in determining whether the exposures and outcomes of interest are truly being measured. In fact, community-based participatory research has emerged as a central concern in public health literature (Green & Mercer, 2001).

To this end, the most basic and simple approach to community participation is simply consulting community leaders or representatives as the research is planned and executed. More formally, community advisory boards are now often constituted as part of the planning and execution of research protocols. Such boards may become the gatekeepers of information and the population. In some cases, formally established bodies, such as Indian tribal councils or formal tribal institutional review boards, may have legally binding precedence over other possible community groups. Open community meetings provide an opportunity to explain the research goals, recruit participants and research assistants, or present results. Community members may also be the best source of project employees, interviewers, service providers in the community, and ethnographic fieldworkers, especially in hard-to-reach populations, such as IV drug users or homeless individuals. One especially successful model is the use of indigenous outreach workers.

However, defining a community and its key stakeholders is often difficult and controversial. Selecting membership on community boards is not a simple question, and likely will entail many complex social and political relationships likely unknown to the researcher. A carelessly created board can seriously compromise how a sample is drawn and how data may be gathered. Relying solely on formal representatives or poorly chosen informal leaders may lead to inappropriate sampling and results with no known generalizability to the population of real interest. Established representatives are not likely to be uncontroversial in communities with histories of internal conflict, and strategies for representing the community in a statistical sense may become difficult. Further, many communities of interest in health research have no formal representation at all, such as poor, urban injecting drug users. For researchers, however, representing the disempowered is both scientifically and ethically imperative. Indeed, research designs must consider not only who is *representative of* a community—a sampling question—but also who *represents* a community in a political sense, both formally (such as tribal councils or urban community organizations) and informally. One is immediately forced to think about the core epidemiological problem of defining the numerators and denominators of rates: Who is at risk for disease? Who develops the disease among those at risk?

Sampling Considerations

Selecting a sampling plan may be the most important design decision for the epidemiologist. To make valid inferences about a population, every individual in a population of inference must have a known, nonzero probability of selection (Levy & Lemshow, 1999). Although sampling statisticians have developed extremely sophisticated techniques for drawing samples and estimating population parameters, getting the appropriate list to start with (of individuals, households, schools, hospitals, etc.) is not a simple task. If a poor sampling plan exists, systematic biases may exclude certain people. For instance, early prevalence rates of chronic fatigue syndrome were believed to be biased because they were conducted in hospitals, so that they likely excluded people of lower socioeconomic status and people of color who were less likely to have access to health care (Richman, Flaherty, & Rospenda, 1994).

Much survey sampling relies on the methods developed by Leslie Kish and others (Kish, 1965) that use the decennial U.S. Census as the list of households from which to start. However, the Census is frequently criticized for missing households, a failing that can be especially acute in poor neighborhoods where people are forced into living arrangement that may elude regulations. Another common technique is the use of random digit dialing where the list is made up of telephone exchanges provided by research companies.

In response to the limitations of these sampling techniques, researchers have begun to use innovative methods to draw samples from which one can more confidently make inferences about populations. Some of these involve active involvement of community representatives whose knowledge is critical to the sampling methodology. For example, a prevalence study of drug use in one Chicago neighborhood drew up its sampling frame using research assistants from the community who knew the residential patterns of the area that could more accurately represent the population of interest (O'Brien, Murray, Rahimian, & Wiebel, 1996). In one investigation into the prevalence of chronic fatigue syndrome (CFS), described later, different methods of contacting people with CFS were pilot-tested. Feedback from the participants themselves were then used to determine which methods might reach the most people with CFS, many of whom are house-bound and unreachable by conventional hospital sampling. A second example is venue sampling. This method has been used, for example, to sample young gay men who do not have a residential base that could be listed using standard approaches. Community members were recruited to draw up a list of places where people in a community gather, such as parks or bars from which research participants were systematically selected (MacKellar, Valleroy, Karon, Lemp, & Janseen, 1996). Still, although this technique can expand the variability in the sample, it remains unclear as to what population such a sample can be generalized.

Measures

In addition to accurate sampling, valid and reliable measurement is crucial for good epidemiological science. Often measures are chosen because they are well-known or standard; using unknown and untested measures may help ensure that results will remain unpublished. Measurement must attend simultaneously to the survey researcher's concerns with generalizability, cross-study comparison, and known sampling error as well as to the psychometrician's concern with measurement error and validity. Ideally, measures should be relatively brief and must efficiently measure constructs of interest. Each item on a survey must be carefully motivated.

Developing new measures is a daunting task requiring a validation component within the larger study. Community participation in the development and selection of measures is simultaneously essential and problematic. Understanding measure development is difficult for graduate students and professionals, and may be even more so for lay people without basic knowledge of test construction and issues of test administration, reliability, and validity. Conversely, a survey cannot usefully be turned into a list of items of what the community "wants to know."

However, in many other respects, community involvement is essential to the development and selection of measures. Focus groups and ethnographers have been critical in determining what questions to ask and how to ask them. Items in a measure must be acceptable to respondents in a general survey across subpopulations. It must be usable in different populations or results will not be comparable with other studies. When determining whether a measures is valid, questions arise regarding which criterion is used to judge the sensitivity and specificity of a measure. The basic methodological research to answer this question represents opportunities and pressing needs for collaboration among survey researchers, epidemiologists, interpretive social scientists, clinicians, and community members. The value of a study and the usefulness of its findings depend on the care with which new measures are constructed.

Although focus groups and ethnographic research are essential to the development of measures, assessing the psychometric properties of measures is no less dependent on choosing an appropriate sample than estimating a mean or proportion. Too often this stage of research is done on convenience samples. Measures tested in patient samples, for example, have poor reliability characteristics in general populations.

Ethnography in Observational Epidemiology

Many components of research design cannot easily incorporate community involvement. Nevertheless, ethnography has increasingly been used successfully in many others. In the old lingo of an earlier generation of anthropology, research participants were "native informants." Activism within and outside of anthropology (as well as other research fields) has highlighted the fundamentally unequal power relationships in research with humans. As a discipline, anthropology with its ethnographic method learned to explicitly incorporate community members as active coinvestigators along with project researchers to investigate what questions to ask, how to ask those questions, and how to interpret findings of quantitative analyses.

By comparison, epidemiology has been slow to rigorously study the members of the social categories that are routinely used as either control variables or as variables across whose levels we might find differential effects of exposure. Epidemiology too easily uses default categories that are implicitly of interest as risk factors, such as age, race, and sex. In contrast, ethnography can provide key information in research contexts as different as the difficult life of the intravenous drug user and the cross-cultural variability in experiencing and interpreting symptoms contributing to depression where the validity of disease entities has not been fully established. Kleinman, a medical anthropologist, cautions that a group of symptoms established in medicine as a valid diagnosis may not translate across cultures and thereby constitute a "category fallacy" (Kleinman & Good, 1985). Ethnographic methods may help elucidate the meaning of a collection of symptoms in a given culture and minimize the occurrence of this type of error.

In addition, the role of community political interests must be acknowledged. A recent cluster analysis aiming to describe community arrived at the following definition: "A group of people with diverse characteristics who are linked by social ties, share common perspectives, and engage in joint action in geographical locations or settings" (MacQueen et al., 2001). It seems, however, that this definition may overstate the importance of social and cultural ties and understate the role of political interests. Important activist movements appeared in the 1960s and 1970s devoted to changes in health care access and delivery. One of the first of these was the Haight-Ashbury Free Clinic, founded in 1967 by Dr. David E. Smith, premised on the belief that "health care is a right, not a privilege. We believe it should be free at the point of delivery, and it should be comprehensive, nonjudgmental, demystified, and humane" (Haight-Ashbury Free Clinic Inc. of San Francisco, California, n.d.). The Boston Women's Health Book Collective, a nonprofit, public interest women's health education, advocacy, and consulting organization began in 1970 with the publication of the influential *Our Bodies, Ourselves* (Boston Women's Health Book Collective, n.d.). About the same time gay men's health clinics were created in a similar spirit, such as Howard Brown in Chicago in 1974 (Howard Brown Health Center, n.d.). These clinics provided the base in turn for the testing of the HBV vaccine and subsequent research on AIDS therapies and behavioral aspects of HIV transmission.

These organizations led the way for the countless patient advocacy organizations one finds today that do not take the good will of the research establishment for granted. Acknowledgment of political agendas, as well as the history of what an organization has experienced when interacting with other researchers, is critically important, as researchers may need to address any concerns or suspicions the organization may have. Ideally, working together with an organization around these issues will help clarify how epidemiological research may serve to advance the goals and agendas of both the researchers and the community organization.

The use of community participation to address these issues has been particularly beneficial in investigating the illness chronic fatigue syndrome (CFS). In the next section, the collaboration between researchers at DePaul University and people within the CFS community to investigate the prevalence of illness will be presented. Specifically, the importance of accurate sampling, sensitive and valid methodology, and the implications of the research findings within the larger sociopolitical climate will be discussed.

The Case of Chronic Fatigue Syndrome

CFS is a controversial illness because the etiology is currently unknown, and large discrepancies exist in perceptions surrounding this illness among researchers, medical professionals, and individuals with CFS. Some medical professionals do not consider CFS to be a legitimate illness or believe it to be a variant of depressive disorder (Abbey & Garfinkel, 1991). Individuals with CFS often face disbelieving attitudes from physicians, family, and friends, in addition to the losses they experience as a consequence of this illness. In a series of studies conducted at DePaul University, including a prevalence study of CFS, community participation has been a key feature of the research team's investigations (Jason, 2001). The use of community participation addressed concerns with previous CFS research. The use of community participation placed the experiences of people with CFS in a sociocultural context, so that the meanings and illness experience of someone with CFS could be acknowledged, understood, and examined. Further, the experiences of people with this illness were used to inform the methodology and measures that are appropriate for use with people with CFS.

Notable in the social history of this illness are the large discrepancies between the perceptions of people within the CFS community and those of the medical research and professional community (Richman & Jason, 2001). Because some physicians and other medical professionals felt that the illness was either psychosomatic or psychiatric—not "real" or imaginary—individuals with CFS were often met with indifference, disbelief, or viewed as malingerers (Wessely, Hotopf, & Sharpe, 1998). Indeed, the delegitimazation of this illness by the medical health establishment, and the subsequent demoralization of people who had this illness, often led to a second victimization for people with this illness (Richman & Jason, 2001). The perspectives of people with CFS and the issues they espoused, like the illness itself, were trivialized, such that these individuals were viewed as lazy, neurotic, or in denial, and their participation in research advocacy or even in conducting research into this illness was viewed as suspect or biased. In response to what was perceived as mistreatment by the medical establishment and the perception that sufferers of this illness had an imaginary illness, self-help and patient advocacy groups were formed to work for improved focus on treatment and to help promote the view that this illness was in fact a legitimate medical condition. These patient groups advocated education of medical professionals and increased biomedical research into this illness (Richman & Jason, 2001).

Methodological issues, including accurate sampling and measurement, were at the heart of the debate between researchers and community members surrounding this illness. One of the basic issues under dispute was the prevalence of CFS. The Centers for Disease Control (CDC) had initially estimated that the prevalence of this illness was 2 to 7.3 persons per 100,000. This estimate was derived from a study conducted in four U.S. cities where physicians identified patients who had unexplained fatigue-related symptoms, and then referred those patients to the study to determine whether they met criteria for CFS (Gunn, Connell, & Randall, 1993). Using data from this and similar

prevalence studies, the CDC published a brochure about this illness that estimated the prevalence of CFS to be 4 to 10 per 100,000 people in the United
States (Centers for Disease Control and Prevention, 1994). If these estimates
were correct, that would have indicated that there were only 20,000 individuals
with CFS in the United States. Subsequently, the perception that CFS was
a relatively uncommon disorder was used to justify not allocating financial
resources for research and treatment (Jason, 2001). These low prevalence numbers, however, contrasted sharply with the interest expressed in information
about this disorder. For example, the high rates of telephone calls to the CDC
seeking information about this illness, up to 3,000 per month, suggested that
this disorder might have been more common than had been reported (Mc-
Cluskey, 1993, p. 288).

Concerns about the sampling practices used in these early prevalence
studies led some to believe that the true prevalence of this disorder had been
severely underestimated. Prevalence data was typically collected in either primary care and hospital-based settings, thus restricting their samples to individuals who had access to health care resources. In particular, people of ethnic
minority status may have been excluded because they tend to have differential
access to health care (Richman, Flaherty, & Rospenda, 1994). Also, previous
studies had found a preponderance of women with this illness. However, this
finding might have arisen because women tend to seek out health services
more often when compared to men (Richman et al., 1994).

In addition, studies relying on physician referral may have underestimated
the prevalence of this illness because some physicians might not have assessed
for the presence of this illness, or did not diagnose this illness because they
did not believe CFS to be a legitimate disorder (Jason et al., 1993). For example,
in the Gunn et al. (1993) study, only 44% of the physicians referred any patients
at all to the study. Some people who actually had the disorder may not have
been diagnosed or treated for this illness (Richman et al., 1994). For example,
people with CFS reported significant difficulty in finding a doctor who would
appropriately diagnose them with the disorder (Feidan, 1990). Also, it was
possible that people with the disorder had either dropped out of the health
care system before receiving a diagnosis because of lack of financial resources
or had dropped out after receiving a diagnosis because they felt that they were
treated badly by medical professionals (David, 1991). Some persons with CFS,
because of skepticism and lack of understanding on the part of medical professionals, may have pursued alternative health care treatments (Jason, Ferrari,
Taylor, Slavich, & Stenzel, 1996).

In response to these concerns about existing epidemiological data, the
research group at DePaul University became involved in multiple studies regarding the prevalence of CFS. A community-based pilot study investigating
the prevalence of this illness was initiated in January of 1993 (Jason et al.,
1993). In this study, 1,031 people in a random community sample were interviewed by telephone using a screening questionnaire. Five percent of the sample
indicated that they had unexplained severe fatigue for at least six months. Of
note is the fact that 64% of the fatigued group reported that they did not have
a medical doctor currently overseeing their fatigue. This finding emphasized
the importance of using community-based prevalence studies, rather than rely-

ing on referrals from physicians or using samples through medical centers. Following medical and psychological evaluations, two patients were diagnosed with CFS, resulting in a point prevalence estimate of 200 per 100,000 for people over age 18 (Jason et al., 1995), a rate considerably higher than the 2 to 10 per 100,000 rate that the CDC had intially found.

Next, a full-scale randomly selected community-based prevalence study was initiated at DePaul University to address past methodological problems (Jason et al., 1999). Community participation was an important feature of the research process. People with CFS were involved throughout the design and implementation of this epidemiology study. These individuals included medical professionals and academic researchers who themselves had been diagnosed with the illness, medical and mental health professionals who treated people with CFS, representatives from the local self-help organizations, and other people with CFS who were known to the researchers. Pilot data were obtained through collaboration between CFS patient organizations and the DePaul research team, and was funded by the CFIDS Association, a national self-help organization. These pilot data, in turn, were used to help secure a National Institutes of Health research grant to conduct a full-scale randomized community-based epidemiological study of the prevalence of this disorder using probability sampling. People with CFS were involved in all phases of the research process, including the development of the study design and methodology, implementation, data analysis, interpretation, and dissemination of the study results.

Research Design and Methodology

Researchers at DePaul University worked to develop the research design, aims, and hypotheses of the large-scale prevalence study in collaboration with CFS community groups and people with CFS. Involvement of community members was critical to the design of the sampling strategies, and assisted researchers in being able to contact a population of persons with CFS. Community members also provided input regarding the validity and appropriateness of the study measures for this population. This was accomplished in several ways. First, people with CFS were present at all research meetings, to aid in the development of the research design, assist in selection of the measures, assist in training of staff interviewers, and engage in problem solving around difficulties encountered in the design and implementation of the research study. Consultation also occurred with other researchers off-site, with persons who both did or did not have this illness. People with CFS helped address specific barriers that arose during the research process, such as transportation difficulties. They assisted in training and education of other staff members about this illness, so that the interviewers were aware of and sensitive toward the needs of people with CFS. Contributions from people with CFS helped ensure that the research team was sensitive to the particular concerns of people with this illness. The methodology of the study was also informed through the feedback from participants with CFS who were assessed in the initial pilot testing.

Using this feedback from multiple sources, the decision was made to use telephone calling and screening as the primary method of recruitment of people into the study. A random sample of households in the Chicago area was selected using procedures developed by Kish (1965). The phone numbers were obtained from Survey Sample Incorporated. This company generated random telephone numbers using valid Chicago prefixes. Both listed and unlisted numbers were included as well as business and nonworking numbers. The sample was stratified to represent several neighborhoods in Chicago that were 10 to 15 minutes from the site of the medical examinations. In all, eight Chicago community areas were sampled, including low socioeconomic areas such as West Garfield Park; middle-class areas such as Bridgeport and Armour Park; gentrified areas such as the near West Side; and high socioeconomic status areas such as the Loop and the near North Side.

A random sample of adults who were 18 years or older were screened between September 1995 and May 1997. Ineligible individuals were those too ill to be interviewed or those not speaking English or Spanish. The response rate was calculated by dividing the number of completed interviews by the number of eligible adults with whom contact was attempted, either successfully or unsuccessfully. Nonrespondents were those calls where an answering machine was reached or where the household or person refused to be interviewed.

Twenty interviewers with past survey research experience were recruited. The interviewers were an ethnically diverse group, including Caucasian, African American, Asian, and Latino male and female interviewers. Training of these individuals took place in three phases, including orientation to technical terms and medical concepts, role-playing sessions with mock interviews conducted, and evaluations and constructive feedback concerning their performance. Weekly meetings were held where all interviewers discussed their progress and problem-solved around any difficulties encountered. Several Spanish-speaking interviewers were recruited, and respondents were offered the option of doing the interview in Spanish. A Latino clinical psychologist translated all instruments for the project into Spanish. When an interviewer reached a person who preferred to be interviewed in Spanish, he or she informed the respondent that a Spanish-speaking interviewer would be contacting the person later. Individuals who did not speak English or Spanish were excluded, but in these cases, the interviewers always tried to contact an English-speaking person in the household to serve as a translator.

Using this procedure, 18,675 people completed the CFS screening interview. Of the 18,675 adults interviewed, 9,717 were Caucasian, 3,692 were African American, 3,450 were Latino, and 1,614 were of other ethnic origins. Of the 18,765 participants who were interviewed, 780 (4.2%) had chronic fatigue. Of these, 408 had chronic fatigue and the concurrent occurrence of four or more symptoms. These participants were defined as CFS-like, and invited to participate in the rest of the study. (The suffix "like" was used to clarify that individuals in this group only met the Fukuda et al. [1994] criteria by self-report and did not necessarily qualify as having a final diagnosis of CFS rendered by a physician.) One hundred sixty-six of the 408 CFS-like participants agreed to complete a structured psychiatric interview (Stage 2) and a comprehensive physical examination (Stage 3). Participants were then classified as having CFS by independent physician consensus. On completion of the study, a team of four physicians and a psychiatrist reviewed each participant's file and made the final diagnoses of CFS, idiopathic chronic fatigue (ICF), or fatigue fully explained by medical or psychiatric condition. These physicians were familiar with the CFS diagnostic criteria and were blinded to the experimental status of the participant (CFS-like versus control). Two physicians independently rated each case to determine whether the participant met the CFS case definition (Fukuda et al., 1994). If a disagreement occurred, a third physician rater was used to arrive at a diagnostic consensus.

Measurement

The measures used in the study were also carefully validated to determine their appropriateness for use with a chronically ill population, as well as a population that was ethnically and socioeconomically diverse. The research team, composed of researchers and community members, worked together to judge the sensitivity and specificity of the study measure for use in a population of people with CFS. For example, one study compared the diagnostic accuracy of the DIS (Diagnostic Interview Schedule; Robins, Helzer, Cottler, & Goldring, 1989) and the SCID (Structured Clinical Interview for the *DSM-III-R;* Spitzer, Williams, Gibbon, & First, 1990) for people with CFS (Taylor & Jason, 1998). This investigation indicated that, when compared to the SCID, the results from the DIS led to inflated rates of psychiatric disorder, primarily because the symptoms of CFS could be considered "medically unexplained" and thus be scored toward meeting criteria for psychiatric disorders (Taylor & Jason, 1998). Therefore, the SCID was used to assess past and current psychiatric disorders in the people who participated in the study, to minimize false positive rates of psychiatric diagnoses.

Another issue regarding the sensitivity and specificity of study measures involved the unique challenges faced by an urban population. For instance, some people had psychological symptoms that, in one context, could have been considered indicative of a psychiatric disorder. However, after further evaluation, these symptoms were consistent with their environmental and cultural context, and thus were not included as indicative of a psychiatric disorder (i.e. severe anxiety following a neighborhood shooting). It was also noted that some ethnic minority group members sometimes did not have a clear understanding of the research process, so that research study was carefully explained until the participant was satisfied that they understood the process. When a difficulty arose and it was suspected that it was related to a cultural issue, resolutions to these problems were sought using feedback from all members of the research team. The inclusion of ethnically diverse research team members facilitated discussion of these cultural issues.

Study procedures were carefully monitored to ensure that specific needs of the populations sampled were not overlooked. For example, there was flexibility in the administration of instruments and in scheduling of participants to be included in the study. This time flexibility arose as it was noted that Latinos were more likely to be out of the country for long periods of time (i.e., some Mexican American participants spent Christmas holidays with family in Mexico for one or two months at a time). Scheduling of appointments took into account the time that they would be gone, and the research team followed up with each participant periodically until they returned and continued with the study.

As the study progressed, feedback was constantly sought from people with CFS regarding the appropriateness of the research design and progress in study implementation. Research teams met weekly to discuss progress toward goals. At all research meetings, people with CFS were present and participated collaboratively on problem-solving. Further, deliberate sampling of neighborhoods near the study site that were ethnically diverse, as well as inclusion of ethnically diverse research team members as interviewers, was used to enhance the cultural sensitivity of the research study. Information regarding the pilot research study design and efforts was published in the *CFIDS Chronicle,* a newsletter that was sent out to members of the CFIDS Association of America, a large self-help organization for people with CFS (Jason et al., 1993).

Finally, there was a strong emphasis on sensitivity to the needs and concerns of the study participants. Each person with CFS was notified of his or her status, and the results of all laboratory tests and the medical examination were sent to the study participants, for them to pass along to their physician if they desired. Participants interacted with people from the research team, including medical professionals, who listened and took their complaints seriously and who provided information and referrals for their illness. While psychological variables were assessed, care was taken to provide the rationale for the administration of these measures and to emphasize the confidentiality of results. By giving participants control of their medical information, being taken seriously by medical professionals, being able to describe their illness in their own words, and receiving information about their illness to be able to manage their illness better, it was expected that participation would ultimately be an empowering experience for the participants.

Results

The results of the prevalence study are reported in Jason et al. (1999). Results indicated that the point prevalence of CFS was estimated at 422 per 100,000. Thus, prevalence estimates indicated that this illness may affect approximately 836,000 people in the United States, a considerably higher figure than the previous CDC estimate of 20,000 individuals. Consistent with previous findings, CFS prevalence rates for women were higher than for men, with 522 women and 291 men per 100,000 having this illness. In addition, rates of this illness were found to be higher in the Latino and African American groups when compared to the Caucasian sample. Rates of illness were 726 per 100,000 for the Latino sample, 337 per 100,000 for the African American sample, and 318 per 100,000 for the Caucasian sample. This investigation found that the occurrence of this illness was independent of the aging process, with peak occurrence during middle age. Highest rates of CFS were among people from middle to low socioeconomic status, with the lowest rates among professionals. People with CFS were more likely to be unemployed, receiving disability, or working part-time compared to healthy controls.

Results of the study indicated that prevalence of CFS was higher than previously estimated. Women, Latinos, middle-aged individuals, and people of middle to lower socioeconomic status were found to be at higher risk for this illness. These results directly contradicted the perception of upper-class Caucasian women as being the primary sufferers of this illness. Results also emphasized that prevalence estimates could vary significantly depending on the methodology used to collect prevalence data. Because only 10% of people with CFS in this sample had actually been diagnosed by a physician before participating in the study, findings highlighted the limitations of hospital- and primary-care-based studies in assessing prevalence of this illness. People included in hospital- and primary-care-based studies may have represented a highly select group of people with CFS who are not representative of all people with this disorder.

Dissemination of Results

Following a participatory action model of research, significant efforts were expended to disseminate the study results to the CFS community. This dissemination of results was facilitated by including people with CFS throughout the research process. Through collaboration with members of the CFS community, key people in the CFS community were aware of and accepted the study. Indeed, leaders in the CFS community helped to fund the pilot study data and were involved throughout the research process. This involvement helped to establish the credibility of this research within the CFS community, and facilitated dissemination of the prevalence study when results were published in 1999 (Jason et al., 1999). In addition, the results of this investigation were used to help inform the goals, political agendas, and public policy surrounding the illness.

Estimates of the prevalence of CFS obtained from this study and others like it helped to inform social policy decisions and allocations of resources. Because the prevalence of CFS is more common than previously thought, the CDC has added CFS to the list of illnesses that are of high priority for research funding. Because the prevalence results appeared to vary widely depending on the sampling methodology used, the CDC recommended that all future epidemiological research involve random community samples, using methodology similar to that conducted by the DePaul research team (Jason, 2001). In this way, the results of the prevalence study were used to address key concerns of the CFS community, to increase biomedical funding for this illness, and led to more appropriate and sensitive methodology for assessment of people with CFS in future research. As a result of this study and the investigations initiated by the DePaul research team, the principal investigator, Leonard Jason, has been invited to serve on the work group of the CFS Coordinating Committee of the Department of Health and Human Services, which coordinates all federal initiatives and policies regarding CFS. In part because of the study, Jason was also asked to become a board member of the American Association of Chronic Fatigue Syndrome, the international research society devoted to investigating CFS.

Issues uncovered by this epidemiological investigation provided a rationale for initiating other community-based interventions for people with CFS. For example, the study data indicated that only 10% of people with CFS had actually received a diagnosis. This finding suggested a lack of knowledge of CFS among medical professionals, with a resulting paucity of health and community resources for people with CFS. Subsequently, in collaboration with the Health Resources and Services Administration (HRSA) and with help from the principal investigator of the study, the CFIDS Association established an education and training program for medical personnel. In this program, Drs. Lapp and Jason trained 50 health care workers and medical personnel in the diagnosis and treatment of CFS. In turn, each of the 50 trained health care workers agreed to train 50 other medical personnel in the diagnosis and management of CFS. In this way, education about this illness incorporating the most recent knowledge will be disseminated throughout the medical community.

Empowerment of People With CFS

CFS is an illness where the experiences, perspectives, and concerns of people with this disorder have been dismissed, ignored, or trivialized by medical professionals (Wessely et al., 1998). An important goal, then, was to include the perspectives of people with CFS through participation of people from the CFS community throughout the research process. Thus, contributions made by people with CFS on the research team were taken seriously and addressed, not trivialized or seen as "biasing" results. In addition to reframing the contributions of people with CFS, the concerns and hypothesis proposed by people with this illness were empirically tested, to confirm the validity and accuracy of these observations and experiences. Efforts were made to provide real benefits to the study participants so that they could gain information about their illness, and ultimately be able to manage their illness better. Thus, participation was used as an opportunity to provide information and to address the needs articulated by participants within the study on an individual level. Finally, the empowerment of individuals with CFS continues to be an important goal as the research team collaborates with the Chicago Chronic Fatigue Syndrome Association and other social service organizations to address issues of concern within the local community.

An important focus of this study was using the results to inform public policy, as well as address the political issues that surrounded this illness and that were put forth by CFS self-help organizations. This epidemiological investigation demonstrated that the prevalence of this illness is significantly higher than was first assumed. It is likely that the empowerment for the CFS community occurred through political decisions in regard to allocation of funding for research and other resources. Empirical information, then, helped validate some of the concerns expressed by people within the CFS community. In addition, knowledge about other issues that were unexpected also helped to inform people within the CFS community, so that they could learn more about how this illness is distributed in communities. Finally, the voices and experiences of people with CFS, a group that have in large part been marginalized by the medical establishment, were included in these studies, and their experiences were used to collaboratively inform a research design that more accurately estimated who met criteria for this illness.

Conclusion

Community participation in health research has the potential to address many difficulties encountered by epidemiological researchers as they develop appropriate research and intervention strategies for chronic illness. Community-based participatory research is a central concern in public health. Community participation can be used to examine the effects of environmental and social variables on disease occurrence and can help elucidate contextual factors on populations at risk for illness, as well as assist in identifying community practices and community resources around a particular illness. Community participation can assist researchers in strengthening research design by addressing sampling issues and by helping ensure that the variables of interest can be accurately and appropriately measured. In addition, ethnographic methods hold much promise to elucidate the meaning of illness and symptoms, as well as practices and experiences of illness, across diverse economic and cultural groups.

In a prevalence study of chronic fatigue syndrome, community participation was instrumental in the development, design, implementation, and use of the study results. Community participation was used to address key epidemiological questions, including the appropriateness of the sampling methodologies to find and count the occurrence of this disorder and the appropriateness of standard measures for both sociodemographically diverse and chronically ill populations. The use of community-based methodology strengthened the research design and allowed for a broader generalization of study results when compared to previous epidemiological investigations. Collaboration with members of the CFS community aided in the credibility of the study results within that community. Using an empowerment framework, these epidemiological investigation results were disseminated to inform social policy and political decisions addressing the previously ignored concerns of people with CFS. The process of collaboration that began with the prevalence study continues today in several initiatives that may benefit people with CFS, as researchers and members of the CFS community have established an ongoing dialogue regarding the needs and concerns of people within the CFS community.

References

Abbey, S. E., & Garfinkel, P.E. (1991). Chronic fatigue syndrome and depression: Cause, effect, or covariate? *Reviews of Infectious Diseases, 13* (Suppl. 1), S73–83.

Berkman, L. F., & Kawachi, I. (2000). *Social epidemiology.* Oxford: Oxford.

Boston Women's Health Book Collective. (n.d.). *History of our bodies, ourselves.* Retrieved April 28, 2002, from http://www.ourbodiesourselves.org/

Breslow, N. E., & Day, N. E. (1980). *Statistical methods in cancer research I: The analysis of case-control studies.* Lyon: IARC.

Centers for Disease Control and Prevention. (1994). *The facts about chronic fatigue syndrome.* Atlanta, GA: U.S. Department of Health and Human Services.

David, A. S. (1991). Postviral fatigue syndrome and psychiatry. *British Medical Bulletin, 47*(4), 966–988.

Feidan, K. (1990). *Hope and help for chronic fatigue syndrome.* New York: Prentice Hall Press.

Fukuda, K., Strauss, S. E., Hickie, I., Sharpe, M. C., Dobbins, J. G., et al. (1994). The chronic fatigue syndrome: A comprehensive approach to its definition and study. *Annals of Internal Medicine, 121,* 953–959.

Gordis, L. (2000). *Epidemiology.* Philadelphia: W.B. Saunders.

Gunn, W. J., Connell, D. B., & Randall, B. (1993). Epidemiology of chronic fatigue syndrome: The Centers for Disease Control study. *Ciba Foundation Symposium, 173,* 83–93.

Haight Ashbury Free Clinics Inc. of San Francisco, CA. (n.d.) *A brief history of the Haight Ashbury Free Medical Clinic.* Retrieved April 28, 2002, from http://www.hafci.org/

Howard Brown Health Center. (n.d.). *HBHC history.* Retrieved April 28, 2002, from http://www.howardbrown.org/

Jason, L. A. (2001). Working with an ambiguous illness. *Psychological Science Agenda, 14*(2), 8–9.

Jason, L. A., Ferrari, J. R., Taylor, R. R., Slavich, S. P., & Stenzel, C. L. (1996). A national assessment of the service, support, and housing preferences by persons with chronic fatigue syndrome. *Evaluation and the Health Professions, 19*(2), 194–207.

Jason, L. A., Fitzgibbon, G., Taylor, R., Taylor, S., Wagner, L., et al. (1993, Summer). The prevalence of chronic fatigue syndrome: A review of efforts—Past and present. *CFIDS Chronicle,* 24–29.

Jason, L. A., Richman, J. A., Rademaker, A. W., Jordan, K. M., Plioplys, A. V., et al. (1999). A community-based study of chronic fatigue syndrome. *Archive of Internal Medicine, 159,* 2129–2137.

Jason, L. A., Taylor, R. R., Wagner, L., Holden, J., Ferrari, J. R., et al. (1995). Estimating rates of chronic fatigue syndrome from a community based sample: A pilot study. *American Journal of Community Psychology, 23,* 557–568.

Kish, L. (1965). *Survey sampling.* New York: Wiley.

Kleinman, A., & Good, B. (1985). *Culture and depression: Studies in the anthropology and cross-cultural psychiatry of affect and disorder.* Berkeley: University of California Press.

Levy, P. S., & Lemeshow, S. (1999). *Sampling of populations* (3rd ed.). New York: John Wiley & Sons.

MacKellar, D., Valleroy, L., Karon, J., Lemp, G., & Janssen, R. (1996). The young men's survey: Methods for estimating HIV seroprevalence and risk factors among young men who have sex with men. *Public Health Reports, 111* (Suppl. 1), 138–144.

MacMahon, B., & Trichopoulos, D. (1996). *Epidemiology: Principles and methods.* Boston: Little-Brown.

MacQueen, K. M., McLellan, E., Metzger, D. S., Kegeles, S., Strauss, R. P., et al. (2001). What is community? An evidence-based definition for participatory public health. *American Journal of Public Health, 91,* 929–1938.

McCluskey, D. R. (1993). Pharmacological approaches to the therapy of chronic fatigue syndrome. In Ciba Foundation Symposium (Ed.), *Chronic fatigue syndrome* (pp. 280–297). New York: Wiley.

O'Brien, M. U., Murray, J. R., Rahimian, A., & Wiebel, W. W. (1996, June). *Household seroprevalence survey in three high-risk Chicago neighborhoods: HIV pathways between high-risk and general populations.* Paper presented at the ninth international conference on AIDS, Berlin.

Richman, J. A., Flaherty, J. A., & Rospenda, K. M. (1994). Chronic fatigue syndrome: Have flawed assumptions been derived from treatment-based studies? *American Journal of Public Health, 84*(2), 282–284.

Richman, J. A., & Jason, L. A. (2001). Gender biases underlying the social construction of illness states: The case of chronic fatigue syndrome. *Current Sociology, 49*(3), 15–29.

Robins, L. N., Helzer, J. E., Cottler, L., & Goldring, E. (1989). *National Institute of Mental Health Diagnostic Interview Schedule, Version Three Revised. DIS–III–R.* St. Louis: Washington University School of Medicine, Department of Psychiatry.

Rothman, K. J. (2002). *Epidemiology: An introduction.* Oxford: Oxford University Press.

Spitzer, D. L., Williams, J. B. W., Biggon, M., & First, M. B. (1990). *Structured Clinical Interview for DSM–III–R—Nonpatient edition (SCID–NP, Version 1.0).* Washington, DC: American Psychiatric Press.

Susser, M., & Susser, E. (1996a). Choosing a future for epidemiology: I. Eras and paradigms. *American Journal of Public Health, 86*(2), 668–673.

Susser, M., & Susser, E. (1996b). Choosing a future for epidemiology: II. From black box to Chinese boxes and eco-epidemiology. *American Journal of Public Health, 86*(2), 675–677.

Taylor, R. R., & Jason, L. A. (1998). Comparing the DIS with the SCID: Chronic fatigue syndrome and psychiatric comorbidity. *Psychology and Health, 13,* 1087–1104.

Wessely, S., Hotopf, M., & Sharpe, M. (1998). *Chronic fatigue and its syndromes.* Oxford: Oxford University Press.

Part II

Creation and Structure of Partnerships

4

Primary Prevention: Involving Schools and Communities in Youth Health Promotion

*Joseph A. Durlak, Roger P. Weissberg,
Elena Quintana, and Francisco Perez*

In the first half of this chapter we introduce the topic of health promotion and its importance, describe some theoretical frameworks that identify critical competencies present at different developmental periods, and briefly summarize the results of outcome research on competency enhancement. Then, in the second half of the chapter we describe approaches that represent collaborative participatory health promotion research occurring either in school settings or in a large urban community.

What Is Health Promotion?

Several terms have been used to refer to various health promotion efforts: wellness, competency, well-being, positive youth development, and empowerment (e.g., Cicchetti, Rappaport, Sandler, & Weissberg, 2000; Cowen, 1994; Weissberg, Barton, & Shriver, 1997). We use the term *health promotion* to refer to all efforts designed to promote specific skills and competencies in young people or to otherwise enhance their overall adjustment and quality of life.

Traditionally, the prevention of problems in young people has focused on the immediate and distal effects of intervention—in other words, on the reduction of negative outcomes and difficulties such as mental health problems, academic failure, drug use, and the like. Of course, demonstrating that such outcomes are achieved is essential for developing credible empirical support for prevention, and there are now plenty of outcome data offering such support (e.g., Durlak, 1997; Durlak & Wells, 1997; Weissberg & Greenberg, 1998). However, a focus on the negative side of adjustment has often obscured the fact that many interventions attempt prevention by promoting skills and developmental competencies—in other words, through the process of health promotion. For example, almost all of the more than 400 drug prevention programs funded by the Center for Substance Abuse Prevention between 1987 and 1995

emphasized skills training of participating youth as a major program component (Sambrano, Springer, & Hermann, 1997).

Pittman, Irby, Tolman, Yohalem, and Ferber (2001) pointed out that there
is something fundamentally limiting about viewing youth in terms of preventing their future problems as opposed to developing their strengths and
potential:

> Suppose we introduced an employer to a young person we worked with by
> saying, "Here's Johnny. He's not a drug user. He's not in a gang. He's not
> a dropout. He's not a teen father. Please hire him." The employer would
> probably respond, "That's great. But what does he know, what can he do?"
> If we cannot define—and do not give young people ample opportunities to
> define—the skills, values, attitudes, knowledge and commitments that we
> want with as much force as we can define those that we do not want, we
> will fail. Prevention is an important but inadequate goal. Problem-free is
> not fully prepared. (p. 4)

Developmental Perspectives on Health Promotion

Several writers have articulated useful frameworks for considering competencies that are important at different developmental periods. For instance, Cowen
(1994, 2000) emphasized that health promotion strategies should be community-
wide, proactive, multidimensional, and ongoing and emphasized that competencies could be promoted via different pathways during childhood—that is,
through wholesome early attachments; acquiring age-appropriate cognitive–
behavioral skills; exposure to environments and settings that facilitate adaptation, autonomy, support, and empowerment; and by encounters with stress
that evoke effective coping strategies. In addition, the optimal development of
competence pathways requires integrated operations involving individuals,
families, settings, community contexts, and macro-level social structures and
policies. Others have focused their attention on specific competencies emerging
during the course of development.

The Early Years

For example, the Carnegie Task Force on Meeting the Needs of Young Children
(1994) presented a model of developmental competence outcomes for 3-year-
olds and also identified policies to foster them. They include being self-confident
and trusting, intellectually inquisitive, able to use language to communicate,
physically and mentally healthy, able to relate well to others, and empathic
toward others. These competencies are believed to result primarily from loving,
caring parent–child interactions that foster healthy attachments, as well as
early experiences with adult caregivers that, in turn, provide a foundation for
intellectual and communicative competence.

Parents who model positive interactions with children and others teach
acceptable behavior, guide healthy habits and routines, and help children to
manage impulses and nurture the development of social and emotional compe-

tence. To increase the number of parents who offer this encouraging milieu for healthy outcomes, the Carnegie Task Force (1994) recommended the following environmental and policy supports:

1. *Promote responsible parenthood* through encouraging planned child-rearing and preconception care; ensuring comprehensive prenatal care and support; and offering parent education and support.
2. *Guarantee quality child care choices* through fostering quality child care, improving parental leave benefits, providing parents with afford-able child care options, and developing family-centered child care programs.
3. *Ensure good health and protection* through the provision of health care services for all infants and toddlers, and creating safe environments for young children that protect them from injury and promote their health.
4. *Mobilize communities to support young children and families* through strengthening community networks, moving toward family-centered communities, and establishing governmental structures that serve children and families more effectively.

Elementary School Years

During the elementary school years, there are substantial changes in children's cognitive and social–emotional growth, as well as in the ways that peer group and the school influence development. A major goal of health promotion during this period is to teach children to use available personal and environmental resources to achieve prosocial goals (Waters & Sroufe, 1983). This also means that the environment should be structured to provide the resources as needed. Modifiable personal resources might include such variables as cognitive, affect-ive, and behavioral skills; realistic self-perceptions of performance efficacy in specific social domains; social awareness and attitudes about others; knowledge about developmentally and culturally relevant social issues and situations; and the ability to elicit the support of parents, teachers, and peers when needed. To enhance children's personal resources for coping adaptively with develop-mental challenges, social interactions, and life stresses, some interventions emphasize the enhancement of social information processing skills such as the capacities to control impulses and manage affect to engage in responsible problem solving; perceive the nature of social tasks and the feelings and per-spectives of the people involved; be motivated to establish adaptive goals to resolve situations; feel confident in the ability to achieve a goal successfully; access or generate goal-directed alternatives and link them with realistic conse-quences; decide on an optimal strategy, and when necessary, develop elaborated implementation plans that anticipate potential obstacles; carry out solutions with behavioral skill; self-monitor behavioral performance and, when needed, abandon ineffective strategies, try alternative plans, or reformulate goals; and provide self-reinforcement for successful goal attainment or engage in emotion-focused coping when a desired goal cannot be reached (Weissberg, Caplan, & Sivo, 1989).

The William T. Grant Consortium on the School-Based Promotion of Social Competence (1992) and Collaborative for Academic, Social, and Emotional Learning (CASEL; Elias et al., 1997) have also offered developmental frameworks for social competencies during the middle childhood years. These groups have proposed that programs educate students to coordinate emotions, cognitions, and behaviors to address developmental tasks in the following six domains of functioning:

1. *Self-awareness and self-management* emphasize issues such as learning about recognizing and labeling feelings; setting goals; understanding the social, legal, and health consequences of risky behaviors; responsible decision making; and managing time effectively to balance study and play time.
2. *Family life* focuses on understanding roles of family members; making contributions at home through chores; relating with siblings; recognizing and accepting different family structures; and developing appropriate intimacy and boundaries with family members.
3. *Peer relations* involves making friends; sharing; taking turns; learning to cope with peer pressure; assertiveness; and handling teasing and aggression.
4. *School-related skills* include accepting responsibility in the classroom; following school rules and respecting authority; setting academic goals and responsibly completing them; working in teams; and accepting similarity and differences in ability levels and appearance.
5. *Community/citizenship* focuses on recognizing that we live in a diverse, pluralistic society; recognizing, accepting, and appreciating cultural differences; assuming responsibility for the environment; helping people in need; and joining prosocial groups or teams outside of school.
6. *Event-triggered stressors* involves coping with events such as family moves, divorce, death, or becoming a big brother or sister.

Hawkins, Catalano, and associates (1992) proposed a social development model for promoting health, social, emotional, and academic development. They contend that children who are bonded to peers, adults, and institutions that promote healthy beliefs and clear prosocial standards are more likely to adopt similar views. Thus, healthy bonding fosters a motivational component that can simultaneously promote positive behaviors and protect children from exposure to risk. According to the social developmental model, three conditions are essential to this bonding process: (a) children must experience challenging and meaningful opportunities to contribute to their family, school, peers, and other institutional and informal settings in ways that are developmentally appropriate and lead to feelings of responsibility and satisfaction; (b) they must be taught skills (e.g., academic, social) that allow them to participate successfully in the opportunities they experience; and (c) they need to receive recognition and acknowledgment for their effective efforts. Appropriate recognition nurtures children's motivation to continue and refine their skilled performances. This tripartite framework of opportunities, skills, and recognition provides a model for establishing supportive processes in the child's environment, and places the motivational component of significant relationships at the center of interventions that provide protection from risk.

Middle School Years

Between the ages of 10 and 14, young people experience many predictable stressors and dramatic life changes. Rapid bodily changes, cognitive maturation, and increased social pressures profoundly influence the functioning of young adolescents. The transition from self-contained, elementary school classrooms to a less protective middle school culture introduces new stresses and challenges to compound those connected with growing up (Carnegie Council on Adolescent Development, 1989). All adolescents face decisions about choosing appropriate friends, resolving conflicts with peers, negotiating increased independence from parents, and making choices about substance use and sexual activity. Despite their normative character, the negative consequences of poor decision making in these areas may lead to serious physical, social, and emotional problems.

Many young adolescents explore new options and possibilities with an exploratory attitude that is common for this age group. Many of these risky behaviors serve functional purposes. However, when carried to extremes, such behaviors can become habitual and produce lifelong negative consequences (Dryfoos, 1990). Early adolescence represents a critical period for the prevention of health-compromising and the promotion of health-enhancing lifestyles before damaging behaviors become entrenched. To become healthy, constructive, productive adults, adolescents on an effective developmental pathway must accomplish the following (Carnegie Council on Adolescent Development, 1995):

> Find a valued place in a constructive group; learn how to form close, durable human relationships; feel a sense of worth as a person; achieve a reliable basis for making informed choices; know how to use the support systems available to them; express constructive curiosity and exploratory behavior; find ways of being useful to others; believe in a promising future with real opportunities; . . . master social skills, including the ability to manage conflict peacefully; cultivate the inquiring and problem-solving habits of mind for life-long learning; become ethical persons; learn the requirements of responsible citizenship; and respect diversity in our pluralistic society. (pp. 10–11)

The Carnegie Council on Adolescent Development (1989, 1992, 1995) has disseminated three informative reports that propose program and policy changes to help adolescents achieve positive developmental outcomes. Core recommendations include reengaging families with their adolescent children through collaborative efforts with schools and community agencies; establishing safe, developmentally appropriate schools that offer challenging, nurturing, and health-promoting learning environments; providing life skills training to foster adaptive behavior; ensuring access to health services; providing growth-promoting, community settings for young people during the nonschool hours; and enhancing the constructive potential of the media.

High School Years and Beyond

Pittman and Cahill (1992) highlighted five core competency domains that define the range of skills and behaviors required for adult success.

1. *Personal/social competence* emphasizes intrapersonal skills such as self-discipline and the capacity to understand personal emotions; interpersonal skills such as the ability to work and develop positive relationships with others through empathy, cooperation, communication, and negotiating; and judgment skills such as the capacity to plan, evaluate, solve problems, and make responsible decisions.
2. *Cognitive/creative competence* focuses on the ability to learn; motivation to learn and achieve; good oral and written language skills; appreciation and participation in different forms of creative expression; analytical and problem-solving skills; and development of a broad base of knowledge.
3. *Health/physical competence* involves good current health status as well as evidence of knowledge, attitudes, and behaviors that will foster future health.
4. *Vocational competence* involves awareness of vocational and avocational options and the steps needed to accomplish goals; understanding the value and function of work and leisure; and adequate preparation for a chosen career.
5. *Citizenship competence* emphasizes knowledge of and appreciation for the history and values of one's community and nation, as well as active participation in efforts that contribute to the community and nation.

Many of the personal, social, cognitive, and health competencies show clear continuities with those in early and middle childhood. In contrast, some of the vocational and citizenship competencies emerge during adolescence. In general, however, these competencies clearly establish a firm foundation for making positive contributions as a member of one's family, peer group, workplace, and community at large. Long-term goals include economic self-sufficiency, healthy family and social relationships, and good citizenship practices.

Positive outcome data are accumulating on the impact of health promotion programs for young people. Although using slightly different methods to identify studies, and thus examining different subsets of programs, the overall consensus from four recent reviews has been that health promotion interventions produce significant positive outcomes (Catalano, Berglund, Ryan, Lonczak, & Hawkins, 1999; Durlak & Wells, 1997; Roth, Brooks-Gunn, Murray, & Foster, 1998; Weissberg & Greenberg, 1998). For example, Catalano et al. (1999) concluded that a "positive youth development approach can result in positive youth behavior outcomes *and* the prevention of youth problems" (p. 95; emphasis added). Similarly, Durlak and Wells (1997), who specifically included health promotion programs in their review of preventive mental health programs for children and adolescents, found that the two types of programs did not produce significantly different outcomes. As the previous discussion has made plain, however, there are different views on which competencies are important and at which developmental periods, suggesting important research questions to be addressed in future work.

There is less specific controlled data on the role of participatory practices on the effects of health promotion interventions. One randomized field test has indicated that having high school students with learning disabilities (and eventually their parents) become actively involved in transition planning by making decisions about what they need for such a step produced significantly better outcomes than for a control group of youth and families who did not have the opportunity to participate actively in the intervention (Powers et al., 2001). Nevertheless, there is growing agreement that participatory research strategies benefit interventions not only by increasing the degree of positive impact but also by increasing the likelihood that interventions will be effectively implemented and sustained over time.

Health Promotion in Schools

The New Haven Social Development Project (NHSDP; Shriver & Weissberg, 1996; Weissberg, Barton, & Shriver, 1997) is one example of a collaborative participatory health promotion effort in schools. NHSDP originated when school staff came to the conclusion that existing treatment and prevention programs in their schools were piecemeal, and probably not very effective because of their lack of comprehensiveness, coordination, and integration. Based on the recommendation of a broadly representative, community-wide task force, the superintendent and board of education decided to establish a new department, the Social Development Department, which would encourage the development of positive student skills and behaviors. Working collaboratively and actively at each stage of the process, the schools developed a K–12 curriculum that requires the active participation and collaboration of multiple stakeholders such as teachers, parents, administrators, pupil support staff, students, and community leaders. Local researchers offered their input, but school staff ultimately decided on the components and operation of NHSDP based on their own priorities and needs. Central to the participatory and collaborative approach was the development of an effective working relationship among related parties so that systemic changes could occur in the schools to support the program. These changes included administrative and organizational changes that created a school-wide climate supportive of NHSDP goals. For example, site-based school planning and management teams were established to develop and monitor strategic plans for identifying and implementing integrated academic, social, and emotional learning programming. Furthermore, building-based staff development facilitators provided training, support, and on-site coaching to classroom teachers and other school staff who implemented new programming to foster a supportive, engaging classroom and school climate. Such changes are particularly important given other findings indicating that a positive climate not only has positive effects on student adjustment but also is related to staff involvement and job satisfaction that, in turn, increases the chances of effective program implementation (Weber et al., 1999). Research findings indicate several significant positive program benefits for NHSDP (Weissberg, 2000).

Another broader, even more ambitious effort focused on schools is the Collaborative for Academic, Social, and Emotional Learning (CASEL, http:// www.casel.org). CASEL is an international consortium of researchers, educators, and citizens dedicated to promoting the social and emotional learning of school children. This type of learning refers to such areas as awareness of self and others, positive attitudes and values, responsible decision making, and social interaction skills (Payton et al., 2000). CASEL's diverse leadership team supports several activities. These include conducting scientific reviews related to social and emotional learning concepts, the publication of helpful guides for educators that emphasize principles for developing effective school-based programs, and disseminating research findings in user-friendly formats to encourage more effective school practices (CASEL, 2002).

Most relevant to the current chapter is CASEL's efforts at consultation with local school districts. CASEL team members work collaboratively with school personnel to help them decide for themselves on the adoption of evidence-based programs that fit the ecology of each school setting, and CASEL personnel also train and collaborate with school staff to enhance the effective implementation of chosen programs. Experiences with several school districts suggest that when community researchers and collaborators work together effectively to conceptualize, design, and implement an intervention, they can encourage each other to think more broadly, ambitiously, systemically, and in evidence-based ways. Second, adopting a health promotion perspective often guides intervention development in ecologically sound ways that are more likely to result in young people who are both problem-free and fully prepared for success in school and life. Collaborative relationships and a health promotion perspective are two foundations for many different types of community intervention research.

Community-Based Health Promotion to Prevent Violence

To foster full development of all youth, communities must have a multidimensional approach to providing services and meeting the needs of young people (Randall et al., 1999). Youth need access to proactive activities such as recreation, education, job training and placement, preventative health care access, and intervention services, such as programs for drop-outs, probation programs, and family counseling (Tolan, 2001). The situation is particularly urgent in high-risk urban settings where repeated exposure to dangerous or illegal activities increases the risk of more children becoming involved in some way in delinquent or violent behavior (Tolan & Guerra, 1994). Others have concluded that offering accurate information, opportunity, training, employment, and social networks is the key to creating comprehensive and effective community programming (Catalano, Loeber, & McKinney, 1999).

An example of a community-based collaborative health promotion effort is the Chicago Project for Violence Prevention (CPVP). CPVP's specific goal is to reduce the most serious forms of gun-related violence that result in injury and death. CPVP's ultimate mission, however, is to work with high-risk communities to build and implement a community-based violence prevention model for reducing violence in all forms, and then to replicate this general model of program development throughout Chicago. CPVP currently works with seven communities that experience approximately 40% of the homicides in Chicago (Chicago Police Department, 2001). CPVP has three specific operational objectives: (a) to aid community-based organizations in their efforts to reduce violence and increase public safety in their communities through the adaptation of nationally recognized best practice methodologies; (b) to work with, and train where needed, community leaders to develop and use comprehensive strategic plans in the reduction of violence; and (c) to evolve a system of collaboration and citizen participation that extends across communities and eventually across the entire city with the goal of enabling communities to foster the development of all resident youth.

Each participating neighborhood in CPVP forms a community coalition promoting nonviolence whose chief responsibilities are to identify problematic areas within neighborhoods and ensure that clergy, youth outreach workers, and police are aware of the areas where the highest risk youth are gathering. This coalition works to implement five aspects of the intervention.

Youth Outreach

This project component supports opportunities for youth to choose constructive lifestyles through interventions and support systems provided through the project. The youth outreach component focuses on two primary activities: reaching out to youth directly who may be in difficult situations to (a) provide safety and assistance in solving conflicts by means other than violence and (b) directly link youth with jobs, job skills centers, GED and literacy training, and other needed services. Youth outreach workers try to develop high levels of trust and flexibility in connecting high-risk youth to local resources and services that can provide them with the skills and nurturing necessary to take advantage of educational and employment opportunities. This outreach model is a youth development approach to providing prevention, intervention, education, employment, treatment, and advocacy and focuses on reducing the barriers that prevent youth from seeking needed services.

Clergy Involvement

Faith leaders are natural community resources who should not be overlooked in collaborative coalitions. CPVP encourages faith leaders to open their houses of worship to youth in an effort to provide resources and safe havens to area youth and to patrol the immediate surroundings of their houses of worship. In an effort to promote clergy involvement, CPVP has developed a Covenant for Peace in Action. This document, signed by participating clergy members, is an agreement to preach the message of peace monthly, to encourage congregants to work for peace, and to bring the call for peace to the street. The Covenant also asks faith leaders to take a leadership role in responding to violent occurrences and to offer positive alternatives and outreach to youth.

The Covenant formalizes the relationship clergy members have with the coalition for nonviolence established in each program neighborhood. In some cases, participating clergy have divided their neighborhoods into small catchment areas, whereby each faith leader pledges to provide outreach, safe haven, distribution of nonviolence messages, and information to all youth in need within his or her area.

Police Participation

Law enforcement officers are key partners for preventing violence. However, CPVP asks police and other law enforcement agents such as those involved in community policing to collaborate closely with other community agents. Law enforcement personnel demonstrate an ongoing presence in response to shootings for an extended period of time and will often participate in vigils. All community coalitions have depended on their close police collaborations to be informed immediately after shootings occur.

Public Education

Because research has confirmed the value of well-crafted mass media campaigns (Backer, Rogers, & Sopory, 1992; Hornick, 2002), there is a major public education component in CPVP. Extensive work concentrates on message development for multiple target audiences, including community residents, clergy, high-risk youth, and parents. Media materials deglamorize violence and glamorize prosocial, nonviolence behaviors to modify the ways society views violence and safety. Public education materials include posters, block club signs, billboards, and leaflets, and materials are designed to mobilize community action and appeal directly to youth.

Community Response

When there is a shooting within a target neighborhood, the community assembles quickly to make a visible public response. Citizens gather with large signs and placards with nonviolent messages in the site(s) where violence was committed. This active response serves as a challenge to the norm of ignoring violent incidences or accepting them as unavoidable. In addition, involving community members in the assembly of responses to violence and in other program efforts increases the number of citizens actively involved in the program.

In sum, CPVP is a multitiered intervention designed to prevent serious violence through various health promotion efforts that arise from community mobilization and coalition activities. It is consistent with other violence prevention programs for youth in that various community stakeholders view the development of positive behaviors in high-risk youth as important or even more important than reducing the incidence of negative behaviors (Lutenbacher, Cooper, & Faccia, 2002).

Evaluation of CPVP

A program evaluation plan was designed to provide ongoing information to city, county, and other partners for use in localized strategic planning. For example, the evaluation team keeps monthly updates of shootings and homicides in target neighborhoods and these data are used by project partners to identify when interventions are needed in key hot spots. In addition, various aspects of subsequent interventions are measured, such as the saturation by law enforcement of a hot spot following a shooting or killing.

CPVP's formal evaluation component has four objectives: (a) to describe the progress of collaborative participatory community activities such as the initiation and development of a local coalition and the instigation and effective implementation of a strategic intervention plan; (b) to measure changes in both proximal and distal indicators of violence in target and comparison communities; (c) to relate levels of community development to changes in outcomes; and (d) to disseminate program findings. A matrix has been developed to provide a quick summary of community factors monitored on a regular basis. The matrix allows quick identification of gaps and strengths in programming in each community area. In addition, the matrix has a scoring element as a means of comparing the level of programmatic implementation with changes in homicide and shooting.

Preliminary Findings

Preliminary findings for CPVP are very encouraging. On average, there have been 24% fewer homicides in targeted neighborhoods compared to no changes over time in comparison neighborhoods. In four of the six target communities, homicides decreased 30 to 40% within the first year. Treating violence as an epidemic and using a coordinated approach that maximizes the contributions of religious leaders, government, community-based organizations, block clubs, politicians, and law enforcement seems to be working. CPVP's ambitious goal is to reduce gun deaths in program communities by 50% over five years.

Conclusion

Collaboration appears to be a crucial element in successful participatory action research. For example, the viability of both CASEL's school-based and CPVP's community-based efforts were determined in large extent by the effective collaborative arrangements that occurred between these university-based initiatives and their host settings (see also chapter 6). Both these projects proceeded similarly by offering a model of intervention that could be flexibly adapted by the local schools or communities. For example, CASEL relied on the advice and input of school staff to carry out the program in a way that made sense to the participatory school staff and their students. CPVP forged a collaborative relationship with key community stakeholders in Chicago neighborhoods, offered a general model of intervention, and then encouraged the community stakeholders to implement intervention tactics and principles in ways that made the most sense for local communities. In each of these projects, the process of collaboration not only created a heightened sense of ownership within the school or community setting but also allowed for tailoring of the intervention in ways that probably increased its effectiveness. In addition, ownership of a given intervention increases the likelihood that the host setting will continue the program after university researchers have left. For example, the New Haven school program has been in operation since 1986.

When designing and implementing programs for young people it is important to understand their needs in terms of the scope of services a given program is able to provide (Spivak, Hausman, & Protrow-Stith, 1989). It may be necessary to build a large network of service providers to offer the full range of opportunities, supervision, and safety that youth need. It can be difficult to broker the kinds of collaborative relationships that are necessary and develop good communication among community partners who have never before had a formal working relationship. This can include, for example, the relationship between clergy and job-training programs, police and outreach workers, or between schools and community service agencies (World Health Organization, 2002). Weak relationships among any of these partners can hamper program effectiveness. If the school or community does not feel a sense of ownership for the given intervention, they may reject or thwart intervention attempts, or simply discontinue the program after researchers leave. Collaboration not only increases community or school buy-in to an intervention, it also models how to broker and negotiate these relationships to the population of youth being served (Zimmerman, 2002).

Depending on the individual and community, there are a wide range of youth risk factors. All youth need opportunities to foster confidence, character, connection to safe places and people. They also need opportunities to develop different competencies and skills at different ages (Pittman, Irby, Tolman, Yahalem, & Ferber 2001). The environment should assist youth by responding to their needs and promoting their strengths and potential. A participatory health promotion orientation can be used effectively to help schools and local neighborhoods develop interventions that are ecologically sound and coordinated. Finding ways to offer an integrated approach to serving the needs of youth in different contexts can be challenging, but as the examples in this chapter suggest, it can be done.

References

Backer, S. P., Rogers, E. M., & Sopory, P. (1992). *Designing health communication campaigns: What works?* Newbury Park, CA: Sage.

Carnegie Council on Adolescent Development. (1989). *Report of the Task Force on Education of Young Adolescents. Turning points: Preparing American youth for the 21st century.* New York: Carnegie Corporation.

Carnegie Council on Adolescent Development. (1992). *Report of the Task Force on Youth Development and Community Programs. A matter of time: Risk and opportunity in the nonschool hours.* New York: Carnegie Corporation of New York.

Carnegie Council on Adolescent Development. (1995). *Great transitions: Preparing adolescents for a new century / Concluding report of the Carnegie Council on Adolescent Development.* New York: Carnegie Corporation of New York.

Carnegie Task Force on Meeting the Needs of Young Children. (1994). *Starting points: Meeting the needs of our youngest children.* New York: Carnegie Corporation of New York.

Catalano, R. F., Berglund, M. L., Ryan, J. A., Lonczak, H. C., & Hawkins, J. D. (1999). *Positive youth development in the United States: Research findings on evaluations of positive youth development programs.* Seattle, WA: Social Development Research Corporation.

Catalano, R. F., Loeber, R., & McKinney, K. C. (1999, October). School and community interventions to prevent serious and violent offending. *Office of Juvenile Justice and Delinquency Prevention Bulletin,* 1–11.

Chicago Police Department. (2001). *Annual compilation of statistics.* Chicago: Office of Research and Development.

Cicchetti, D., Rappaport, J., Sandler, I., & Weissberg, R. P. (2000). *The promotion of wellness in children and adolescents.* Washington, DC: Child Welfare League of America.

Collaborative for Academic, Social, and Emotional Learning (CASEL). (2002). *Safe and sound: An educational leader's guide to evidence-based social and emotional learning programs.* Chicago: University of Illinois at Chicago.

Cowen, E. L. (1994). The enhancement of psychological wellness: Challenges and opportunities. *American Journal of Community Psychology, 22,* 149–178.

Cowen, E. L. (2000). Psychological wellness: Some hopes for the future. In D. Cicchetti, J. Rappaport, I. Sandler, & R. P. Weissberg (Eds.), *The promotion of wellness in children and adolescents* (pp. 477–503). Washington DC: Child Welfare League of America Press.

Dryfoos, J. G. (1990). *Adolescents at risk: Prevalence and prevention.* New York: Oxford University Press.

Durlak, J. A. (1997). *Successful prevention programs for children and adolescents.* New York: Plenum Press.

Durlak, J. A., & Wells, A. M. (1997). Primary prevention mental health programs for children and adolescents. *American Journal of Community Psychology, 25,* 115–152.

Elias, M. J., Zins, J. E., Weissberg, R. P., Frey, K. S., Greenberg, M. T., Haynes, N. M., et al. (1997). *Promoting social and emotional learning: Guidelines for educators.* Alexandria, VA: Association for Supervision and Curriculum Development.

Hawkins, J. D., Catalano, R. F., & Associates. (1992). *Communities that care: Action for drug abuse prevention.* San Francisco: Jossey Bass.

Hornick, R. C. (2002). *Public health communication: Evidence for behavior change.* Mahwah, NJ: Erlbaum.

Lutenbacher, M., Cooper, W. O., & Facccia, K. (2002). Planning youth violence prevention efforts: Decision-making across community sectors. *Journal of Adolescent Health, 30,* 346–354.

Payton, J. W., Graczyk, P. A., Wardlaw, D. M., Bloodworth, M., Tompsett, C. J., et al. (2000). Social and emotional learning: A framework for promoting mental health and reducing risk behavior in children and youth. *Journal of School Health, 70,* 179–185.

Pittman, K. J., & Cahill, M. (1992). *Pushing the boundaries of education: The implications of a youth development approach to education policies, structures, and collaborations.* Washington, DC: Council of Chief State School Officers.

Pittman, K. J., Irby, M., Tolman, J., Yohalem, N., & Ferber, T. (2001). *Preventing problems, promoting development, encouraging engagement: Competing priorities or inseparable goals.* Tacoma Park, MD: International Youth Foundation.

Powers, L. E., Turner, A., Westwood, T., Matuszewski, J., Wilson, B., & Phillips, A. (2001). TAKE CHARGE for the Future: A controlled field-test of a model to promote student involvement in transition planning. *Career Development for Exceptional Individuals, 24,* 89–104.

Randall, J., Swenson, C., Cupit, H., & Scott, W. (1999). Neighborhood solutions for neighborhood problems: An empirically based violence prevention collaboration. *Health Education and Behavior 26*(6) 806–820.

Roth, J., Brooks-Gunn, J., Murray, L., & Foster, W. (1998). Promoting healthy adolescents: Synthesis of youth development program evaluations. *Journal of Research on Adolescence, 8,* 453–459.

Sambrano, S., Springer, J. F., & Hermann, J. (1997). Informing the next generation of prevention programs: CSAP's cross-site evaluation of the 1994–1995 high risk youth grantees. *Journal of Community Psychology, 25,* 375–395.

Shriver, T. P., & Weissberg, R. P. (1996, May 15). No new wars! *Education Week, 15,* 33, 37.

Spivak, H., Hausman, A. J., & Prothrow-Stith, D. (1989). Practitioners forum: Public health and the primary prevention of adolescent violence—The violence prevention project. *Violence and Victims, 4,* 203–212.

Tolan, P. (2001). Youth violence and its prevention in the United States: An overview of current knowledge. *Injury Control and Safety Prevention, 8,* 1–12.

Tolan, P., & Guerra, N. (1994, July). *What works in reducing adolescent violence: An empirical review of the field.* Boulder, CO: Center for the Study and Prevention of Violence.

Waters, E., & Sroufe, L. A. (1983). Social competence as a developmental construct. *Developmental Review, 3,* 79–97.

Weber C. K., Baranowski, T., Baranowski, J., Hebert, D., deMoor, D., et al. (1999). Influence of school organizational characteristics on the outcomes of a school health promotion program. *Journal of School Health, 69,* 376–380.

Weissberg, R. P. (2000). Improving the lives of millions of school children. *American Psychologist, 55,* 1360–1373.

Weissberg, R. P., Barton, H. A., & Shriver, T. P. (1997). The Social-Competence Promotion Program for Young Adolescents. In G. W. Albee & T. P. Gullotta (Eds.), *Primary prevention exemplars: The Lela Rowland Awards* (pp. 268–290). Thousand Oaks, CA: Sage.

Weissberg, R. P., Caplan, M. Z., & Sivo, P. J. (1989). A new conceptual framework for establishing school-based social competence promotion programs. In L. A. Bond & B. E. Compas (Eds.), *Primary prevention and promotion in the schools* (pp. 255–296). Newbury Park, CA: Sage.

Weissberg, R. P., & Greenberg, M. T. (1998). School and community competence-enhancement and prevention programs. In W. Damon (Series Ed.) & I. E. Sigel & K. A. Renninger (Vol. Eds.), *Handbook of child psychology: Vol. 4. Child psychology in practice* (5th ed., pp. 877–954). New York: John Wiley & Sons.

William T. Grant Consortium on the School-Based Promotion of Social Competence. (1992). Drug and alcohol prevention curricula. In J. D. Hawkins, R. F. Catalano, & Associates (Eds.), *Communities that care: Action for drug abuse prevention* (pp. 129–148). San Francisco: Jossey-Bass.

World Health Organization. (2002, April). *Report of the second WHO/UNICEF meeting on Programming for adolescent health and development: What should we measure and how.* Chinang Mai, Thailand: Author.

World Health Organization. (2002). *World report on violence and health.* Geneva: Author.

Zimmerman, M. A. (2002). Empowerment theory: Psychological, organizational, and community levels of analysis. In J. Rappaport & E. Seidman (Eds.), *Handbook of community psychology* (pp. 43–63). New York: Plenum Press.

5

Prevention Science: Participatory Approaches and Community Case Studies

Steven B. Pokorny, Donna R. Baptiste, Patrick Tolan, Barton J. Hirsch, Bruce Talbot, Peter Ji, Roberta L. Paikoff, and Sybil Madison-Boyd

Introduction

This chapter explores the integration of academic and community responses and approaches to preventing the social problems of youth. We present case studies to illustrate our belief that scientific principles and community interests can be productively integrated and that the resulting merger is a valuable aspiration for prevention science. We view this issue as part of an ongoing conversation in community psychology where the goal is to refine our questions and demonstrate a fit between prevention science and utility (Tolan, Chertok, Keys, & Jason, 1990).

The increasing scope and intensity of youth problems influenced concerned citizens and groups in communities around the United States to demand greater attention to preventing and reducing them. Similarly, prevention scientists are engaged in experimental studies of interventions that are developmentally and contextually attuned, and there is evidence that systematically implemented interventions focused on enhancing youth development, and the multiple factors that influence it, can be useful in prevention (Tolan, Gorman-Smith, & Henry, in press). However, despite the existence of both community and academic responses to problems involving youth, there is little integration between the two. Research findings explaining youth's vulnerabilities and

Funding for this manuscript was made possible, in part, by a grant from the Robert Wood Johnson Foundation to Leonard Jason at DePaul University. We acknowledge the extensive contributions of Leonard Jason, who played a major role in overseeing the two case studies presented in this chapter. We also acknowledge the efforts of key community members (city leaders, police officials, public health workers, and school administrators) who collaborated with the DePaul University research team to develop, implement, and assess the intervention presented in these case studies.

interventions that may address them are rarely integrated into social and policy-related actions undertaken by individuals and groups in communities. As a result, prevention science has limited impact on community efforts to deter young people from engaging in risky behavior, and innovative community-initiated messages and outreach programs also designed to affect youth are not evaluated for effectiveness (Tolan & Brown, 1998).

This chapter presents an organizational framework that, in our view, improves the likelihood that this gap between academic and community approaches to prevention can be bridged. Our perspective assumes that the two are not inherently incompatible nor are they simpatico. We believe that the knowledge base of prevention science can be integrated with community initiatives to address, reduce, and even prevent the problems of youth (Learner, Fisher, & Weinberg, 2000). But the level of integration may depend on the nature of the scientific question or investigation, the focus of prevention initiatives, researcher and community values, and the intended outcome of prevention activities. To illustrate our ideas we present two case studies from a program of tobacco prevention research conducted at the Center for Community Research at DePaul University. This program is an example of research built on university–community partnerships to prevent youth tobacco use.

A Rationale for Integrating Academic and Community Approaches in Prevention

We offer three arguments for valuing community involvement and community influence in prevention research generated within the academy. First, scientific information and activities related to prevention are typically aimed at meeting the needs and challenges of communities (Lerner, Fisher, & Weinberg, 2000). Second, there are questions about the generalizability and soundness of risk models and intervention principles generated and refined within the laboratory-like approach in which many academic preventive efforts are grounded (Kellam & Rebok, 1992). Third, an increasing number of prevention theorists suggest that the impact and sustainability of interventions meant to affect youth problems are enriched by both academic and community theories and interventions (Schensul, 1999). These arguments focus on integrating academic and community understandings of prevention to narrow the gap between the research process and community action, the researcher and those researched, theoretical models of development and appreciation of context, and theory and application (Butterfoss, Goodman, & Wandersman, 1993; Schenshul, 1999). Therefore, we advocate for developing academic–community partnerships and present the key principles that may facilitate their effectiveness. We attempt to identify a connection between the nature of the prevention task at hand and the level of academic–community linkage that may be sought.

Defining Collaborators and Collaborations in Prevention

The wide use of the term *academic–community collaboration* without specification of its necessary features makes for uncertainty. In this chapter we use the term to specifically refer to a joint enterprise between academic prevention researchers and persons or institutions or other constituents within a community or population in which the prevention work is focused. *Academic* will refer to the individual or group of individuals who have formal scientific training and may be affiliated with a college, university, or private research institution. *Community* will refer to self-identified as well as officially designated representatives of a setting or population that is the focus of the scientific study. These people are thought to be representative of and understanding of the local ecology, norms, values, and needs and to be able to speak with and manage relationships with academic researchers. Our definition of community allows for individuals acting from self-motivations, designation by communities informally or formally engaging in the collaboration, action to represent cultural expressions and views, and a diverse set of perspectives from within a given community. These representatives may act independently and pluralistically or be under the watch of a central entity. In the first case study presented later in this chapter, the academic was Leonard Jason, a researcher at DePaul University; and the community was Bruce Talbot, a police officer in the town of Woodridge, Illinois (i.e., a suburb of Chicago) concerned about youth tobacco use in his community. In the second case study, the academic was a team of researchers led by Leonard Jason; and the community was represented by city leaders, police officials, public health workers, and school administrators in eight suburban Illinois communities involved in the collaborative efforts to prevent youth tobacco use.

Differentiating Collaboration

Although there are examples of academic–community collaborations operating as full partnerships from the outset and continuing well beyond a funding cycle or leadership regime, these may be rare. Most of these collaborations appear to grow out of academic-instigated, theoretically driven interests in a prevention science question or problem. Most are multiphasic and grow over time, not necessarily in a straightforward fashion; they are often multifaceted and influenced by persons, circumstances, and emerging changes in the science or community needs. In the first case study (i.e., that which occurred in Woodridge), a member of the community initiated contact with the researcher and the relationship began as a full partnership based primarily on community needs. In contrast, the researchers initiated contact with the eight communities in the second case study and the relationships were based largely on scientific needs. Over the life span of a collaborative venture, researchers and communities may be involved in differential roles and relationships based on the focus of prevention initiatives, researcher and community values, the nature of the scientific question or investigation, and the intended outcome of prevention activities. These factors may lead to variations in the nature of the collaborative relationship over time.

Evans, Rey, Hemphill, and Perkins (2001) differentiated five types of academic–community collaborative relationships noting differences in purpose, structure, and process for each level of linkage. Organized from lowest to highest community involvement, the types are: (a) networking, (b) cooperation or alliance, (c) coordination or partnership, (d) coalition, and (e) collaboration. The two case studies described later in this chapter would be classified at different levels of community involvement. The first case study could be considered at the highest level—collaboration (i.e., citizens are equally involved in decisions to define and develop the research project) because the community, represented by Officer Talbot, had an important role in every stage of the project from problem definition to program implementation. In contrast, the second case study could be considered at the middle level—coordination or partnership because the research team was identified as the leadership, but partnered with citizens to provide them with opportunities to engage in a collaborative effort that allowed both parties to tailor an innovation to the unique terrain of each community. These relationships also tend to differ on multiple dimensions, usually depending on the scientific tasks involved.

Types and Their Relation to the Prevention Science Task

We discussed that over the course of a program of research the nature of the collaboration and the relationships between the academic and community collaborators may develop and shift. We believe that this may be related to the several interdependent levels of knowledge that are needed to build an effective prevention program of research. These include: (a) generative studies of epidemiology and risk patterns, (b) theoretical formulations of the malleable predisposing and precipitating influences on risk or enhanced functioning in the face of risk, (c) tests of the interventions that might affect these potentially malleable factors, and (d) studies related to robustness and generalizability of the findings (Kellam & Rebok, 1992). It is very likely that academic–community linkages may vary over the life of the collaboration—operating at high intensity in some of the aforementioned levels of a prevention research program but low intensity levels in others. The two examples presented in the case study had very different scientific tasks, and consequently different levels of community involvement. The work in the first case study (i.e., Woodridge) was relatively small in scope and focused on developing and testing an intervention for a local problem, hence the collaboration involved a full partnership between a university researcher and one community police officer. In contrast, the work in the second case study (i.e., eight communities) was large in scope and focused on testing an existing intervention in multiple settings, hence the partnerships centered on adapting and implementing the intervention within each community, and the research team had primary responsibility for the larger study across communities.

   To illustrate how academic–community collaborations can differ in levels of community involvement and how the level of involvement may depend, in part, on the nature of the scientific task, we present two case studies from a program of prevention research built on university–community partnerships to prevent youth tobacco use. In providing both examples we illustrate that although collaboration may not be consistently used over the life of a prevention enterprise it can still be beneficial to the entire prevention process.

Case Studies: University-Community Collaborations to Prevent Youth Tobacco Use

The following two case studies presents a program of research by an academic team from the DePaul University in Chicago to develop and test an intervention to prevent youth tobacco use. This process involved two phases of university–community collaboration: (a) development and documentation of an innovation to reduce youth access to retail sources of tobacco as described in the first case study, and (b) assessing the effectiveness of that innovation in other communities by testing it in a random community trial with eight communities as described in the second case study. We will describe the program of research and highlight some of the methods used in the second phase to increase community participation with a random community trial.

Youth Tobacco Use

Smoking is the leading preventable cause of death in the United States, killing more than 400,000 people each year. This is more people than die each year of AIDS, homicide, suicide, automobile accidents, illegal drug use, and fires combined. In the United States, first use of tobacco almost always occurs during adolescence, typically before high school graduation (Centers for Disease Control [CDC], 1998). Youth who begin smoking at earlier ages are more likely to use larger amounts of tobacco, over longer periods of time, and have more difficulty quitting than are youth who begin smoking later in life. All of these factors place such youth at increased risk for developing long-term serious health consequences. Recent population estimates for persons under the age of 18 indicate that every day 5,500 youth try cigarettes for the first time, and nearly 3,000 more youth become established smokers (Gulpin, Choi, Berry, & Pierce, 1999). Even though these rates decreased somewhat in the past few years, rates of smoking among American youth remain unacceptably high. The 2000 National Youth Tobacco Survey indicated that rate of current smoking was 11% among middle school students in grades 6 to 8 and 28% among high school students in grades 9 to 12 (CDC, 2001). It is estimated that one out of every three youth who become regular smokers will die prematurely from tobacco-related illnesses. If the trend of early tobacco use does not change, approximately 5 million youth currently under the age of 18 years will die prematurely from smoking-attributable diseases.

Unfortunately, the majority of adolescent smoking preventive interventions used over the past few decades focused on individuals and produced mixed results with only modest gains for short periods (Lantz et al., 2000). These interventions do not address environmental factors that may induce youth to begin using tobacco. Youth access to tobacco may be an important environmental factor that contributes to the prevalence of youth tobacco use. In 1988, a research team led by Leonard Jason at DePaul University found about 80% of the tobacco retailers in the greater Chicago area sold cigarettes to minors despite a state law that prohibited such sales (Jason, Ji, Anes, & Xaverious, 1992), and the local media extensively publicized these findings. The Illinois state tobacco minimum-age-of-sales law was not effective primarily because of the procedures required to enforce the law. To enforce the tobacco sales law, a police officer would have to witness the minor purchasing cigarettes, and then would need to take the store owner to the police station to process the complaint. The complaint would ultimately result in a court trial, which made the enforcement process very time-intensive for police officers.

Case Study 1: Developing a University–Community Partnership to Prevent Youth Tobacco Use

After the tobacco access study was publicized, Officer Talbot of the Woodridge Police Department contacted Dr. Jason to indicate that his community solved the problem of retailers selling tobacco to minors. The chief of police sent a letter to local merchants informing them of the law and instructing them not to sell cigarettes to minors. The DePaul researcher countered that a letter, in and of itself, might not change the merchants' behavior, as merchants made considerable income from these sales, and the probability of being caught in this illegal activity was unlikely. Following these initial conversations, the DePaul researcher and the police officer decided to collaborate to further investigate problems and solutions related to preventing youth access to tobacco in this community. The first step in this process was to determine whether or not merchants were selling minors tobacco in Woodridge. To determine this, Officer Talbot was trained to conduct compliance checks, which involved sending minors into all the community's stores to assess the merchant's compliance with the tobacco sales law (i.e., to determine the extent to which merchants illegally sold cigarettes to minors). Subsequently, Officer Talbot recruited, trained, and supervised youth who participated in the study. It is noteworthy that all the resources for conducting these compliance checks came from the community and not the DePaul researcher. The mayor, community board, and police chief approved the allocation of personnel and financial resources from the police department budget to cover the associated costs (e.g., the police officer, the youth, wages, and money for the cigarette purchases). This decision helped to establish local ownership of the process. When the initial assessment revealed that 70% of the vendors sold cigarettes to minors, it was decided that a local tobacco-control ordinance should be developed to solve this problem. The local ordinance was designed to address the shortcomings of the state law and embrace an ecological perspective by targeting youth (e.g., prohibiting possession of tobacco by minors) and their environment (i.e., prohibiting tobacco sales to minors).

The collaboration between Officer Talbot and the DePaul researcher influenced drafting of Woodridge's tobacco licensing and enforcement law, which passed on May 1, 1989. This law was modeled after the local liquor control laws and contained several important features designed to decrease youth's access to retail sources of tobacco and to prevent youth tobacco use. The new law required each tobacco retailer to obtain a license to sell tobacco. This requirement helped to identify all local tobacco retailers, and the money generated from the license fee was used to repeatedly monitor whether the stores were in compliance with the law. Another provision specified that the licensee would be issued a citation every time store employees sold tobacco to minors. By holding store owners accountable for the actions of their employees, they would be more vigilant in training their employees not to sell tobacco to minors.

The new tobacco-control law established regular checks for retailer compliance with the law through unannounced inspections. During these inspections, underage youth would be sent into stores to attempt to purchase tobacco. The proactive compliance checks makes retailers more vigilant about preventing tobacco sales to minors and eliminates the problem of police officers having to wait to witness violations. Retailers found in violation of the law were reported to the mayor, who had the authority to suspend the tobacco sales license. Finally, the new law included a provision that prohibited the possession and use of tobacco by minors. Violations of this provision were considered civil rather than criminal offenses that result in a ticket carrying a $25 fine and parental notification of the incident. The possession provision was created to send a clear message that youth could not purchase or use tobacco in the community. Officer Talbot believed that this provision was important because he often observed youth congregating and smoking in front of the entrance to youth events (e.g., school dances), and he was powerless to stop them from modeling this negative behavior in front of other impressionable youth. He also felt that the presence of these groups contributed to the misperception that the majority of youth smoked and suggested that it was an acceptable community norm for youth to use tobacco. Officer Talbot wanted the authority to intervene and stop groups of youth using tobacco at local events because he believed that his actions could help to change community norms regarding youth tobacco use.

Evaluating the Initial University–Community Intervention

The Woodridge Police Department planned to enforce the new tobacco-control law through quarterly compliance checks with all tobacco retailers. Before beginning enforcement activities, Officer Talbot personally visited each tobacco retailer to provide information and answer any questions about the new law. In June of 1989, the compliance checks indicated that the rate of illegal tobacco sales to minors had fallen from 70 to 35%. In accordance with Woodridge's new tobacco-control law, violators were issued first-offense warnings. The remaining stores that were compliant with the law received letters from the Police Department thanking them for refusing to sell tobacco to minors. In August of 1989, the second round of compliance checks indicated that the rate of illegal tobacco sales to minors increased from 35 to 36%, and half of these stores were repeat offenders from June. The repeat offenders received a one-day tobacco license suspension and a $400 fine. None of these merchants contested the penalty. The new violators were issued first-offense warnings. The remaining stores that complied with the law received the police thank-you letter. At this point, Officer Talbot contacted Dr. Jason to indicate that the problem of youth access to tobacco was solved as they had documented a 50% reduction in illegal sales of tobacco to minors. The DePaul researcher suggested that the rates would quickly rise unless Woodridge continued to conduct the compliance checks. The community agreed and continued unannounced compliance checks. In November of 1989, the third round of compliance checks indicated that the rate of illegal tobacco sales to minors decreased from 36% 0%. Over the subsequent four compliance checks (i.e., a one-year period), the rate of illegal tobacco sales to minors was maintained below 5%. In addition, 50 minors were cited for possession of tobacco during this time, and they were each assessed a $25 fine (four of these youth were repeat offenders within this time period).

Woodridge was the first community in the United States to establish documentation showing that legislation and enforcement could produce sustained reductions in illegal cigarette sales to minors. In addition, the creation and enforcement of the new tobacco-control legislation was related to lower rates of regular smoking among youth in Woodridge. Nearly two years after passage of this legislation, the percentage of seventh- and eighth-grade regular smokers was reduced from 16% to 5% (Jason, Ji, Anes, & Birkhead, 1991). Seven-year follow-up data (Jason, Berk, Schnopp-Wyatt, & Talbot, 1999) with a sample of high school youth indicated that youth who lived in two communities with regular enforcement of tobacco sales laws (i.e., one of which was Woodridge) compared to youth living in three communities without regular enforcement of tobacco sales laws had significantly fewer regular smokers (8.1% vs. 15.5%, respectively) and used significantly less smokeless tobacco (8.7% vs. 16.7%, respectively).

Implications of the Collaboration for Social Change

The extent of minors' easy access to retail tobacco helped motivate federal legislators to establish a national policy to prevent youth access to tobacco. In the spring of 1990, Health and Human Services Secretary Louis Sullivan proposed a national legislative initiative to reduce cigarette sales to minors. Several important features of this proposed legislation followed recommendations derived from the Woodridge study. In 1992, Congress enacted the Alcohol, Drug Abuse and Mental Health Agency Reorganization Act, which mandated that states pass and enforce laws to prohibit the sale and distribution of tobacco products to minors (Jacobson, Wassermen, & Anderson, 1997). In 1996 the Department of Health and Human Services finalized and implemented this law, which was referred to as the Synar Amendment, which required states to both reduce illegal sales of tobacco to youth to less than 20% and to regularly enforce laws through the types of compliance checks that had been used in Woodridge. Key features of this law were similar to the Woodridge model, and this model provided states with a road map for implementing the federal mandate.

Reflections on the Collaborative Process

The police department in Woodridge was meaningfully involved in the development, implementation, and assessment of the intervention. Moreover, Officer

Talbot fostered acceptance of this program among his police force and the broader community. After two years of working on the project, he transferred all responsibilities for the program to other members of the police force. The partnership led to an assessment of the nature and extent of a local problem, the development an intervention informed by local knowledge and scientific methodology, an evaluation of the impact of this intervention, and a sustained community effort to prevent youth tobacco use. For example, the Woodridge Police Department continues to consistently implement the program today. Overall, the partnership resulted in the development and documentation of a new intervention strategy to address the problem of youth tobacco use.

From a prevention science viewpoint, several important questions remained unanswered. Because the Woodridge model used both tobacco sales laws and tobacco possession laws, it was unclear if the documented decrease in regular smokers could be attributed to the restriction in retail sources of tobacco, the enforcement of the tobacco possession law, or both. In addition, it was not clear if this finding could be replicated in other communities.

Case Study 2: A Broader Application of the University–Community Intervention

To answer the important questions remaining after the Woodridge study and affect broader social change through policy research and advocacy, the DePaul University research team decided to test the intervention in a random community trial. However, the purpose of this task differed considerably from that in the Woodridge study and consequently presented unique challenges to involving the community (i.e., city leaders, police officials, public health workers, and school administrators) in the process of adapting and implementing the intervention. The Youth Tobacco Access Project (YTAP) was a three-year project funded by The Robert Wood Johnson Foundation. YTAP occurred from 1999 until 2001, and involved a randomized community trial to test the hypothesis that the combined enforcement of tobacco sales laws and tobacco possession laws would be more effective in reducing youth tobacco use than enforcement of tobacco sales laws alone.

A random sample of towns in northern and central Illinois, each with a population between 5,000 and 100,000, were initially contacted to participate in the study. Recruited towns met specific inclusion criteria: (a) the community was willing to help investigate the impact of tobacco-control policies on youth tobacco use; (b) if there was a local tobacco possession law, the police were enforcing it at a relatively low rate because it would be inappropriate to ask police departments to decrease or stop their enforcement efforts; (c) community officials were willing to be randomized into one of two experimental conditions, and the police department agreed to implement the enforcement strategy specified by the assigned condition; and (d) school superintendents and principals were willing to help the project obtain outcome data through annual student self-report surveys.

Eight towns met the selection criteria and were matched for population size and median family income and then randomly assigned to one of the two conditions: possession (P)—enforcement of tobacco possession and sales laws; or nonpossession (NP)—enforcement of only the tobacco sales law. Police departments in both conditions checked retailer compliance with local tobacco sales laws two to three times a year. Retailers who violated the sales laws were issued citations and were fined by the court. For towns in the P condition, we worked with police departments to increase enforcement of tobacco possession laws so that minors were issued citations for possession or use of tobacco products in public locations. The university–community partnerships worked together to assess the prevalence of youth tobacco use and attitudes toward tobacco-control laws (i.e., through an annual self-report student survey) and the rate of illegal tobacco sales to minors (i.e., through independent compliance checks on tobacco retailers).

Findings from this study (Jason, Pokorny, & Schoeny, 2003) suggest that the combination of local enforcement of the tobacco sales law and tobacco possession law reduced the incidence and prevalence of youth tobacco use. Because a large proportion of children get tobacco from social sources (Harrison, Fulkerson, & Park, 2000), efforts focused only on eliminating retail sources of tobacco may not be sufficient to reduce tobacco use among youth. However, these efforts combined with possession bans may make it harder for minors to get tobacco from other minors, because fewer minors may be willing to risk the consequence of being caught with tobacco. Possession bans also make it easier to reduce subtle peer pressure when students congregate at social events and publicly smoke and encourage others to engage in this behavior.

Assessing Community Readiness for Youth Tobacco Prevention

Many community psychologists embrace the ecological perspective that necessitates the modification or adaptation of preventive interventions to fit the unique characteristics of a community. A related but less explored perspective extends this conceptualization to include an assessment of the community's readiness for the intervention itself. Some of the most carefully adapted interventions may fail when members of the community are not brought into a dialogue about the nature and implementation of an intervention. The DePaul University research team adapted a model, the Community Readiness Theoretical Model (Donnermeyer et al., 1997), to bring multiple parties into the process of assessing community readiness for the tobacco-control intervention using behaviorally based criteria. After baseline data were collected, the research team conducted semistructured interviews with police officials to assess community readiness for the intervention. It was very clear from reviewing these data that each community was at a different point in their understanding and motivation to think about the issue of youth access to tobacco. The research team involved the police officials in the process of assessing community readiness by having them rate their own level of readiness as well as the level they wanted to be at a year later. The self-assessment and goal-setting activity fostered dialogue between the researchers and the community about the necessary steps to achieve the stated goals.

In addition, the community readiness data provided a framework to focus the collaborative efforts to implement the intervention in a way that was

compatible with the unique characteristics of each community. When the research team worked with a community that had little recognition that there
was a local problem, it was important to first have a dialogue with them about
their perceptions of the problem and share with them data collected from the
schools and merchants who sold tobacco illegally. In this process, the research
team and the community developed a better understanding of the problem (i.e.,
youth access to tobacco and youth tobacco use) in their community. Increasing
awareness of the local problem helped to set the stage for more conversations
about what might need to be done to deal with these problems. In contrast,
when the research team worked with communities in the preparation stage
(i.e., community recognizes the local problem, is aware of the pros and cons of
different efforts to address the problem, and is making decisions about what
will be done and obtaining the required resources), police officials found the
self-assessment of community readiness useful because it helped inform decisions about what needed to be done and provided a benchmark to assess
progress toward their stated goals. The very process of discussing these issues
in a safe and collaborative setting often helped the team to prepare for change
and take action. In some of the communities the research team learned that
there was a need for a stronger tobacco-control ordinance, and in these situations the research team worked with towns in developing new ordinances.

Enhancing Community Involvement and Benefit

The case studies present two examples of university–community collaborations
that attempted to give citizens meaningful involvement in the research process
but differed in the levels of community involvement. We believe that the level
of collaboration should be guided by careful consideration of the scientific task.
In the Woodridge study, this task involved assessing the nature and extent of
a local problem, developing an intervention informed by local knowledge and
scientific methodology, and evaluating the impact of this intervention. In contrast, the scientific task of YTAP was to answer important questions about
Woodridge's intervention components and to determine if the documented effects could be replicated in other communities. Moreover, the nature of these
tasks dictated how the initial relationship between the community and the
researcher was formed. In the first example, the community approached the
research team. In the second example, the research team approached the communities. Both initiatives provided excellent opportunities to identify critical
elements to building partnerships, which we explore in detail next.

Building Collaborations: Critical Elements

As we have previously indicated, researchers and communities may not always
pursue a high level of collaboration in every aspect of the research process.
Indeed, partnerships may begin at a low level of intensity and progress to more
egalitarian structure over time. Notwithstanding, because we view community
involvement as a critical community empowerment process that can positively

affect prevention, we offer guidelines for how it can be enhanced in university-sponsored prevention research and programs. The extant literature offers some important principles and strategies that should inform and enhance the development of academic–community collaborations. We briefly summarize the accumulated guidelines to illustrate the potential benefits as well as challenges that may occur in the collaborative prevention process. Examples are presented from the second case study, YTAP, because the nature of this prevention task presented the greatest challenges for a high level of community involvement.

Work Across Systems

There is increasing evidence that preventive efforts that focus on multiple aspects of the developmental ecology and link across settings and systems impinging on youth and families are the most effective. Therefore, we recommend collaborations that reflect the multifactorial risk and protective influences on youth by developing multisectoral/multisystemic approaches involving focused interventions targeting youth at risk. In YTAP, the research team worked across community systems by developing partnerships with city leaders, police officials, public health workers, and school administrators to adapt and implement the intervention.

Balance and Integrate Service and Science Goals

Often at the outset of prevention work tensions may arise because academics are more focused on the scientific goals while the community members and many of the prevention staff may be more oriented toward the service interests. We view these tensions as inevitable aspects of collaborative work versus making value judgments as to which should be primary and which is the more important. Schensul (1999) advocates that researchers collaborate with community to balance and integrate service and science goals. For example: (a) developing a clearer understanding of youth and their issues (e.g., formative or basic research); (b) identifying messages and strategies that may reduce youth's behavior problems (e.g., intervention research); (c) using ideas and strategies in preexisting programs for a new setting (e.g., dissemination research, building intervention theory, and translation research); (d) improving the quality of a program and staff (e.g., process evaluation and building treatment integrity); (e) determining if a program is effective (e.g., outcome research and efficacy research); (f) changing an existing program to meet the needs of a specific population or setting (e.g., piloting and building on intervention theory); (g) developing a new program from an old program (e.g., building on outcome research); and (h) influencing local and state policies and policy makers (e.g., policy research). In the Woodridge study, the nature of the prevention task as well as the shared leadership and decision-making process permitted a natural balance between science and service goals. In YTAP, the nature of the prevention task required considerably more effort from the university–community partners to balance science goals (i.e., goals focused on dissemination research, building intervention theory, and outcome research) with service goals (i.e., goals focused on developing a clearer understanding of youth tobacco use, perceptions of tobacco-control laws, and youth access to tobacco and then to provide the community and policy makers with this information to shape local policy and enforcement efforts).

Build the Collaboration on Sound Management Principles

Sustainability and enhanced community capacity are related to the collaboration structure. We suggest adopting time-honored principles that facilitate coalition building in public and private sectors, at national and international levels (Butterfoss et al., 1993). These principles include: (a) involving all partners early, (b) bringing the entire coalition together on a regular basis to exchange information and to participate in key decisions, (c) defining roles and responsibilities clearly and repeatedly, (d) addressing conflicts honestly, (e) preparing for the future early and often, (f) phasing prevention activities to maximize capacity for a mutual transfer of skills and information, (g) identifying benchmark goals to be accomplished, and (h) attending to human resource concerns. These principles were critical for the development of partnerships with communities in YTAP. Two of these principles were particularly essential and deserve mention. Early in the process, the research team spent a considerable amount of time identifying key community members interested in tobacco control and establishing networks among these individuals and the research team and defining roles and responsibilities among these partners.

Maintain Openness and Transparency at Every Level of the Collaboration

Collaboration suggests an egalitarian approach, but it is common that one agency assumes final responsibility for some aspects (e.g., fiscal policies and the institutional review processes). Thus power and decision making may not be equally shared over the course of a partnership. This reality does not preclude the existence of a high level of collaboration with a community (Schensul, 1999). The existence of ambiguities around power-sharing and decision making requires transparency on the part of the leading partner, who must openly and regularly discuss external constraints that may hamper the collaborative process and solicit recommendations from communities about specific issues (e.g., hiring, informed consent). In YTAP, for example, a parent in one community was upset about the passive consent procedure for the student survey, which led the research team to switch to active consent procedures (Jason, Pokorny, & Katz, 2001). Because the research team developed a strong partnership with each of the schools, team members were able to discuss this decision openly and solicited their recommendations to develop a range of more active consent procedures that did not strain school or project resources (e.g., attaching the consent form to report cards that had to be signed and returned to the school). However, two of the schools were unwilling to change the procedures, and the research team continued to use passive consent with them. Because schools were involved in developing the new procedures, the research team was able to obtain extremely high participation rates during our second wave of data collection, and there were no significant sociodemographic differences between the two waves of data collection (Pokorny, Jason, Schoeny, Townsend, & Curie, 2001).

Attend to the Leadership and Organizational Structure

Academic–community partnerships may be unusual types of organizations requiring innovative or multilayered organizational structures and decision-making processes. This may not be given much consideration by academics or community collaborators. Direct and careful discussion and formulation of the leadership and organizational structure becomes critical for managing the challenges and the complex demands of the collaboration. We suggest talking early, openly, and honestly about the optimal leadership and organizational structure that will work in the best interests of fulfilling the prevention mission (Evans at al., 2001). In YTAP, the partnerships developed unique organizational structures with each community based on competencies and needs. For example, one school system was highly organized and preferred to assume the leadership role for completing the student survey; whereas another school system, which had few resources and many demands, wanted the research team to take the lead role in planning and conducting the survey. At the same time, however, the research team was required to maintain a certain level of leadership with all communities for the multisite prevention trial, but this was discussed openly and honestly with communities.

Acknowledge and Manage Agendas

Tensions between academic and community interests during collaborations may arise because of differences in initial agendas, subgroup agendas, individual needs and expectations, and also differences in interpretation of incidents during the course of the intervention. Given that these agendas cannot always be reconciled, it is critical to develop mechanisms for balancing the interests posed by each. We believe that the greater the collaborative involvement in such decision making, the greater the likelihood that the complexities involved in reconciling competing agendas will be addressed fully and with circumspection, rather than resorting to unilateral decisions or decisions that emphasize one agenda with no regard for the another. For example, the YTAP research team frequently found that working with multiple subsystems in our target communities required a commitment to continual negotiation. There were essential criteria that had to be met for the larger study, but the specific methods for accomplishing these objectives were negotiated with members of each community.

Prepare for Inevitable Changes

The inevitability of midcourse changes in project strategies, responsibilities, and occasionally objectives can test the metal of a collaborative venture (Evans et al., 2001). Planning for change must be conducted on every level of the partnership so those community members are apprised about the present and future status of the initiative. Undertaken early, this step may prevent disruptions and decreased morale related to a sense of broken promises, abandoned commitments, lapsed leadership, and tokenism. In addition, transitions and changes within the partnership can also be viewed as opportunities for the emergence of collaborative problem solving, reevaluation of work and mission, and in the end create new opportunities for reflection and action. For example, the YTAP research team had to develop strategies for handling changes in school administrations. In one community, the entire school district was reorganized, resulting in the consolidation of two participating schools and the appointment of a new principal and assistant principal. The research team met with the superintendent and the new administration over the summer break to reevaluate the mission of the project, including the roles and responsibilities, and establish a plan so that the new school could continue participating in the study.

Plan for Dissemination

Academic researchers and community partners often have different priorities and agendas regarding how results related to the work should be managed and disseminated. Academicians may be interested in using scientific journals and professional meetings. Community members and agencies may be interested in bringing results to the attention of their board of directors, local school councils, the community at large, local politicians, and policy makers. We suggest that dissemination of data should be handled carefully with all agendas on the table. Attention to outcomes (e.g., changes in youth behavior over time) as well as process findings (e.g., progress and mechanisms of collaboration) may generate information that can be useful to the academic community as well as to policy makers, community program developers, and local leaders and residents. For example, the YTAP research team created a report based on the student survey data for each school and asked if the principal and superintendent would agree to share this information with the police and broader community. Typically schools agreed to share this information. However, in one community the principals of the two participating schools did not want the information disseminated outside of the individual schools. Apparently, one of the schools had problems with student behavior, and as a consequence, the principal was concerned about releasing information that might reinforce negative stereotypes about this school and its students. The research team was sensitive to these concerns and negotiated a compromise with school administrators so that only aggregate data (i.e., including both schools) were summarized and shared with the police and broader community.

Strengthen Community Capacity to Participate

Attention to small details of collaboration can go a long way in enhancing community involvement. These include: (a) using a meeting location that facilitates the members' attendance, (b) maintaining an agenda informed by community interests and needs, (c) scheduling meetings when the community can attend, (d) offering infrastructure to support attendance, (e) promoting openness in language and feedback, (f) facilitating equal access to information, and (e) managing group processes to create a community-friendly atmosphere. In YTAP, for example, members of the research team always met with partners in their communities at times that were convenient for the partners, even when this meant that the researchers had to leave the office at 4:00 a.m. to drive to the community for a 7:00 a.m. meeting.

Promote Mutual Respect and Transfer of Knowledge and Skills

The skills and competencies of each partner must be mutually respected and applied in the collaborative process. This may require a paradigmatic shift in individual epistemologies about knowledge and its application. Ideally, over the life of a partnership a transfer of knowledge and skills will occur that builds the competencies of each partner. Such transfer can only occur if there is a mutual recognition of and respect for the existence of academic and community knowledge bases and their value for the development of effective prevention science. For example, the YTAP director collaborated with communities to obtain grants from the Illinois Liquor Control Commission (ILCC), so that police departments were paid by the ILCC for conducting three rounds of compliance checks on their tobacco retailers. This collaborative process helped police departments to learn how to complete the grant process, and these communities were able to get additional grants from the ILCC on their own after the formal research process ended.

Address Barriers to Sustainability

In our view, the organizational and leadership structure on which the collaboration rests is perhaps the most critical factor in sustainability. We suggest that incorporation of community empowerment goals into the mission of the collaboration will enhance the partnership's flexibility and ability to survive if new leadership emerges, mission and goals evolve, prevention focus shifts, or grant support ends. A coalition in which community citizens own and manage the process can survive, even after academic constituents move on. Indeed, the energy of citizens and agencies to keep the work going may be the most vital forces in achieving a sustained response over time. In YTAP, for example, an important part of the intervention was building networks of concerned community members and raising community awareness of a narrowly defined problem by providing specific feedback on the prevalence of youth tobacco use and the rate of illegal tobacco sales to minors. Moreover, the community (i.e., police department) delivers the intervention rather than the research team. These components help to create a momentum in the community focused on youth tobacco use, transfer of skills required to address the problem, and feedback on community efforts to address the problem. This combination resulted in communities sustaining the program well beyond the formal research process.

Conclusion

We discussed the reality that community members may only be partially involved in academic research and programs, but even limited involvement can have beneficial effects on prevention science. Two contemporary trends may propel researchers to seek higher levels of collaboration with community members, beginning early and operating over the entire life span of a prevention initiative. First, there are converging trends in policy, funding, citizen interests, and prevention science for community involvement and responsibility for addressing social and health problems (Kreuter et al., 2000). Second, there is a growing recognition that when community members and groups are involved early and extensively in the prevention process there is an increased likelihood that what is implemented will be applicable to that community and will be sustained (Beeker, Gunthier-Grey, & Raj, 1998). This collaboration may act as a catalyst to structural change in both community organization and in academic thinking and organization (Freudenburg & Manoncourt, 1998). As a consequence, academic–community collaborations may lead to infrastructure, risk specification, and intervention approaches that are most promising, have some scientific basis, and are more likely to be used.

Academic–community collaborations such as those discussed in this chapter can indeed be an efficient approach to understanding and preventing problems of youth. In addition, the increasing interest in decentralization of control and resources to solve community problems, and the growing interest in complex ecologically based prevention models, may increase the demand for academic–community linkages. However, we are mindful that, at the moment, there is woefully little information about the efficacy of high-intensity collaborations over noncollaborative approaches in prevention. Future research should systematically examine the effects of different levels of community involvement on program efficacy to provide prevention science with guidelines for program development, implementation, and assessment. Nevertheless, we believe that the synergy created by academic–community collaboration can be transformational, where the collaboration itself can affect deeper structures of change and produce the most promising practices to help youth and their families.

References

Beeker, C., Guenthier-Grey, C., & Raj, A. (1998). Community empowerment paradigm drift and the primary prevention of HIV/AIDS. *Social Science Medicine, 46,* 831–842.

Butterfoss, F. D., Goodman, R. M., & Wandersman, A. (1993). Community coalitions for prevention and health promotion. *Health Education Research, 8,* 315–330.

Centers for Disease Control. (1998). Incidence of initiation of cigarette smoking—United States 1965–1996. *Morbidity and Mortality Weekly Report, 47,* 837–840.

Centers for Disease Control. (2001). Youth tobacco surveillance—United States 2000. *Morbidity and Mortality Weekly Report, 50,* 1–86.

Donnermeyer J. F., Oetting, E. R., Plested, B. A., Edwards, R. W., Jumper-Thurman, P., et al. (1997). Community readiness and prevention programs. *Journal of the Community Development Society, 28,* 65–83.

Evans, G. D., Rey, J., Hemphill, M. H., & Perkins, D. (2001). Academic–community collaboration: An ecology for early childhood violence prevention. *American Journal of Preventive Medicine, 20,* 22–30.

Freudenburg, N., & Manoncourt, E. (1998). Urban health promotion: Current practices and new directions. *Health Education & Behavior, 25,* 138–145.

Gulpin, E. A., Choi, W. S. Berry, C., & Pierce, J. P. (1999). How many adolescents start smoking each day in the United States? *Journal of Adolescent Health, 25,* 248–255.

Harrison, P. A., Fulkerson, J. A., & Park, E. (2000). The relative importance of social versus commercial sources in youth access to tobacco, alcohol, and other drugs. *Preventive Medicine, 31,* 39–48.

Jacobson, P. D., Wassermen, J., & Anderson, J. R. (1997). Historical overview of tobacco legislation. *Journal of Social Issues, 53,* 75–95.

Jason, L. A., Berk, M., Schnopp-Wyatt, D. L., & Talbot, B. (1999). Effects of enforcement of youth access laws on smoking prevalence. *American Journal of Community Psychology, 27,* 143–160.

Jason, L. A., Ji, P. Y., Anes, M., & Birkhead, S. H. (1991). Active enforcement of cigarette control laws in the prevention of cigarette sales to minors. *Journal of American Medical Association, 266,* 3159–3161.

Jason, L. A., Ji, P. Y., Anes, M., & Xaverious, P. (1992). Assessing cigarette sales rates to minors. *Evaluation & the Health Professions, 15,* 375–384.

Jason, L. A., Pokorny, S., & Katz, R. (2001). Passive versus active consent: A case study in school settings. *Journal of Community Psychology, 29,* 53–68.

Jason, L. A., Pokorny, S. B., & Schoeny, M. (2003). The effects of enforcements and possession laws on youth prevalence. *Critical Public Health, 13,* 33–45.

Kellam, S. G., & Rebok, G. W. (1992). Building developmental and etiological theory through epidemiologically based preventive intervention trials. In J. McCord & R. Tremblay (Eds.), *Preventing antisocial behavior: Interventions from birth through adolescence* (pp. 162–195). New York: Guilford Press.

Kreuter, M., Sabol, B., O'Donovan, A., Donovan, J., Klein, L., et al. (2000). Commentaries on Fawcett et al.'s proposed memorandum of collaboration. *Public Health Report, 115,* 180–190.

Lantz, P. M., Jacobson, P. D., Warner, K. E., Wasserman, J., Pollack, H. A., et al. (2000). Investing in youth tobacco control: A review of smoking prevention and control strategies. *Tobacco Control, 9,* 47–63.

Lerner, R. M., Fisher, C. B., & Weinberg, R. A. (2000). Toward a science for and of the people: Promoting civil society through the application of development science. *Child Development, 71,* 11–20.

Pokorny, S. B., Jason, L. A., Schoeny, M., Townsend, S. M., & Curie, C. J. (2001). Do participation rates change when active consent procedures replace passive consent. *Evaluation Review, 25,* 567–580.

Schensul, J. J. (1999). Organizing community research partnerships in the struggle against AIDS. *Health Education & Behavior, 26,* 266–283.

Tolan, P. H., & Brown, C. H. (1998). Methods for evaluating intervention and prevention efforts. In P. K. Trickett & C. Schellenbach (Eds.), *Violence against children in the family and the community* (pp. 439–464). Washington, DC: American Psychological Association.

Tolan, P. H., Chertok, F., Keys, C., & Jason, L. (1990). Conversing about theories, methods, and community research. In P. H. Tolan, C. Keys, F. Chertok, & L. Jason (Eds.), *Researching community psychology: The integration of theories and methods* (pp. 3–8). Washington, DC: American Psychological Association.

Tolan, P. H., Gorman-Smith, D., & Henry, D. (2003). The developmental-ecology of urban males' youth violence. *Developmental Psychology, 39,* 274–291.

6

University–Community Partnerships: A Framework and an Exemplar

*Yolanda Suarez-Balcazar, Margaret I. Davis,
Joseph Ferrari, Philip Nyden, Bradley Olson,
Josefina Alvarez, Paul Molloy, and Paul Toro*

University–community partnerships are at the heart of community research and action. In these partnerships, university researchers work in collaboration with a variety of settings and programs, involving community leaders, agency staff, or members of grassroots and self-help groups. This chapter reviews the literature on university–community partnerships and provides a framework of 10 characteristics that are typical of successful partnership endeavors. We illustrate these principles with an example of a collaborative research project undertaken by a DePaul University research team that has engaged in a 10-year partnership with a community-based, self-run, residential substance abuse recovery program called Oxford House. Through a review of this collaborative effort, the authors examine the distinct opportunities and constraints in adopting unconventional methods of inquiry and action, highlighting a number of practical and theoretical issues that have been raised as the research team has striven to maintain a mutually beneficial alliance throughout the endeavor. The experience of the research team demonstrates the benefits to be gained from cultivating and maintaining collaborative university–community partnerships.

The past 10 years have been marked by a new vision of how universities and communities work together. Institutions of higher education have become more concerned with providing learning experiences that link theoretical

Funding for the Oxford House research projects was made possible, in part, by grants awarded to Leonard Jason from the National Institute on Alcohol Abuse and Alcoholism (Grant #AA12218) and the National Institute on Drug Abuse (Grant #DA13231). The authors express special gratitude to Dr. Jason, who has been critically involved in all phases of the Oxford House project and has provided invaluable feedback on sections of this manuscript. The authors thank the men and women of Oxford House who devoted time and interest to participate in each of the research projects, as well as the numerous students and volunteers who have participated in this collaboration, including Kathy Erikson, Bertel Williams, and Leon Venable for sharing their stories, insights, and experiences in this collaborative process.

principles and real-life situations. In addition, some universities want to build bridges to bring their local communities and their institutions closer together. University–community partnerships depart from traditional research endeavors in a variety of important ways. Within collaborative partnerships, communities are not merely seen as an extension of the laboratory experience. The traditional researcher's role of consultant or expert changes to collaborator and partner, and the research endeavor becomes a participatory process that is not necessarily under the control of the researcher (Connors & Seifer, 2000; Nyden, Figert, Shibley, & Burrows, 1997).

As suggested by Mattessich and Monsey (1992), "Collaboration is a mutually beneficial and a well-defined relationship entered into by two or more organizations to achieve common goals" (p. 11). In university–community partnerships, faculty and students work in collaboration with a variety of community settings and programs from grassroots groups and community-based organizations, to human service agencies and schools. Concepts that guide these partnerships include one articulated by sociologist Philip Nyden (Nyden et al., 1997) as *adding chairs to the research table* and the concept of empowerment (Fawcett et al., 1994; Rappaport, 1981, 1987). Based on these concepts, in collaborative partnerships community leaders, residents, or members of a community-based organization become active members of the research team. The research agenda is decided in collaboration and is guided by the needs of the community, rather than the needs of the researcher (Balcazar, Keys, Kaplan, & Suarez-Balcazar, 1999; Bond & Keys, 1993; Fawcett et al., 1994; Rappaport et al., 1985; Selener, 1997; Serrano-Garcia, 1990).

Working in collaboration with the community provides unique opportunities to identify and build on the assets and resources that exist within the community, allowing for a more accurate analysis of their social reality and an increased likelihood that programs will be used to greater benefit (Jason, 1997; Ostrom, Lerner, & Freel, 1995). Experiential knowledge is brought to the research process when participants can articulate their issues and concerns, assist in the development of materials, and participate in the process of facilitating change. Community members are then more likely to develop a sense of ownership of the research effort and more likely to act on the findings of the research (Fawcett et al., 1994; Serrano-Garcia & Bond, 1994; Suarez-Balcazar, Balcazar, & Fawcett, 1992). Within these mutually beneficial alliances, partners engage in joint reflection and analysis of the needs and values of the community, collaborate in the research endeavor, and use findings to support social change efforts (Jason, 1997; Roussos & Fawcett, 2000).

Descriptions of partnership principles and conceptual analyses of collaboration are available in a variety of fields and disciplines, including community psychology (see Bond & Keys, 1993; Harper & Salina, 2000; Kaftarian & Hensen, 1994; Suarez-Balcazar, Harper, & Lewis, 2002); public health (Connors & Seifer, 2000; Kreuter, Lezin, & Young, 2000; Roussos & Fawcett, 2000); and sociology (see Park & Lee, 1999). Furthermore, there are many model centers dedicated to this work (e.g., the HUD's office of University Partnerships, the Loka Institute, Comm-Org: The On-line Conference on Community Organizing and Development, Loyola Center for Urban Research and Learning [CURL], and the San Francisco Community-Campus Partnerships for Health). Based on a review of this literature and these models, it is evident that a number of principles are shared across disciplines that seem to best characterize the development and maintenance of collaborative partnerships. What follows is a review of 10 common characteristics and an illustration of these principles in the DePaul University–Oxford House research project.

Ten Characteristics of Collaborative University– Community Partnerships

The following characteristics provide a framework for building and sustaining mutually beneficial and truly collaborative partnerships between universities and communities.

1. *Develop a relationship based on trust and mutual respect.* The development of a collaborative relationship between two different entities takes time and commitment to the partnership (Mattessich & Monsey, 1992). Partnerships with the community imply a diverse set of stakeholders (from funders, executive directors, members of the board of directors, and program staff, to community leaders and residents and participants) and, thus, it is paramount to identify early on all of the constituents who will participate in the endeavor. Partnerships call for flexibility in working with these multiple layers of decision makers (Mattessich & Monsey, 1992), who might be invested and more intimately involved in different stages and aspects of the collaborative endeavor. However, all interested potential partners should be involved and informed throughout the partnership-building process.

   Establishing trust is a necessary foundation for creating a successful partnership and involves appropriate entry into the setting and taking time to get to know and understand the setting and the different stakeholders. To establish trust, partners identify a common vision and goals for the partnership, clarify expectations, and discuss time commitment and resources needed to develop ownership over the collaboration.

2. *Maximize, use, and exchange resources.* Each of the partners brings to the relationship a set of resources and strengths that need to be recognized and valued (Connors & Seifer, 2000; Mattessich & Monsey, 1992). Typically, faculty and students bring access to resources (e.g., grant funding), knowledge of research literature and research methods (e.g., research-trained student personnel), and knowledge and access to technology (e.g., computer software). Community partners bring knowledge of the specific area or population of interest, experiential knowledge of the issues involved, as well as knowledge of the cultural and contextual characteristics of the setting and community (Bond, 1990; Jordan, Bogat, & Smith, 2001). They also provide access to key informants, community leaders, and networks in the community as well as program participants (Suarez-Balcazar et al., 2002). Because there is often a difference in the resources contributed by

the two sets of partners, access to resources might create an unequal, unbalanced relationship of power and control, which one needs to be aware of and willing to address with the partners (Nelson, Prillettensky, & MacGillivary, 2001).

3. *Build a two-way learning relationship.* Ideally, each partner comes to the partnership ready to learn, as well as ready to guide. Collaborative partnerships for research recognize that there is knowledge in both the university and the community. It challenges and eliminates false boundaries between the knowledge residing in academia and knowledge existing in the community. Community members' knowledge is often devalued by an illusion of superiority of academic expertise, when in fact one knowledge set is not superior to the other. Indeed, experiential knowledge and academic knowledge may complement each other (Bond, 1990; Serrano-Garcia, 1990).

4. *Establish open lines of communication.* Establishing a good communication system is at the heart of collaborative partnerships. This involves what is communicated, how it is communicated, and the style and language used in such communications. Partnership goals, expected roles, and outcomes are agreed on early in the process (Connors & Seifer, 2000; Panet-Raymond, 1992). Given the complex nature of partnerships, goals and expectations may change throughout the process, and they need to be discussed and negotiated openly using both formal and informal channels of communication. Being sensitive to the communication mode and style of the setting may imply using modes of communication that work for the setting, including formal memos, regularly scheduled meetings, e-mail messages, phone calls, and one-on-one visits (Suarez-Balcazar et al., 2002). For a relationship to be successful it is essential to establish open and frequent communication by providing updates, discussing issues openly, and conveying all information to one another as well as to others outside the team (Mattessich & Monsey, 1992).

5. *Respect and celebrate diversity.* Human diversity characterizes these partnerships, and respecting and celebrating diversity becomes essential to relationship building (Bond & Keys, 1993; Jordan et al., 2001; Nelson et al., 2001; Trickett, 1994; Trickett, Watts, & Birman, 1994). Most community settings in urban areas, from schools to agencies and community-based organizations, serve a diverse population, based on characteristics such as ethnicity, race, sexual orientation, and ability level. Celebrating and respecting diversity involves recognizing that people have the right to be different from one another (Nelson et al., 2001; Rappaport, 1981). Respecting diversity also includes the development and use of culturally sensitive and appropriate research instruments and protocols (Marin, 1993).

6. *Learn about the culture of the organization.* Culture is a dynamic concept, which evolves in transaction with the context and ecology of the organization and its people (Trickett, 1994). It is important to respect and understand the culture of the organization and give special attention to how people relate to one another with their celebra-

tions and idiosyncratic behaviors. Each community organization has its own cultural features particular to the setting, its members' background, ethnic group, education, areas of expertise, and the community to which they belong. Academic institutions also have their own cultural identity, values, and traditions. To develop an understanding and respect for the culture of a setting, partners need to devote sufficient time to listening to one another, volunteering in the organization or community, and getting to know the community by touring it and visiting with its different constituents (Suarez-Balcazar et al., 2002).

7. *The research collaboration is based on the needs of the community,* University–community partnerships work toward problems and issues identified by the community and of relevance to participants. The research agenda is guided by the community members' concerns. For the partnership to be successful, it needs to be beneficial to the community. It also must meet a need for the organization, which is likely to result in increased utilization of findings and social action (Panet-Raymond, 1992; Perkins & Wandersman, 1990; Selener, 1997). However, researchers also bring to the partnership their own agendas and needs such as theses, dissertations, and publications. Both researchers and community partners need to be clear about their goals and commitment to the alliance, as well as the potential uses of the data and knowledge gathered from their collaborative project. Often this requires good negotiation skills and compromise (Mattessich & Monsey, 1992).

8. *Understand the multidisciplinary nature of partnerships.* University–community partnerships often comprise engaging individuals from different disciplinary backgrounds, as well as individuals from different cultural and historical backgrounds. The diversity of the partners that come together in the collaborative effort provides an opportunity to benefit the partnership given that community members often bring diverse skills, different perspectives, and a variety of experiences that are typically distinct from those of academic researchers. For example, community leaders may possess years of experience dealing with the social and political impact of the issue of interest. Researchers (e.g., Solarz, 2001) have indicated the advantages of multidisciplinary research teams in addressing and studying complex social issues.

9. *Use both qualitative and quantitative research strategies.* Both qualitative and quantitative strategies complement each other and provide the research agenda with multiple levels of analysis. Using multiple methodologies also allows partners to obtain information on an ongoing basis and remain invested. At the same time that quantitative methodologies have enjoyed a long history in the field of psychology, qualitative methods have had a long history in the social sciences (Stewart, 2000). As community researchers, we are not only interested in numerical data descriptive of participants but also the rich stories and voices that help explain or illustrate those numbers. In fact, listening to the voices of the people of concern is consistent with the key principles of the field of community psychology (Rappaport, 1981;

Serrano-Garcia & Bond, 1994; Trickett, et al., 1994). Qualitative methodologies underscore the development of trust and rapport with participants to gain access to their personal experiences (Tandom, Azelton, & Kelly, 1998). In addition, community partners appreciate the use of both strategies and are likely to have previous experience with public forums, focus groups, listening sessions, personal interviews, and other qualitative methods.

10. *Share accountability of partnership success and opportunities.* In true partnerships, as leadership and control of the process and structure are shared among members (Mattessich & Monsey, 1992), so ought the responsibility for successes and failures be shared. As successes are celebrated, failures need to be viewed as opportunities to reflect and learn. In partnerships developed with low-income communities or grassroots groups where levels of resources are disparate, sharing the credit for accomplishments and successes is even more important (Blake & Moore, 2000). This might be done by writing reports in collaboration with the group, sharing publicity about the partnership within the academic institution and local community and sharing responsibility for problems, misunderstandings, and conflicts that may happen throughout the process.

These 10 characteristics of collaborative university–community partnerships provide a framework for partners to consider to protect the nature of collaboration as well as the interests of the community. The following case study describes a partnership between researchers from DePaul University and a self-help grassroots organization called Oxford House.

A University–Community Partnership at Work: The Oxford House Project

Oxford House is a network of self-supported, democratically operated homes that offer residents a mutual-help setting, established and maintained by recovering substance abusers living together to develop long-term abstinence skills (Ferrari, Jason, Olson, Davis, & Alvarez, 2002; Jason, Davis, Ferrari, & Bishop, 2001; Jason, Olson, Ferrari, & Davis, 2001). The first Oxford House was founded in 1975 by Paul Molloy and a group of peers who were recovering from alcoholism and decided to take on the responsibilities of maintaining their recovery home when it was faced with closure because of lack of funding. They named their community Oxford House after the Oxford Group, a religious organization that influenced the founders of Alcoholics Anonymous (St. Pierre, 1991). Since 1991, a DePaul University-based research team and the community-based organization Oxford House have developed a long-term collaborative partnership. Throughout this partnership, the Oxford House community has continued to provide not only a powerful opportunity for individuals and families who are in need of a safe and supportive environment to recover from their addiction and rebuild their lives but an exciting opportunity for the DePaul research team to explore the processes of recovery and the growth of a healing community.

One of the goals for initiating the relationship between the researchers and Oxford House was to facilitate the assessment and evaluation of this innovative model of recovery. Over the course of the 12-year partnership the ongoing intent has been to foster a positive alliance that benefits both the researchers, who are interested in investigating the dynamics and efficacy of the Oxford House model as an alternative to traditional models of substance-abuse recovery, and the community participants, who see the university connection as a way to validate, expand, and support their self-help organization through the research effort.

The Adoption of a Participatory Action Research Agenda

From the beginning of the partnership the DePaul team adopted a participatory action research agenda. As community psychologists, the team maintains that research endeavors should directly benefit both participants and practitioners—the actual, as well as the academic, community—and believes that research should not only be seen as a process of creating knowledge but simultaneously as education and development of consciousness and of mobilization (Gaventa, 1988). In addition, the team believes that the adoption of a participatory action research agenda is in line with the principle that the people who are to be the direct beneficiaries of relevant research must be involved to help inform and direct the work, monitor it, and make the best use of it for creating social change (Chesler, 1991). The team also realized that participation by activists and members of the Oxford House community could provide specific insight into appropriate skills and applicable techniques for gathering and analyzing information, thus complementing the researcher's knowledge and improving the team's strategic decision-making ability (Chesler, 1991). Therefore, active collaboration with the Oxford House community was (and is) not viewed as supplementary but as an integral and necessary component of the knowledge generation process.

Collaborative Research Meetings

Since the foundation of Oxford Houses in the Chicago area and the establishment of the collaborative partnership, the weekly Oxford House research meetings held at the university have been open to Oxford House residents, providing a forum for community members to learn about our interests, provide feedback, and maintain an ongoing exchange of ideas. Maintaining such open lines of communication has facilitated the development of collaborative research and action agendas, as well as served to cultivate greater trust and understanding. For example, when DePaul researchers began conducting qualitative pilot studies to learn more about the nature of Oxford Houses and the experiences of its residents, the research team wanted to tape-record the interviews to ensure accuracy of the data. Coincidentally, a representative from an Illinois Oxford House noted that they were interested in learning about the data collection process and asked to tape-record the university-based research meetings to share with other members of Oxford House. We welcomed this process of mutual recordings, demonstrating that we had nothing to hide and were invested in promoting an atmosphere of open communication and trust.

Although they no longer tape-record research meetings, to this day Oxford House representatives continue to attend weekly research team meetings. An Illinois Oxford House facilitator and alumnus (i.e., former resident) also regularly attends these meetings, where he provides feedback, insight, and direction for on-going studies and keeps us informed of relevant issues within Illinois Oxford Houses.

Attendance at Oxford House Meetings

Over the years, Oxford House residents have likewise opened their meetings and homes to members of the team from the university, appearing to have grown as accustomed to our interest and visitations as we have grown to theirs. Similar to the comfort that Oxford House members evidence during attendance at our meetings, members from DePaul consistently report experiencing a high level of ease and comfort when in attendance at House meetings. At these meetings, residents have openly interviewed potential new members and discussed sensitive House matters (e.g., conflicts among members and financial information). As this example evidences, attendance at House meetings also offers a forum to gain critical insight into the processes that operate within these homes and provides an opportunity to learn more about the residents as individuals rather than as "research participants." Obviously, access to this level of discourse would not be possible without having developed a high level of trust between the research team and community members.

Collaboration as a Forum for Research

Because an ultimate joint goal of the partnership is the assessment of the innovative Oxford House model, efforts to gather data via multiple methods have been ongoing. In keeping with the principles of collaboration, community members and other relevant parties have consistently been engaged to inform and actively shape these endeavors to our mutual benefit. Simultaneous to efforts to gain external funding, the DePaul team proceeded to conduct a number of smaller scale studies of Oxford House. During the first year in working with Oxford Houses in Illinois, the research team had student volunteers who went to the houses to get to know the residents. Each volunteer was assigned to a specific house and visited that house on a monthly basis for a year. During this time, they collected qualitative data regarding why residents sought out this setting and residents' expectations of and experiences in Oxford House. That qualitative work became an important foundation for later quantitative work and demonstrates how both qualitative and quantitative methods play an important role in doing this type of research.

In addition, throughout these projects and in the implementation of two larger scale grant-funded studies (one an accelerated longitudinal study funded by National Institute on Drug Abuse [NIDA] and the other a 5-year randomized outcome study funded by the National Institute on Alcohol Abuse and Alcoholism [NIAAA]), Molloy's support and insights have been invaluable, as has the input of Oxford House residents. For example, in the researchers' efforts to secure an NIAAA grant, the scientific review committee felt strongly that the most effective way to study Oxford House was through a randomized outcome study. Although, from a research perspective, the utility of the design cannot be questioned, the research team was hesitant to advance a methodology that could potentially upset the natural process of self-selection that occurs within Oxford House. That is, members of each House interview, discuss, and vote on whether an applicant should be admitted as a resident in their house. As this democratic process is an important cornerstone to the Oxford House approach of recovery, we did not want to disrupt that process, because it would fundamentally change the structure of how Oxford House operates (see also Humphreys & Rappaport, 1994, for an explanation of the problems related to randomized outcome studies with mutual-help groups). However, Molloy and Oxford House staff supported a random assignment design and in fact expressed a desire for the most rigorous outcome study, regardless of its outcome.

Throughout the process and through frequent discussions between team members from the university and Oxford House, we have together been better able to identify the strengths and possible difficulties with adopting various research designs (including random assignment) and to develop protocols that accommodate more rigorous methodologies within Oxford House's philosophy and democratic system of operation.

Involving Community Members Throughout the Research Partnership

Since the initial contact with Oxford House founders, the university team has consistently worked to build mutual trust and dispel misconceptions. The development of trust was aided by including recovering individuals on the research team, who were able to more easily access and establish rapport with Oxford House members based on their shared understanding of addiction and recovery processes and, in general, facilitated a greater openness to dialogue. In addition, Oxford House members have actively participated in shaping research activities such as the development of the methods and measures used, as well as in collecting data. In both the NIAAA and NIDA projects, the individuals responsible for recruiting participants and collecting data were hired through associations with Oxford House. In the recruitment of these key staff positions, Molloy and his associates provided advice and recommendations, and all of the individuals hired have either historically resided or currently reside in an Oxford House and have successfully remained abstinent. Recognizably, these individuals have expertise to offer with respect to the Oxford House model and best understand the recovery process, as well as have greater access to networks within the Oxford House community. These individuals have provided, and continue to provide, invaluable feedback regarding how to best sensitize research efforts to ensure that measures are composed to best capture the realities of Oxford House members in the most respectful and effective manner, that scale items are worded clearly and appropriately, and that methods are most successfully implemented.

Over years of collaborative interaction, the expertise of Oxford House members has been welcomed and appreciated, and the research team has made many substantial revisions based on their opinions. For example, in the NIDA-funded study, the grant application proposed that interviews to House members across the country would be conducted via telephone. However, based on pilot data and feedback from Oxford House staff on the NIAAA project, the research team learned that residents were more willing to participate and responded more favorably to personal methods of data collection. Based on the recommendation of the Illinois recruiters and other Oxford House residents, we revised the proposed methodology and hired field-based recruiters to visit each house and collect the data in person. Again drawing on Molloy's knowledge of the Oxford House network across the country, we were able to identify outstanding candidates for these positions in specific geographic locations that have high concentrations of houses. In addition, Oxford House officials are allowing and encouraging the university research team to use existing modes of communication within the national Oxford House community (e.g., their newsletter) to facilitate participant recruitment and retention and to disseminate information and results to residents.

Although the involvement of community members is integral to the development of appropriate research protocols, it is important to remain appreciative of the dynamics of role evolution as community members become more immersed in the research endeavor and to accept responsibility for providing necessary support for the development of new skills that may be needed and guidance if possible role conflicts arise. For example, at the beginning of the NIAAA project, the two participant recruiters—one who is an Oxford House alumni and the other who is a current House resident—had only minimal experience with computers and no experience with research methodology nor psychological constructs. However, because the project required that they administer survey interviews on laptop computers, they needed to receive appropriate technical training, as well as training in the administration of standardized clinical interviews. With proper training and support, they quickly became proficient in these programs and procedures. In fact, they not only entered the scale items into a data processing program, but also suggested ways to better express and capture issues of interest. Similarly for the NIDA project, the recruiters have required training and support to gain relevant knowledge and skills in technological resources and survey administration protocol, but the personal knowledge and skills that they have contributed to the process in exchange has been immeasurable.

Since their involvement on the projects, the recruiters, as well as other Oxford House members involved with the research team, have become quite knowledgeable of psychological terminology and methodological issues—occasionally now challenging the academic members of the team to become even more rigorous in protocol and procedures. Furthermore, when the recruiters initially joined the research team, they strictly identified with the Oxford House community, but through their work on the project and support of the research agenda have broadened their perspectives to identify themselves both as community members and members of the DePaul research team. Likewise, we, as researchers, have become more knowledgeable of the issues and concerns that matter most to Oxford House members. Such knowledge has subsequently shaped research endeavors.

The University–Community Collaboration as a Forum for Action

The DePaul team not only worked extensively to cultivate collaborative relationships with Oxford House members but also became committed to active involvement in the process of creating change. These commitments led the team to adopt roles beyond those of the traditional researcher—functioning also as occasional consultants, support system, and advocates for Oxford House. On multiple occasions, circumstances have required that the research team decide with some urgency whether or not, and how best, to adopt these diverse roles. Decisions necessarily were founded on critical reflection and deliberation of how each action on the part of the researchers would affect the Oxford House community, the research venture, and the relationship between the community and the researchers. Examples of some of the action endeavors that the research team has undertaken in collaboration with Oxford House include the team's involvement in the establishment of both the first men's and the first women's and women with children's Oxford Houses in Illinois, as well as historical and ongoing involvement in advocacy activities that support the growth of Oxford House nationally. Overall, throughout the 12 years of partnership, DePaul team members have been sensitive to putting into practice the 10 characteristics highlighted in this chapter.

Challenges and Lessons Learned

The development of successful university–community partnerships presents its own challenges, opportunities, and lessons. The following is a brief discussion of some thought-provoking conceptual issues apparent in university–community partnership work.

Linear Thinkers, Beware

Truly collaborative research partnerships require a high tolerance for complexity and ambiguity. The collaborative partnership road is not well mapped and indeed is almost always in a state of continuing construction. As more perspectives engage around the research table, the process becomes more interesting and often more complex. In the course of the project, priorities and needs of the organization are likely to change. The organization might experience staff turnover and conflicts of interest. In addition, delays may occur in obtaining funding, gaining access to community data, developing protocols, and collecting data. Furthermore, one needs to recognize the multiple layers of decision makers evident in every organization who may want to have a say in the process or be involved at different points and to various degrees (Mattessich

& Monsey, 1992). This often requires the accommodation of diverse agendas. In the Oxford House research project, the ongoing dialogue and open communication provided the opportunity to learn the varied views of diverse parties and through a series of accommodations diverse agendas were able to be reconciled.

Defining and Redefining Boundaries Between Roles

In collaborative partnerships, researchers need to be ready to play different roles such as learner, facilitator, researcher, and advocate (Connors & Seifer, 2001). Likewise, community partners may play similar varied roles at different points in the process. In the case of Oxford House, DePaul researchers and community partners play the roles of researchers, consultants, and advocates seeking support for Oxford House.

Addressing the Entrenched Conservatism of Discipline-Defined Research

Researchers working in partnerships with communities know that community participants and leaders bring to the table knowledge and experience that can more effectively shape and guide the research process. However, despite the benefits to be gained by both researchers and community members, there are certain costs that may be associated with electing to disregard a more conventional research paradigm. For example, it has been noted that methodological prejudice in favor of positivist and quantitative methods often makes it difficult for researchers wishing to use qualitative or collaborative methods to gain access to funding agencies and publish in scientific journals (Lidz & Ricci, 1990). In addition, the scientific community frequently voices concern regarding the possible negative consequences of conducting research without adequate detachment and disengagement from participants. Although it is becoming more widely recognized that the adoption of a nonconventional research strategy can yield insights and systematic understanding as valid as that obtained by conventional detached research methods (Kingry-Westergaard & Kelly, 1990; Tebes, 2000), action-oriented researchers may still experience efforts from more conservative researchers to diminish or devalue a partnership approach to conducting research.

   Community researchers recognize that the adoption of a collaborative approach is not only most congruent with our personal values, the goals of communities (such as Oxford House's) participation, and the philosophical and sociopolitical interests of community psychology (Kingry-Westergaard & Kelly, 1990) but is also appropriate for generating both academic and practically useful knowledge for both researchers and participants (Chesler, 1991). Collaborative research provides a rich context for gaining critical understanding of phenomena of interest. With the Oxford House research project, the research endeavor continuously benefits from the involvement of and feedback from members of the community to generate the most relevant and useful research topics and questions, clarify concepts, and validate results. Presenting collaborative research findings at disciplinary conferences and faculty forums, and publishing results in collaboration with partners, help inform others of the value of collaborative partnership research.

Conclusion

This chapter provides an outline of the general principles of effective university–community partnerships and provides an example of these principles in action. Although there have been many examples of university–community collaborations from different community sites over the years, it is only recently that there has been widespread interest in such collaborations. Pioneers such as Seymour Sarason (1972) often engaged in such collaborations, with little recognition coming from university colleagues. Many universities, including a growing number of urban research institutions, have now made their interest in such collaborations explicit in mission statements and other public documents as well as through actual deeds of their faculty.

The first part of this chapter provides a thorough cataloging of ingredients commonly seen in successful collaborations. Although these ingredients may come as no surprise to most community researchers, it is rare to have them all laid out in such a straightforward fashion. For the researcher wishing to embark on a new community partnership, the 10 characteristics discussed in this chapter will provide a solid framework to guide efforts.

In this chapter it is clear that significant time must be devoted if one is to develop collaborative partnerships. It is also clear that there must be real benefits for both the university and community partners. One way that university faculty can benefit community groups is by bringing "legitimacy" to the work these groups do, often on behalf of a particular marginalized group such as recovering substance abusers, as in the case of Oxford House. It is our experience that the expectation of such legitimacy is often an important concern for community agencies and others interested in university collaborations. However, it is important that researchers not merely promise legitimacy, relying on the university's prestige. Rather, researchers must also deliver legitimacy in various ways such as those delivered by the DePaul team in participating, volunteering, seeking funding, and advocating for the community.

An important way that community members can benefit researchers, aside from access to participants, is to offer relevance to the research. Working intimately with a community or community organization forces the researchers to consider the impact of their work and to consider divergent methodologies and interpretations of findings. Community members can also provide an antidote to the burn out seen among many professionals by providing a refreshing view on human problems.

This chapter also highlights the need to identify partners in a university–community collaboration. Very often, community researchers collaborate with administrators of human service organizations, government officials, and other policy makers. Collaboration with the community members is less common. The Oxford House project illustrates how to collaborate simultaneously with both leaders and participants. Most important, community partners are not only participants but also consultants on research design and interpretation of findings. The Oxford House research project has worked to foster such full participation, with the regular inclusion of members in all research meetings, as well as in research planning and implementation. This project truly exemplifies the 10 characteristics of collaborative partnerships. Without the trust that has been nurtured between the university and Oxford House leaders and residents, such an intensive and high quality research endeavor as described would not have been possible.

Community researchers still have a long way to go in adopting and validating the utility of engaging in truly collaborative community partnerships. The result of such efforts, responses to these challenges, and lessons learned to date have laid an important foundation for advancing this mutually beneficial form of participatory methodology. In all, university–community partnerships are at the heart of community research and action. By working together, faculty, students, community leaders, and community residents increase their skills and enhance their ability to study, understand, and address issues that matter to our communities.

References

Balcazar, F., Keys, C., Kaplan, D., & Suarez-Balcazar, Y. (1999). Participatory action research and people with disabilities: Principles and challenges. *Canadian Journal of Rehabilitation, 12,* 105–112.

Blake, H., & Moore, E. (2000). Partners share the credit for the partnership's accomplishments. In K. Connors & S. D. Seifer (Eds.), *Partnership perspectives* (Vol. 1, pp. 65–70). San Francisco: Community-Campus Partnerships for Health.

Bond, M. A. (1990). Defining the research relationship: Maximizing participation in an unequal world. In P. Tolan, C. Keys, F. Chertok, & L. Jason (Eds.), *Researching community psychology* (pp. 183–185). Washington, DC: American Psychological Association.

Bond, M. A., & Keys, C. B. (1993). Empowerment, diversity and collaboration: Promoting synergy on community boards. *American Journal of Community Psychology, 21,* 37–57.

Chesler, M. (1991). Participatory action research with self-help groups: An alternative paradigm for inquiry and action. *American Journal of Community Psychology, 19,* 757–768.

Connors, K., & Seifer, S. D. (2000). *Partnership perspectives* (Vol. 1). San Francisco: Community-Campus Partnerships for Health.

Fawcett, S. B., White, G. W., Balcazar, F., Suarez-Balcazar, Y., Mathews, M. R., et al. (1994). A contextual–behavioral model of empowerment: Case studies involving people with disabilities. *American Journal of Community Psychology, 22,* 471–496.

Ferrari, J. R., Jason, L. A., Olson, B. D., Davis, M. I., & Alvarez, J. (2002). Sense of community among Oxford House residents recovering from substance abuse: Making a house a home. In A. Fisher, C. Sonn, & B. Bishop (Eds.), *Psychological sense of community* (pp. 109–122). New York: Kluger/Plenum Press.

Gaventa, J. (1988). Participatory research in North America. *Convergence, 21*(2/3), 41–46.

Harper, G. W., & Salina, D. (2000). Building collaborative partnerships to improve community-based HIV prevention research: The university-CBO collaborative (UCCP) model. *Journal of Prevention and Intervention in the Community, 19,* 1–20.

Humphreys, K., & Rappaport, J. (1994). Researching self-help/mutual aid groups and organizations: Many roads, one journey. *Applied and Preventive Psychology, 3,* 217–231.

Jason, L. A. (1997). *Community building, values for a sustainable future.* Westport, CT: Praeger.

Jason, L. A., Davis, M. I., Ferrari, J. R., & Bishop, P. D. (2001). Oxford House: A review of research and implications for substance abuse recovery and community research. *Journal of Drug Education, 31,* 1–27.

Jason, L. A., Olson, B. D., Ferrari, J. R., & Davis, M. I. (2003). *Substance abuse: The need for second order change*. Manuscript submitted for publication.

Jordan, L. C., Bogat, A. G., & Smith, G. (2001). Collaborating for social change: The Black psychologist and the Black community. *American Journal of Community Psychology, 29*, 599–620.

Kaftarian, J., & Hansen, W. B. (Eds.). (1994). Community Partnership Program [Special issue]. *Journal of Community Psychology, 22*.

Kingry-Westergaard, C., & Kelly, J. G. (1990). A contextualist epistemology for ecological research. In P. Tolan, C. Keys, F. Chertok, & L. Jason (Eds.), *Researching community psychology: Issues of theory and methods* (pp. 23–31). Washington, DC: American Psychological Association.

Kreuter, M., Lezin, N., & Young, L. (2000). Evaluating community based collaborative mechanisms: Implications for practitioners. *Health Promotion Practice, 1*(1), 49–63.

Lidz, C., & Ricci, F. (1990). Funding larger-scale qualitative sociology. *Qualitative Sociology, 13*(2), 113–126.

Marin, G. (1993). Defining culturally appropriate community interventions: Hispanics as a case study. *Journal of Community Psychology, 21,* 149–161.

Mattessich, P., & Monsey, B. (1992). *Collaboration: What makes it work*. St. Paul, MN: Amherst Wilder Foundation.

Nelson, G., Prillettensky, I., & MacGillivary, H. (2001). Building value-based partnerships: Toward solidarity with oppressed groups. *American Journal of Community Psychology, 29*, 649–677.

Nyden, P., Figert, A., Shibley, M., & Burrows, D. (1997). *Building community: Social science in action*. Thousand Oaks, CA: Sage.

Ostrom, C. W., Lerner, R. M., & Freel, M. A. (1995). Building the capacity of youth and families through university-community collaborations: The development-in-context evaluation (DICE) model. *Journal of Adolescent Research, 10,* 427–448.

Panet-Raymond, J. (1992). Partnership: Myth or reality? *Community Development Journal, 27,* 156–165.

Park, P., & Lee, W. L. (1999). A theoretical framework for participatory evaluation research. *Sociological Practice: A Journal of Clinical and Applied Sociology, 1*(2), 89–100.

Perkins, D. D., & Wandersman, A. (1990). "You'll have to work to overcome our suspicions": The benefits and pitfalls of research with community organizations. *Social Policy, 20,* 32–41.

Rappaport, J. (1981). In praise of paradox: A social policy of empowerment over prevention. *American Journal of Community Psychology, 9,* 1–25.

Rappaport, J. (1987). Terms of empowerment/exemplars of prevention: Toward a theory of community psychology. *American Journal of Community Psychology, 15,* 121–148.

Rappaport, J., Seidman, E., Toro, P., McFadden, L., Reischel, T., et al. (1985). Collaborative research with a mutual help organization. *Social Policy, 15,* 12–24.

Roussos, S. T., & Fawcett, S. B. (2000). A review of collaborative partnerships as a strategy for improving community health. *Annual Review of Public Health, 21,* 369–402.

Sarason, S. B. (1972). The creation of settings and the future societies. San Francisco: Jossey-Bass.

Selener, D. (1997). *Participatory action research and social change*. Ithaca, NY: Cornell Participatory Action Research Network.

Serrano-Garcia, I. (1990). Implementing research: Putting our values to work. In P. Tolan, C. Keys, F. Chertok, & L. Jason (Eds.), *Researching community psychology: Issues of theory and methods* (pp. 171–182). Washington, DC: American Psychological Association.

Serrano-Garcia, I., & Bond, M. (1994). Empowering the silent ranks: Introduction. *American Journal of Community Psychology, 22,* 433–446.

Solarz, A. (2001). Investing in children, families, and communities: Challenges for an interdivisional public policy collaboration. *American Journal of Community Psychology, 29,* 1–14.

Stewart, E. (2000). Thinking through others. In J. Rappaport & E. Seidman (Eds.), *Handbook of community psychology* (pp. 725–736). New York: Kluwer Academic.

St. Pierre, S. (Executive Producer). (1991, May 5). "60 Minutes/Oxford House" [Television broadcast]. New York: CBS Worldwide.

Suarez-Balcazar, Y., Balcazar, F., & Fawcett, S. B. (1992). Problem identification in applied social research. In F. Bryant, J. Edwards, R. S. Tindale, L. Health, E. L. Posavac, et al. (Eds.), *Social psychological methods applied to social issues* (pp. 25–42). New York: Plenum Press.

Suarez-Balcazar, Y., Harper, G., & Lewis, R. (2002). *An interactive and contextual model of university–community partnerships.* Manuscript submitted for publication.

Tandom, S. D., Azelton, S. L., & Kelly, J. G. (1998). Constructing a tree for community leaders: Contexts and process in collaborative inquiry. *American Journal of Community Psychology, 26,* 669–696.

Tebes, J. K. (2000). External validity and scientific psychology. *American Psychologist, 55,* 1508–1509.

Trickett, E. (1994). Human diversity and community psychology: Where ecology and empowerment meet. *American Journal of Community Psychology, 22,* 583–592.

Trickett, E. J., Watts, R. J., & Birman, D. (Eds.). (1994). *Human diversity: Perspectives on people in context.* San Francisco: Jossey-Bass.

Part III

Power Sharing in Participatory Research

7

Self-Help Research: Issues of Power Sharing

Daryl Holtz Isenberg, Colleen Loomis, Keith Humphreys, and Kenneth I. Maton

Few published articles or chapters delineate the complexities confronting researchers and self-help group (SHG) members involved in collaborative research. This chapter articulates limitations to reliance on collaborative (power sharing) and participatory action research (PAR) methods as the sole or primary methods for SHG research. It examines (through an empirical study of 17 self-help groups) the conditions under which SHG members and researchers have positive and negative experiences with collaborative and PAR approaches.

Some scientists are open to power sharing with SHGs (and self-help clearinghouses as well) and to an action research orientation in general. However, other researchers trained in traditional research methods are unfamiliar or uncomfortable with collaborative research approaches. They debate whether professionals should "assist" SHGs through collaborative action research because of the possibilities of inhibiting the group's sense of self-responsibility or of losing scientific rigor. Although Borman (1979) and others have clearly outlined professional roles that support SHG autonomy, many of which include participatory or action research, the extent of power sharing varies across and within research projects.

The following organizations generously provided information for this chapter: Al-Anon Family Groups; Epilepsy Self-Help Groups, a program of the Epilepsy Foundation, Greater Chicago; GROW Illinois; Let's Breathe-Sarcoidosis Self-Help Group; Men Overcoming Violence; Recovery, Inc; Rainbows; Resolve of Illinois; Test Positive Aware; ToughLove©, International; Tourette Syndrome Association; United Ostomy Association; Parents Care & Share; Anorexia Nervosa and Associated Disorders, Y-ME National Breast Cancer Organization; Cancer Wellness Center; and Women Employed.

The Researcher Perspective on Sharing Power in Self-Help Group Research

Collaborative projects between SHGs and researchers have been conducted for more than 40 years (see, e.g., Trice, 1957). Because collaborative and PAR approaches focus on equal sharing of power and on practical, action-oriented outcomes, some community psychologists argue that these methods are best for SHG research. However, in our view, blanket endorsement of fully collaborative, participatory methods is built on underlying assumptions about power sharing that do not hold true all the time across all conditions. We therefore offer for consideration alternative premises to conventional beliefs about collaboration in SHGs.

Conventional Premise 1: Sharing Power Is Inherently Socially Just

Nelson, Ochocka, Griffin, and Lord (1998) conveyed this assumption in their article, "Nothing About Me Without Me." From the article's title, we might infer that SHG research methods that share power are preferable and a decision to collaborate applies in all situations.

The relationship between researcher and researched always includes a third interested party, namely the society at large that may be affected by the study's results. In the case of SHGs, these stakeholders include people thinking of joining an SHG if there is evidence of its effectiveness, health care providers who might refer patients to it, and policy makers who might include referrals to self-help in the programs they promote.

At times, a collaborative relationship between researcher and researched is at odds with the interests of the broader society. For example, some organizations that are helpful in certain ways have also been found to treat women members in a sexist manner. In such a situation, the researcher is faced with a problem because his or her collaborator, the organization, may not want the data on sexism made public. If the information is withheld, however, it would be a betrayal of those women who might join the group, unaware of the organization's sexist views.

Thus, we propose an alternative premise: *There are times when power must not be shared in the interest of the social good that transcends the researcher and the researched.* When deciding when to collaborate, Price (1989) reminded us that "intergroup conflict is largely muted in the empowerment perspective. Hard choices about who should be empowered and to what end are not yet part of the implicit agenda of empowerment theorists" (pp. 166–167). We do not have an easy, universal solution to propose, but that is, in fact, our point: A collaborative relationship can be at odds with social justice.

Conventional Premise 2: Sharing Power Necessarily Improves the Quality of Science

Some SHG researchers believe that if ethical and respectful power sharing occurs, the quality of the science conducted will necessarily be enhanced. However, there is no evidence within the history of SHG research to support the viewpoint that collaboration also makes inherently better science. For example, the visibility and credibility of SHGs have been raised in recent decades by some high-quality longitudinal studies demonstrating the positive impact of groups on a variety of health and social outcomes (Kurtz, 1990). Although some of these projects were research collaborations, most were not; yet this fact did not stop researchers from producing high-quality science that aided SHGs. Here, collaboration was not required to ensure the quality of the science.

It may sound good to say that collaboration improves science and saying so may even reduce criticism of the researcher who has to defend his or her approach (e.g., the tenure-track assistant professor). But, as we have mentioned, collaboration is only one approach and should not preempt other legitimate research methods.

We therefore propose an alternative premise: *The decision to collaborate should be recognized as values-based, rather than for the sake of science.* We agree with Nelson et al. (1998) that the decision to share power between researcher and researched is political and values-based. We also agree with them that when community psychologists work with oppressed groups, the values should be completely consistent with sharing power as much as possible. And, more particularly, all the values associated with SHGs—the importance of experiential knowledge, the concept that even the most troubled person has positive things to offer, egalitarianism—are also in strong alliance with power sharing. For us, values considerations are enough to make collaboration worthwhile in itself with no further rationale needed.

Conventional Premise 3: Sharing Power Is a Noble Sacrifice

An alternative premise would be: *Collaboration is easier than noncollaboration in many cases.* An often-heard lament among academic community psychologists is how much harder their research is than that conducted in other fields because they have to engage in relationship building and collaboration with those they want to study. This makes power sharing sound like a noble sacrifice by the researcher and gives the impression that noncollaborative researchers are somehow less committed to social justice because they do not do the hard work of collaboration.

The early phase of collaboration may give some researchers the sense that collaborating is hard work that must be endured to achieve some virtuous end. Yet, in many projects, collaboration greatly facilitates important tasks, such as asking the right questions, formulating research procedures, gaining entrée, and gathering and interpreting data. A number of surveys of self-help organizations have received extremely high response rates (e.g., Galanter, Egelko, & Edwards, 1993; Kaskutas, 1992; Klaw & Humphreys, 2000). These studies share a collaborative context: In each case, the organization worked on the survey from the beginning, felt it had some ownership of the survey, and strongly endorsed the survey to its members. Although building collaborative relationships does require some start-up work, the effort is probably less than that involved in coping with the more typical, quite low, survey response rate attained in a noncollaborative project (e.g., it is harder to figure out what the data mean and to convince others of their value). Thus, over the course of a collaborative research project, researchers can and should get significant rewards from collaborating. Indeed, if only the community is benefiting, then by definition the relationship is not collaborative and equitable.

Conventional Premise 4: Sharing Power Ensures Conflict-Free Relationships Between Researchers and Community Members

We have observed some psychologists equating polite interchanges with collaborations. A polite relationship is not the same as a collaboration. If two parties cannot disagree, they are not sharing power. When SHG members suggest what a researcher believes to be a bad or impracticable idea, the researcher should feel at liberty to say that it *is* a bad idea, as he or she would do with any collaborator with whom there was genuine power sharing.

In the same vein, we should not idealize SHGs to the point where we believe that if only researchers would decide to collaborate, then SHGs will naturally be wonderful collaborators. We have observed several studies in which researchers were severely exploited by self-help organizations. In one case, a self-help organization approached a researcher and asked to be the subject of a study. The researcher conducted, at considerable expense and time, a pilot study of the organization. The study was designed in collaboration with the organization, and was conducted with its full consent, on the assumption that the survey results would form the basis of a larger project. After the pilot study was done, the organization took the pilot data for its own purposes and refused to let the researcher even see the results. As no subsequent grant for a larger study was possible, thousands of dollars of the researcher's resources, invested in a spirit of trust, were essentially stolen by the self-help organization.

Therefore, we propose the alternative premise: *Collaboration necessarily includes conflicts, not all of which can be easily resolved.*

Conventional Premise 5: Sharing Power Is Necessary for the Exchange of Valued, Mutually Exclusive Resources

In general, researchers assume that they have a unique set of resources (e.g., social status, skills in the form of technical assistance, connections to power) that research participants need and want and are unable to achieve on their own. Collaboration implies the reciprocal exchange of presumed valued and relatively exclusive resources.

This may be true in some instances, such as when an SHG's collaboration with researchers leads to increased recognition of or legitimization for a group, access to valuable technical assistance, and growth in membership. On the other hand, community members may have access to their own resources without academics' help, or may not find the academics' resources valuable. For example, a researcher's ability to write grants to obtain funding is not always valued or desired by self-help organizations. Perhaps a professional's credentials may be a source of stigma rather than legitimization. For example, some individuals in the mental health consumer movement believe that trained psychiatrists are a source of oppression of mentally ill individuals (Chamberlin, 1978). Being a psychiatrist is a considerable disadvantage for attaining trust from such organizations. The general public often has more skepticism of credentialed mental health professionals than it does of people who are solving emotional difficulties in a mutual help group setting.

The conventional premise that research participants and their organizations need recognition or connections to power may be a projection of researchers' needs onto research participants. This premise has some echoes of premise number 3 in that it casts the researchers as "nobly" sharing their many resources with the dispossessed. We must prevent researchers from deluding themselves or misleading others that we have something to offer when we do not.

We suggest, then, a final alternative premise: *Access to and value of participants' and researchers' resources are varied.*

Our reflections on power sharing experiences with self-help group research helps us to remain mindful. Many successful power-sharing research projects conducted with SHGs have yielded valuable results. We caution, though, that the widespread interest in research collaborations, although exciting, should not lead researchers to simplify the problems or the solutions.

The Self-Help Perspective on Sharing Power in Self-Help Group Research

An empirical investigation to explore self-help participants' perspectives of research was conducted as part of a larger study (Isenberg, 2003). One-on-one interviews focusing on common practices in community research were carried out with 25 self-helpers and 7 researchers from 17 self-help groups (see Table 7.1). The results of the interviews provide useful and informative information about the varied experiences of self-help groups and researchers, and suggest directions for fruitful research approaches in the SHG area.

Many of the SHGs in this study are grassroots, peer-governed, voluntary organizations, operating without much professional involvement. Volunteer facilitators spend most of their energy responding to a member's crisis or the crisis of organizing group meetings. In general, these self-help organizations, selected from the Illinois Self-Help Coalition (ISHC)[1] database, vary in size, peer or professional facilitation roles (with the professional serving as a consultant), growth patterns, and structure. Some organizations with a single focus begin with one group and grow into a national organization with many groups. Other organizations beginning with a single focus develop over time into multi-focused organizations.

---

[1]The ISHC is an SHG clearinghouse that has provided workshops for and consultation to more than 400 SHGs in the Chicago area.

Table 7.1.   Participating Self-Help Organizations (N = 17)

Peer-run SHGs or associations (n = 11)	Peer-run SHG programs of professional agencies (n = 2)	Peer-run & professionally facilitated group services of health associations (n = 2)	Professionally facilitated group services of a community-based organization (n = 2)
1. Al-Anon Family Groups	1. Epilepsy SHGs	1. Anorexia Nervosa and Associated Disorders	1. Cancer Wellness Center
2. GROW Illinois	2. Parents Care & Share		2. Women Employed
3. Let's Breathe–Sarcoidosis		2. Y-Me National Breast Cancer Organization	
4. Men Overcoming Violence			
5. Recovery, Inc.			
6. Rainbows			
7. Resolve of Illinois			
8. Test Positive Aware Network			
9. TOUGHLOVE©			
10. Tourette Syndrome Association			
11. United Ostomy Association			

Twelve of the 17 organizations in our interviews discussed previous or current research projects that were participatory. Seven SHGs initiated and partially or completely funded their own research (Al-Anon Family Groups, Anorexia Nervosa and Associated Disorders [ANAD], Cancer Wellness Center, Parents Care & Share [PC&S], Rainbows, Recovery, Inc., Test Positive Aware Network [TPAN], and Women Employed). In instances when external researchers initiated SHG research projects, they solicited government research funding (Epilepsy Self-Help Groups, GROW, and Y-Me National Breast Cancer Support Organization). ToughLove© (TL), and Resolve of Illinois discussed the impact of unfunded research that is initiated by graduate students.

Interview findings revealed what SHGs perceive as negative and positive aspects of collaborating with researchers, as well as what SHGs want from research. With regard to social justice, which was not part of the interview, some of the groups have an explicit agenda to create a more just society, particularly for individuals who share the focal concern of the group (e.g., reducing stigmatization of persons with a mental illness).

Lessons Learned From Self-Helpers: Negative Experiences With Collaborative Approaches

Self-help groups reported limitations of past collaborations with researchers frequently resulting from unresolved conflicts or lack of clear communication between researchers and SHGs.

NEGATIVE EXPERIENCE 1: FAILURE TO DEVELOP TRUSTING WORKING RELATIONSHIPS. Collaboration is difficult when, for various reasons, the researcher does not develop a relationship based on trust and equality. Chesler, who has done extensive research with childhood cancer self-help organizations, has observed that researchers are uncomfortable with the lack of group structure, commenting that "some researchers believe SHGs should be more corporate, more organized, and have by-laws. That is partly because they are used to formal organizations and because it is easier to study these systems than SHGs where there is shifting leadership, more caring" (M. A. Chesler, personal communication, January 22, 2002).

Attempts by researchers trained in hierarchical organizations to solicit the participation of SHG members may therefore be frustrating to both the researcher and the SHG. The Recovery, Inc., executive director reported that the researcher's hierarchical mentality made it "difficult to translate the survey findings into an appropriate area leaders' training manual that was easy to understand and to use." Recovery, Inc., informants further explained that gathering information for a leader training manual welcoming newcomers required hiring a technical writer better adapted to the egalitarian decision-making culture of self-help.

One Epilepsy Foundation of Greater Chicago SHG leader involved in a national study felt the research process was mysterious and questioned why researchers met apart from group members. Self-helpers interpreted this to mean that they were not valued or trusted. Group leaders were informed only about the timeframes in the research process and received research results after they were published. In the meantime, self-helpers reported that they felt locked out of the process.

A Recovery, Inc., group leader stated that researchers should use less jargon and, rather than send students, come themselves to participate in SHG activities. The SHGs interviewed reported that mistrust developed when researchers did not give research information in plain words, clearly explain the research process, provide feedback in person, or invite the SHG to comment on research results or share control of the research products.

Hearing that SHGs reported interest in learning research methods, two researchers conjectured that some groups might want to learn research methods themselves because they lack faith in outside researchers to conduct research that is fair to their group. GROW's president responded that the desire of groups to learn how to conduct research themselves is related to communication gaps that would or could create confusion, which leads to mistrust. She felt that if SHGs understood research methods and knew how to participate in the research design and review reports, they could help capture the full essence of the subject, its purpose or goals. Several groups suggested that researchers should assist self-helpers to become knowledgeable about research before such struggles occur.

NEGATIVE EXPERIENCE 2: DIFFERING RESEARCHER AND SELF-HELP GROUP/COMMUNITY OBJECTIVES. Differences in basic objectives can directly contribute to the perception that research is not relevant. During its Inner City Project, the Illinois Self-Help Center learned that researchers and the community might differ in their primary group objective when opposing views developed over the exchange of resources. After Jason's (1988) two-year process documenting the involvement of community gatekeepers and local professionals in building the concept of inner-city SHGs, it became clear that there was a mismatch in objectives between community leaders, who wanted economic development self-help, and the self-help leaders on the committee, who wanted peer support groups. Differing opinions between community leaders and SHGs can confound research objectives.

NEGATIVE EXPERIENCE 3: EXPLOITATION. Six of the 12 SHG organizations interviewed, including Anorexia and Associated Disorders, Recovery, Inc., ToughLove©, Epilepsy SHGs, Rainbows, and Resolve of Illinois, reported one or more research experiences in the past that detracted from the SHG's purpose or did little to enhance the organization in the long run. These SHGs claimed that researchers "exploited" information from their membership and contacts, attempted to add additional program components to make it easier to obtain information, and, without appropriate permission, studied local or online groups and sometimes posted their research findings on Web sites. In addition, they claimed that researchers did not check with or credit the SHG in the final report, or coopted the group itself as a hospital-based professional program.

NEGATIVE EXPERIENCE 4: LACK OF PERCEIVED VALUE IN RESEARCH. Frontline SHG leaders, in contrast to administrators, frequently report that they see research as an unwelcome burden. Consumed by serving members, they did not readily see how they would have the time, resources, or expertise to focus on a research component. Recovery, Inc., and GROW report that some leaders are skeptical of the value of research. They viewed anecdotal testimony as sufficient evidence of the beneficial services of the group. A ToughLove© (TL) leader responded that she did not see the need for research to evaluate TL because "TL kept my son from driving me crazy and it costs me only $5 a week."

NEGATIVE EXPERIENCE 5: CONSTRAINTS IN THE UNIVERSITY SETTING. Rainbows' researchers reported that the organization was not set up to participate in research because of overextended or volunteer staff and nonhierarchical leadership. As a result, the researchers and groups differed in the desired time frame for the research. A 1-year project had to be extended to 3 years, which caused a problem for the student researcher expecting to complete his dissertation in less than 18 months and for a faculty member applying for tenure. Rainbows's experience suggests difficulties in collaborative research may be a result in part to inadequate funding and pressures exerted within universities (G. Laumann, personal communication, May 30, 2002).

Lessons Learned From Self-Helpers: Positive Experiences With Collaboration

Self-helpers also reported many benefits of past collaborations with researchers.

POSITIVE EXPERIENCE 1: DEVELOPING SHARED GOALS. SHGs rate the research experience highly (mean = 9, on a 10-point scale) when researchers work hard to develop shared goals with the group. For example, P. Corrigan reported (personal communication, January 10, 2002) that although the early partnership-building period with GROW took far longer than expected, the result was well worthwhile. The GROW research involves a 120-page interview protocol taking 4 to 5 hours to complete. Also, GROW coordinators are able to track down and complete interviews with 90% of the study participants at 3, 6, and 12 months. After 24 months the GROW study lost only 20% of the original interviewees. GROW research coordinators who have been part of designing the research repeatedly make efforts to recontact those who did not respond initially. Similarly, the research of Recovery, Inc., with a university-based disability research organization familiar with PAR yielded a high return (85%) of surveys and follow-up interview of all registered Recovery, Inc., group leaders.

POSITIVE EXPERIENCE 2: RESEARCHERS WITH A PERSONAL CONNECTION TO THE SHG. The decision to use PAR in a research project is based on the value that members should have the opportunity to participate maximally. In some cases, sharing power is a consequence of the researcher's history of interest in and experience with the group.

Six of the 12 SHGs have participated in university research collaborations: Cancer Wellness Center; Epilepsy SHGs; GROW, Rainbows; Recovery, Inc.; and Y-Me National Breast Cancer Organization. Academicians serve on the professional advisory committees of these self-help organizations, linking groups to university researchers. Several researchers are involved in SHG research because they have a personal connection with a particular group or area. One such researcher, Mark A. Chesler (personal communication, January 22, 2002), has a daughter who had a childhood cancer. He has been an SHG member, board member, researcher, and resident scholar, and is currently generating research findings about international cancer parent groups. Another researcher, Leonard D. Jason (personal communication, December 22, 2001), has personal experiences with Chronic Fatigue Syndrome (CFS) that have led him to study two organizations: a support group for people with CFS and a housing model, Oxford House, which might be applicable to people with CFS. Researcher Gary Laumann (personal communication, May 30, 2002) was a Rainbows facilitator for many years before beginning his research with Rainbows as a doctoral candidate. For their master's theses or doctoral dissertations, student researchers often collaborate in research projects with groups in which they are personally involved in some way. Personal connections to the SHG help researchers remain involved while contributing principled and scientifically sound research.

POSITIVE EXPERIENCE 3: FINANCIAL AND DECISION-MAKING EQUALITY. In examples of successful financial collaborations, financial and decision-making equality are interrelated. A 4-year, $20,000,000 research project of the Substance Abuse and Mental Health Services Administration that investigated mental health consumer groups requires that the seven-state research team collaborate on a standardized randomized design. The GROW president meets regularly in Washington, DC, with its seven university and eight consumer group research team. The grant terms give 51% of decision-making power to the eight consumer groups. The regulation allows GROW to receive a maximum of up to 40% of the University of Chicago research funds for service enhancement. Corrigan supported giving the maximum funds to self-helpers because "this gets us beyond good intention to true participation" (P. Corrigan, personal communication, January 10, 2002). In turn, GROW staff rate highly (mean = 9.5, on a 10-point scale) their current power in decision making, cooperation of the researcher, and expectation that the research will be useful to the group.

POSITIVE EXPERIENCE 4: LEARNING ABOUT AND INITIATING RESEARCH. Frustration resulting from the use of researcher jargon during the GROW research was resolved by introducing self-helpers to a glossary of common research terms (Rittenhouse, Culter, & Campbell, 1999). More generally, Chesler (personal communication, January 22, 2002), Corrigan (personal communication, January 10, 2002), and Jason (personal communication, 2001) each reported the importance of teaching research skills to SHG members on the research team. Chesler reported, "I am less interested in how we help researchers work more productively with SHGs than how we can help SHGs learn research skills. If self-helpers learn research techniques, they can meet researchers on the same playing field and a more even playing field, rather than being mystified or shoved around by them." Six of the 12 SHGs that learn about or initiate their own research place a high value on the research (mean = 8, on a 10-point scale).

POSITIVE EXPERIENCE 5: DISSEMINATING THE RESULTS TO THE SHG. Although attention to disseminating research results is frequently short-lived, some collaborative research results have been appropriately disseminated. Chesler's (1991; personal communication, January 22, 2002) focus on one disease entity, childhood cancer, gives him more leverage to disseminate collaborative research results through presentations about SHG programs and organizational processes.

Jason has suggested that researchers can involve SHGs in dissemination activities by creating a media plan (Jason, 1985). Researchers can invite stakeholders to participate together in media activity to bring the information in the research report to the attention of the public. Jason advised brainstorming with stakeholders about what they want from the effort and what they can do to get it.

In addition, researchers report SHGs appreciate assistance when they follow up their research by creating Internet interactive self-help message boards and discussion groups. Phone conferencing with self-help leaders to discuss research related to issues such as recruitment and retention also facilitates collaboration.

Lessons Learned From Self-Helpers: Differing SHG/Researcher Perspectives

Results from the SHG interviews indicate that researchers sometimes have research objectives that SHGs do not share. Self-help groups that participate in research hope to achieve practical knowledge, self-applied research tools, and resources. One primary type of help would enhance internal operations. The second type of help is external, in terms of relations with funders, professionals, and the larger public.

DIFFERING PERSPECTIVE 1: PRACTICAL KNOWLEDGE TO IMPROVE PROGRAM FUNCTIONING. In contrast to researchers' interest in good science requiring long-term study, SHG representatives report current and future interest in short-term research focused on program functioning and member recruitment and retention, as in the following examples:

- An epilepsy self-help leader with the Epilepsy Foundation, Greater Chicago, was interested only in research that contributes to the group's ability to recruit members, resolve conflicts, and involve members in assuming responsibility.
- Recovery, Inc., wanted research that leads to increased membership, to stop a significant decline in the number of its groups from 1,000 to 650 in the past decade.
- The United Ostomy Association (UOA) executive director wanted to (a) conduct a satisfaction survey of UOA magazine readers, (b) use the Internet to email surveys to younger members, and (c) develop benchmarks and show trends involving UOA membership.
- The UOA, Chicago, chapter president was concerned about recruitment and diversity and cultivating hospital relationships in rural hospitals.
- In 1992, Oxford House founder Paul Malloy encouraged researcher Leonard Jason to document the process of Oxford House with the hope that the data would help the organization understand the results of member participation.
- Rainbows wanted clear data about its program; the Rainbows' vice president wanted to study different age groups and follow over time children who have been in Rainbows' programs.
- The president of Resolve of Illinois was interested in identifying needed services Resolve was not providing; the hotline coordinator wanted to evaluate services.
- The GROW program coordinator wanted to develop a random design process in which fieldworkers coordinate GROW members in 12-step work with the purpose of engaging people receiving mental health services in GROW.

DIFFERING PERSPECTIVE 2: LEGITIMACY AND CREDIBILITY, QUALITY ASSURANCE, FUNDING. All groups express one primary hoped-for gain from research: to enhance legitimacy and credibility. For example, a Recovery, Inc., leader stated, "It is important for a group like Recovery to obtain research in order to get the ear of the professionals who don't seem to trust what they see anecdotally unless someone tells them through research that it works." A Cancer Wellness Center cofounder believed that "having a researcher of David Cella's caliber is very validating to a fledgling organization. Professionals began to take the organization seriously. They no longer thought of the Cancer Wellness Center as run by three women who were volunteers." According to the Al-Anon Family Groups associate director of public outreach to professionals, Al-Anon employs a survey research organization to learn what is important to members from a random survey of 3% of its adult participants. They also learn from a survey of 10% of the Alateen sponsors how sponsors and other Alateen programs are working within their organization. The surveys are useful in part to inform members and their board, as well as to provide objective information to professionals.

Interest in conducting research is also driven in some cases by SHG funders, boards, and credentialing agencies. SHGs dependent on external funding or sponsored by host organizations are asked to document change in group members' behavior as a result of attending the group. For example, since 1992, the research information gathered from Parents Care & Share (PC&S) surveys assures the board that the PC&S model is being used properly and that members report change in parenting behavior. To comply with PC&S Council on Accreditation (COA) requirements, PC&S has recently licensed a take-home survey instrument geared to parent educational groups. Similarly, Test Positive Aware Network (TPAN), with help from the Public Health Department, satisfies requirements for quality assurance and for funding by administering a self-assessment component to determine knowledge gained about HIV.

Groups also hope positive research results will allow them to attract more funding. For example, Y-Me's director of patient services expects the result of current research to be valuable to Y-Me because, even if there are negative findings, "The analysis will educate and inform and will be helpful in explaining the process." Although many SHGs eventually figure out how to market their groups, most believe (as do GROW, Recovery, Inc., Rainbows, Epilepsy Self-Help Groups, TPAN, PC&S, and UOA) that their groups are underused, especially as part of a continuum of health or mental health care. The group representatives interviewed hoped research would result in increased funding. Interestingly, they ultimately accepted the fact that positive research findings did not directly result in such funding.

Conclusion

The conventional and alternative research premises, as well as the findings from the empirical study of SHGs together illustrate a basic tension between research and SHG perspectives. Specifically, researchers generally view power sharing as one option among many in the research repertoire, with various styles and stages for sharing; collaboration is not always the method of choice. In contrast, SHGs tend to view equal sharing of power, along with action-oriented goals (PAR), as the preferred method for their involvement in research.

We delineated problematic assumptions that hinder determination of when to use power sharing and offered alternative premises. These problematic assumptions include the view that power sharing necessarily contributes to social justice, necessarily improves the quality of the science, is a researcher's noble sacrifice, ensures conflict-free relationships between researchers and SHG members, and necessarily involves the exchange of equally valued resources. Under some conditions, power sharing and PAR would not be a researcher's method of choice—such as when the greater social good is not served by power sharing because an SHG's practices are counter to important social values or when high quality science is pursued most effectively in the absence of full power sharing.

The study of 17 self-help organizations indicated that respondents assume that power sharing consists of mutual decision making about the research design, process, and dissemination of products. It involves the researcher sharing his or her expertise about the research process and methods while inviting or funding insiders from the organization to participate in the research project. In addition, power sharing involves SHG members sharing their experiential knowledge. Collaborative action steps preferred by SHG members include the following: listening and feedback, problem solving, frequent communication about the project from researcher to SHG, helping secure funds, initiatives that increase community and media awareness of the group, converting technical research instruments to user-friendly evaluation tools, writing training manuals, presenting findings to stakeholders and professionals, identifying other volunteer/consultant expertise, and informing policy. (See Chesler's 1991 report.)

We also learned from the SHG interviews that SHGs have a unique culture that researchers must work to become familiar with, that both the goals of research and the division of labor for the research evolve through dialogue, that both tensions and positive collaborations coexist, and that the possibility of misunderstandings during the research endeavor necessitate ongoing dialogue and negotiation. In addition to wanting researchers to learn how their groups function, self-helpers ultimately want to know that researchers are working to identify creative formats for disseminating findings and better informing policy makers about self-help organizations.

Not surprisingly, the research experiences of the SHGs studied are quite mixed. Positive experiences appear most likely when the researcher and the self-help organization have congruent priorities and a stake in each other's goals. This outcome appears especially likely with "insider" research (when the researcher is a member of the group or a member of the advisory board).

The presence of a perceived power differential and lack of equity are primary obstacles to successful collaboration. To reduce the power differential, we suggest that researchers commit themselves to helping SHGs understand the research process and methods, provide groups with funding for collaborating in the research, and allow substantial voice for groups in making research decisions. Finally, most important is assurance that the SHG will be an equal partner on the research project team.

The researcher and SHG perspectives underscore both the complexities and the potential of collaboration in self-help research. The complexities begin, as noted earlier, with potential differences in the primary goals of many researchers (e.g., to conduct high quality research) and self-help participants (e.g., to help their groups succeed). Furthermore, the great diversity in orientations and personalities of researchers, in types of research questions, and in critical dimensions of self-help organization (i.e., focus problem, group ideology, organizational structure, stage of development) underscore the critical nature of the match of researcher, research question, and self-help organization, for the success of a collaborative effort.

Given both the complexity and the positive potential of participatory self-help research, where do we go from here? One primary need is a greater understanding of the conditions under which different types and levels of collaboration result in research of empirical or practical value in the self-help area. There is no easy way—and no single way—to achieve such understanding.

In part, we need further articulation of the underlying assumptions both of researchers and of SHG members of the nature and anticipated value of collaborative, participatory research. The ensuing dialogue will help make explicit some of the key dimensions that need to be taken into account in examining, and fashioning, future research in the area. It should also help delineate the different meanings of terms such as *collaboration, participatory, power sharing, action,* and *research,* as well as the range of roles and meanings of the terms *researcher* and *SHG.* The participation of researchers from different disciplinary backgrounds and self-help participants from a range of SHGs will enhance the value of such a dialogue.

We also need additional systematic empirical examination of the experience of self-help researchers and self-help organizations who have participated in collaborative, participatory research. This will shed light on key factors and processes leading to both positive and negative outcomes of the research experience. Ideally, a range of methods varying in types and levels of research collaboration and in extent of focus on research versus action goals will be encompassed. Furthermore, a range of research questions, research disciplines, and types of self-help organizations will be captured. Especially rich data would emerge from well-designed prospective studies focused explicitly on the collaborative processes and outcomes of new or ongoing participatory research studies. Interdisciplinary teams of self-help researchers and self-help members ideally would contribute to such an examination.

References

Borman, L. D. (1979). Characteristics of development and growth. In M. A. Lieberman & L. D. Borman (Eds.), *Self-help groups for coping with crisis* (pp. 13–42). San Francisco: Jossey-Bass.

Chamberlin, J. (1978). *On our own: Patient controlled alternatives to the mental health system.* New York: McGraw-Hill.

Chesler, M. A. (1991). Participatory action research with self-help groups: An alternative paradigm for inquiry and action. *American Journal of Community Psychology, 19,* 757–768.

Galanter, M., Egelko, S., & Edwards, H. (1993). Rational recovery: Alternative to AA for addiction? *American Journal of Drug and Alcohol Abuse, 19*(4), 499–510.

Isenberg, D. H. (2003). Report on self-help group research. In D. H. Isenberg (Eds.), *The insiders' guide to self-help groups in Illinois.* Chicago: Self-Help Coalition.

Jason, L. A. (1985). Using the media to foster self-help groups. *Professional Psychology: Research and Practice, 16,* 455–464.

Jason, L. A., Tabon, D., Tait, E., Iacono, G., Goodman, D., et al. (1988). The emergence of the inner city self-help center. *Journal of Community Psychology, 16,* 287–295.

Kaskutas, L. A. (1992). Beliefs on the source of sobriety: Interactions of membership in Women for Sobriety and Alcoholics Anonymous. *Contemporary Drug Problems,* 631–648.

Klaw, E., & Humphreys, K. (2000). Life stories of Moderation Management mutual help group members. *Contemporary Drug Problems, 27,* 779–803.

Kurtz, L. (1990). The self-help movement: Review of the past decade of research. *Social Work With Groups, 13,* 101–115.

Nelson, G., Ochocka, J., Griffin, K., & Lord, J. (1998). "Nothing about me, without me": Participatory action research with self-help/mutual aid organizations for psychiatric consumer/survivors. *American Journal of Community Psychology, 26,* 881–912.

Price, R. (1989). Bearing witness. *American Journal of Community Psychology, 17,* 151–167.

Rittenhouse, T., Culter, S., & Campbell, J. (1999). *Dressed-down research terms: A glossary for nonresearchers.* St. Louis: Missouri Institute of Mental Health.

Trice, H. M. (1957). A study of the process of affiliation with Alcoholics [sic] Anonymous. *Quarterly Journal of Studies on Alcohol, 18,* 39–54.

8

Empowerment Evaluation: Principles and Action

Abraham Wandersman, Dana C. Keener,
Jessica Snell-Johns, Robin Lin Miller,
Paul Flaspohler, Melanie Livet-Dye, Julia Mendez,
Thomas Behrens, Barbara Bolson,
and LaVome Robinson

Empowerment evaluation (EE) aims to increase the likelihood that programs will achieve results by increasing the capacity of program stakeholders (any individual, group, or organization that has an important interest in how well a program functions) to plan, implement, and evaluate their own programs. This chapter defines EE, proposes a set of principles for the theory and practice of EE, and presents a case example to illustrate EE in action.

Getting to Know Empowerment Evaluation

Although EE is relatively new (it was introduced in 1992), it is gaining acceptance in mainstream evaluation circles. Since the publication of the seminal book on EE (Fetterman, Kaftarian, & Wandersman, 1996), much work has been done in the name of EE. In addition to scholarly contributions and numerous evaluations that labeled themselves as EE, the creation and establishment of the American Evaluation Association's Collaborative, Participatory, and

The evaluation of the Night Ministry was made possible by an evaluation team from the University of Illinois at Chicago, which was made up of Robin Miller and several graduate students: Barbara J. Bedney, Terri Bicok, Khari Hunt, Mary Murray, Bernadette Sanchez, and Dana Wardlaw. In addition, we acknowledge leaders and staff from the Middle Tyger Community Center and the Foundation for the Future Initiative—both of Spartanburg, South Carolina—who through their collaboration and commitment to evaluation greatly informed our ability to identify and articulate the empowerment evaluation principles. Finally, we are grateful to Rebecca Campbell, Margaret Davis, David Fetterman, Miles McNall, and Shakeh Kaftarian for their valuable feedback on the chapter.

Empowerment Evaluation topical interest group has provided fertile ground for extended debate and discussion about the EE approach.

Definitions of Empowerment Evaluation

Fetterman (2001) defined EE as "the use of evaluation concepts, techniques, and findings to foster improvement and self-determination" (p. 3). Although this definition of EE has remained consistent since the onset of the approach, the methods and principles of EE have continued to evolve and become more refined over time. Wandersman's description of EE places an explicit emphasis on results:

> The goal of empowerment evaluation is to improve program success. By providing program developers with tools for assessing the planning, implementation, and evaluation of programs, program practitioners have the opportunity to improve planning, implement with quality, evaluate outcomes, and develop a continuous quality improvement system, thereby increasing the probability of achieving results. (1999, p. 96)

Purposes of Empowerment Evaluation

EE expands the purpose, roles, and potential settings of evaluation beyond that of traditional evaluation approaches.[1] However, this does not preclude the need or diminish the importance of more traditional evaluation approaches (Fetterman, 2001). The type of evaluation selected for a given program is best determined by the goals and purposes of the evaluation. Therefore, neither EE nor traditional evaluation is inherently a "better" approach. Instead, each evaluation approach is valuable when applied for purposes that are well-suited to the strengths and intentions of the given approach (Chelimsky, 1997; Patton, 1997).

Chelimsky (1997) described three purposes of evaluation, including: (a) evaluation for development (information collected to strengthen institutions); (b) evaluation for accountability (measurement of results or efficiency); and (c) evaluation for knowledge (acquisition of a more profound understanding in some specific area or field; p. 10). EE is especially appropriate for the purpose of development, because it actively seeks to develop people, programs, and institutions. In addition, EE can also be used effectively for the purpose of accountability, as stated in Wandersman's definition of EE. The frameworks and methodology (e.g., Prevention Plus III, Getting to Outcomes) created and used by Wandersman and colleagues (e.g., Linney & Wandersman, 1991; Wandersman, Imm, Chinman, & Kaftarian, 2000) are designed not only to improve programs but to measure the results of programs (accountability). Although it

---

[1]Traditional (or independent) evaluation is characterized by greater autonomy of the evaluator, the use of controlled research methods, and is most often used for the purpose of accountability (Rossi, Freeman, & Lipsey, 1999).

Table 8.1. Ten Principles of Empowerment Evaluation

Core values	Principle 1. EE aims to influence the quality of programs.
	Principle 2. In EE, the power and the responsibility for the evaluation lies with program stakeholders.
	Principle 3. EE adheres to the evaluation standards.
Creating a culture that is ready and interested in improvement	Principle 4. Empowerment evaluators demystify evaluation.
	Principle 5. Empowerment evaluators emphasize collaboration with program stakeholders.
	Principle 6. Empowerment evaluators increase stakeholders' capacity to conduct evaluation and to effectively use results.
	Principle 7. Empowerment evaluators use results in the spirit of continuous quality improvement.
EE is a cyclical and developmental process	Principle 8. EE is helpful at any stage of program development.
	Principle 9. EE influences program planning.
	Principle 10. EE institutionalizes self-evaluation among program staff.

is not a current emphasis of EE, in the future we hope to systematically explore the potential usefulness of EE for the third purpose of research knowledge.

Guiding Principles of Empowerment Evaluation

EE is characterized by principles that represent EE's stance on evaluation ideology and practice. Table 8.1 represents one way to organize the guiding principles of EE. The first category consists of core values that are central to the philosophy and practice of EE. The second category consists of principles that relate to creating a culture that is ready and interested in improvement. The third category includes principles that illuminate how EE is a cyclical and developmental process. It is important to note that: (a) the principles represent ideals; (b) the individual principles are not exclusively associated with EE; and (c) it is the set of principles, taken as a whole, that distinguishes EE from other approaches.

Core Values of Empowerment Evaluation

When selecting any evaluation approach, it is important to ensure that the core values of the selected approach match the needs of the program and its stakeholders. The core values of EE are that it aims to influence the quality of programs, that the power and the responsibility for the evaluation lies with the program stakeholders, and that it adheres to the evaluation standards.

PRINCIPLE 1: EMPOWERMENT EVALUATION AIMS TO INFLUENCE THE QUALITY OF PROGRAMS. EE values program success. Accordingly, the EE approach seeks to increase the likelihood that programs will achieve their desired outcomes. This is in contrast to traditional evaluation, which values neutrality and objectivity and wants to examine programs in their "natural state." A traditional evaluator tries to avoid influencing a program's outcomes, and an empowerment evaluator strives to positively influence a program's degree of success. Some argue that because empowerment evaluators are not neutral, evaluation findings are more likely to be inaccurate because of the misrepresentation of data, biased research questions, or misinterpretation of results. It is important to recognize that the integrity of an evaluation can be compromised in any setting (e.g., the 2002 ENRON scandal) or evaluation approach. Practitioners working with empowerment evaluators may actually be less likely to misrepresent data than practitioners who feel threatened by evaluation. Empowerment evaluators propose that because they strive for program improvement, they may actually be *more* critical than traditional evaluators (Fetterman, 2001).

PRINCIPLE 2: IN EMPOWERMENT EVALUATION, THE POWER AND RESPONSIBILITY FOR EVALUATION LIES WITH THE PROGRAM STAKEHOLDERS. Typically in traditional evaluation, decisions regarding the purpose, design, and use of evaluation results are made by the evaluator and the funder. Alternatively, empowerment evaluators work to blur boundaries that traditionally separate funders, practitioners, and evaluators (Yost & Wandersman, 1998) by giving each group a voice in the decision-making process. Although empowerment evaluators share ideas and provide expert guidance, the stakeholders ultimately make critical decisions about the evaluation, conduct the evaluation, and put the evaluation findings to use. In participatory evaluation designs, decision making is shared by both evaluators and practitioners (Cousins & Whitmore, 1998), whereas in EE, the practitioners are explicitly the ones with the decision-making power.

PRINCIPLE 3: EMPOWERMENT EVALUATION ADHERES TO THE EVALUATION STANDARDS. Although the philosophical underpinnings of EE are quite distinct from traditional evaluation approaches, the principles of EE are fully consistent with the standards of evaluation set forth by the Joint Committee on Standards for Educational Evaluation (1994; Fetterman, 2001). The standards serve to provide a common language and set of values for the field and ensure quality across all evaluation philosophies and methodologies. The utility standards are designed to ensure that evaluation serves the information needs of the intended users. The feasibility standards are designed to ensure that evaluation is realistic, prudent, diplomatic, and frugal. The propriety standards are designed to ensure that evaluation is conducted legally, ethically, and with due regard for the welfare of those involved in the evaluation, as well as those affected by the results. The accuracy standards are designed to ensure that evaluation will reveal and convey technically adequate information about the features that determine worth or merit of the program being evaluated.

Creating a Culture That Is Ready and Interested in Improvement

One of the central aims of EE is to create a culture that is ready and interested in improvement. In EE, teaching stakeholders to value opportunities for program improvement is as central to building capacity and achieving results as teaching stakeholders' specific evaluation skills (e.g., logic modeling, survey administration, data entry). Fetterman stresses the importance of "creating a dynamic community of learners—a community where people are willing to share both successes and failures, to be honest, and to be self-critical" (2001, p. 6). We believe that this type of evaluation culture is established when evaluators demystify the process of evaluation, work collaboratively with stakeholders, build stakeholders' capacity, and emphasize that results will be used in the spirit of continuous quality improvement.

PRINCIPLE 4: EMPOWERMENT EVALUATORS DEMYSTIFY EVALUATION. Before specific steps can be taken to increase stakeholders' capacity and to influence programming, explicit attention must be given to stakeholders' concerns about evaluation. The Northwest Regional Educational Laboratory (1999) highlights common fears about evaluation, including general anxiety among program staff, uncertainty about how to conduct evaluation, and misuse and misunderstanding of evaluation findings, especially by program opponents. Program stakeholders often have good reason to be fearful of evaluation when they lack a role in the evaluation process or when their survival depends on the outcome (e.g., Bicknell & Telfair, 1999). Such fears lead practitioners to feel uneasy about revealing problems and challenges they inevitably face in implementation, which potentially compromises the accuracy and utility of the evaluation results.

The effective empowerment evaluator seeks to overcome these fears and concerns by demystifying evaluation. This is accomplished by using a structured framework to explain the logic and process involved in evaluation. The three steps proposed by Fetterman (2001, pp. 23–33) and the 10 accountability questions proposed by Wandersman et al. (2000) are examples of question-based frameworks that guide stakeholders to make critical decisions about essential elements of effective programs (including evaluation). By translating evaluation methods into specific questions that can be considered by stakeholders, the complex process of evaluation is made concrete. Empowerment evaluators believe that practitioners are more trustful of evaluation results—whether they are positive or negative—when they share ownership of the information and have both the ability and responsibility to use the information to improve their programs.

PRINCIPLE 5: EMPOWERMENT EVALUATORS EMPHASIZE COLLABORATION WITH PROGRAM STAKEHOLDERS. One way empowerment evaluators reduce fears and facilitate stakeholders' interest in evaluation is by explaining that EE is not something done by someone, to someone else. Rather, EE is a process in which evaluators work side by side with program stakeholders to implement and evaluate a program in a way that meets the stakeholders' needs. The nature of this collaboration is such that the boundaries traditionally separating funders, practitioners, and evaluators are intentionally blurred (Yost & Wandersman, 1998). Empowerment evaluators and stakeholders are seen as sharing a common purpose, and all stakeholders are seen as contributing something unique and valuable to that common purpose.

PRINCIPLE 6: EMPOWERMENT EVALUATORS BUILD STAKEHOLDERS' CAPACITY TO CONDUCT EVALUATION AND TO EFFECTIVELY USE RESULTS. EE is an ongoing process of building stakeholders' capacity. EE creates a culture that is ready and interested in improvement by tailoring support to the current capacities of stakeholders. Stakeholders come to trust that if they need assistance, their empowerment evaluators are available to guide them. At the same time, empowerment evaluators are eager for stakeholders to operate independently.

Empowerment evaluators teach stakeholders to use techniques that lead to the design and implementation of more effective programs. It is assumed that developing practitioners' abilities to use evaluation to inform decision making will later translate into the use of evaluation to benefit all program activities. Patton (1997) summarized capacity-building as "individual changes in thinking and behavior, and program or organizational changes in procedures and culture, that occur as a result of the learning that occurs during the evaluation process" (p. 90). Snell-Johns and Keener (2000) defined evaluation capacity as the ability to understand and perform skills related to assessing the implementation and effectiveness of a given program and the ability to make changes to this program based on the information gained. Empowerment evaluators believe that when stakeholders know the steps involved in conducting a high-quality evaluation, they are in a better position to understand and use evaluation results, which makes them ready and interested in program improvement.

PRINCIPLE 7: EMPOWERMENT EVALUATORS USE EVALUATION RESULTS IN THE SPIRIT OF CONTINUOUS QUALITY IMPROVEMENT. Empowerment evaluators encourage stakeholders to value both positive and negative results; positive results are celebrated and negative results are seen as crucial for additional program development. Negative results are not to be feared, especially in circumstances where the funder also values EE. Because EE emphasizes the use of process and outcome data for program improvement, rather than simply for auditing purposes, practitioners are better able to trust that negative results will not be used arbitrarily or to punish them. By emphasizing that evaluation results will be used for continuous quality improvement, evaluators are able to help establish a dynamic community of learners. Stakeholders learn the value of being honest with one another and with evaluators, and they come to respect and admire others' willingness to be self-critical, perhaps as much as they may have initially valued the discovery of positive results.

Empowerment Evaluation Is a Cyclical and Developmental Process

If one considers evaluation and evaluation capacities as existing along a logical developmental continuum, it becomes clear why it is not only possible but necessary for empowerment evaluators to take on different roles and incorporate various techniques at different points in the life cycle of a program (Fetterman & Eiler, 2001). A key task in implementing EE involves assessing the evaluation capacity of program personnel and their readiness for change. This awareness sets the stage for an empowerment evaluator to choose particular methods to move the program from its current status to the next step along the developmental continuum. Progress along this continuum occurs each time a stakeholder takes greater control over the evaluation design, process, or use of evaluation results.

PRINCIPLE 8: EMPOWERMENT EVALUATION IS HELPFUL AT ANY STAGE OF PROGRAM DEVELOPMENT. EE has the explicit value of working with people and programs "where they are at" to move them forward. For example, if a program's staff has never conducted an evaluation before, getting the staff to simply identify their program's target population, goals, and desired outcomes is seen as a legitimate step toward better programming and evaluation. Although it is optimal to begin EE during the early stages of program development, EE can benefit mature programs as well. For example, if a program is in the middle of implementation, EE methods and tools can be used to help assess the quality of implementation. If a program has already been completed and an empowerment evaluator is hired, the evaluator can teach the program stakeholders how to understand the results and how to translate these results into plans for improving the program the next time it is offered. Ideally, empowerment evaluators work with programs and organizations for several years so that a cycle of improvement can be created.

PRINCIPLE 9: EMPOWERMENT EVALUATION INFLUENCES PROGRAM PLANNING. It is a truism that programs that are planned better work better. Planning is a necessary, although not sufficient, element of an effective program. The most important questions to answer when developing a good program plan are also relevant to program evaluation. For instance, both a program plan and an evaluation process should identify the goals, target populations, and strategies of a given program. The unfortunate reality is that programs are frequently implemented without giving adequate attention to clearly identifying the needs, target populations, and goals. Often programs are chosen just because they seem like a good idea and not because they are addressing a specific, identified need. Thus, under ideal circumstances, EE begins as soon as an agency decides it wants to address a problem in the community. This means that empowerment evaluators can play a role as early as the grant-writing stage (Yost & Wandersman, 1998). EE can examine the logic or theory of a program before it even gets off the ground, saving time and energy that might be misguided or misused. In doing this, the evaluation process serves as a guide not only for evaluating the program but also for program planning and implementation.

PRINCIPLE 10: EMPOWERMENT EVALUATION INSTITUTIONALIZES SELF-EVALUATION AMONG PROGRAM STAFF. As the capacities of the program grow and develop, empowerment evaluators shift from the role of teacher to more of a "critical friend" in the evaluation process (Fetterman, 2001). If EE is successful, the techniques of evaluation become a part of regular program activity and influence the overall quality of programming. For evaluation to have its optimal impact, it needs to be an ongoing process, which allows EE to become a part of the culture and daily life of a program. In other words, the goal is for EE to eventually become institutionalized within the program setting (Fetterman, 2001). By participating in EE, program stakeholders learn to see the intervention from an evaluator's perspective. This can have a greater, and more durable, impact than the results of a particular evaluation. Fetterman (2001) suggested that institutionalization and the development of a dynamic community of learners allows EE to accommodate changes in the program environment caused by shifting populations, goals, knowledge, and external forces impinging on the program.

Case Example

The principles of EE are inherent in the ideals of EE, but what does EE really look like? The growth in EE's popularity has resulted in its application in a wide variety of settings (e.g., school readiness initiatives, family resource centers) and with programs of differing scales, ranging from well-funded evaluations of multi–million-dollar, statewide initiatives (e.g., Wandersman et al., 2001) to unfunded evaluations of small local community agencies and programs.

In January 1996, Robin Lin Miller began working as an evaluator with the Night Ministry, a unique faith-based organization located in Chicago. Miller's experience is presented as an illustration of EE's application in a real-world setting. Following is a description of the Night Ministry organization, the conditions that led the evaluation team to choose an EE approach (Fetterman, 1994, 1996; Vanderplaat, 1995), and the process of conducting the evaluation. To conclude, the evaluation effort is examined in terms of the extent to which it conforms to the 10 defining principles of EE.

The Night Ministry: The Organizational Setting

Founded in 1976, the Night Ministry is a nondenominational church-based organization that provides physical, emotional, and spiritual services to Chicago's nighttime street communities. Male and female prostitutes, homeless adults and youth, chronically mentally ill individuals, disenfranchised sexual minorities, and substance users are among the Night Ministry's congregants. Locations such as bars, restaurants, liquor stores, street corners, adult bookstores, bathhouses, and parks are its parishes. The Night Ministry reaches out to individuals at the margins of society through three programmatic efforts: (a) a street and health outreach program (the Outreach Health Ministry); (b) a 16-bed emergency shelter for youth and their children (the Open Door Youth Emergency Shelter); and (c) a city-wide partnership of organizations providing emergency shelter to youth (the Youth Shelter Network).

The evaluation activities described in this example were focused on the Outreach Health Ministry (OHM). In OHM, ministers have street parishes in several communities throughout the greater Chicago area. Ministers spend time in local parishes (e.g., bars, strip clubs, street corners) providing companionship, support, counseling, and referrals to parishioners. The program also operates a bus that travels to each parish between 7 p.m. and 2 a.m. offering hospitality, condoms, clothing, toiletries, health care, STD screening, counseling, and companionship. A minister, a nurse, and a cadre of volunteers staff the bus that travels to about three parishes each night on a regular schedule known to parishioners.

The Outreach Health Ministry is based on the idea that promoting personal and spiritual growth will lead to improved quality of life. Quality of life improvements can be psychological, spiritual, physical, or circumstantial (e.g., getting a job). The program seeks to improve quality of life outcomes by developing relationships with nighttime community members that are characterized by respect and dignity and that provide people with a sense that they are valued and supported. The development of these relationships occurs over long periods of time—in some cases many years. OHM seeks to empower its parishioners through a process of personal transformation and validation. Interactions among community members, staff, and volunteers are reflexive in nature. In other words, staff members believe that personal and spiritual growth evolves through a constant process of reflection and reassessment.

According to the program's proponents, the Night Ministry and its Outreach Health Ministry program represent a radical vision of ministry. OHM puts its faith into action in the nonjudgmental way that they believe Christ might have if He were alive today—going to the people, tailoring ministry to the individual and his or her context, and transforming the role of the minister to that of a mutual learner who is equal to parishioners. Although the program has much in common with traditional outreach and other faith-based initiatives, the Night Ministry asserts that the way it has brought these elements together is unique. It is this nontraditional, fresh approach to pastoral care— an approach that departs from business as usual within the church—that defines the organization's identity.

The Empowerment Evaluation

The EE project with the Night Ministry began in response to the ministry's desire to improve the evaluation process of its Outreach Health Ministry as well as the evaluation skills of its staff. The organization was greatly dissatisfied with the type of data they were previously required to collect, because they believed that the data failed to communicate the program's identity and practice in a meaningful way. In March 1996, Miller attended a meeting of board members and staff to identify the organization's evaluation needs and the target audience of the evaluation results. Later, an evaluation team was formed to include Miller, a team of graduate students from the University of Illinois at Chicago (UIC), ministers, nurses, and divinity student interns. By group consensus, parishioners were not included in the evaluation team, although they were integral to the evaluation process.

A notable feature of this evaluation was that it was a volunteer effort (i.e., not funded). This is despite the fact that funding was offered by a foundation midway through the project. In this case, the evaluation team chose to decline the funding offer so that the project could proceed unfettered by the timelines and accountability requirements often dictated by funding institutions.[2]

When considering the type of evaluation to use for this project, the EE approach emerged as most consistent with the Night Ministry's culture, values, and practices. By matching the evaluation approach to the values and practices of the program, the evaluation team established a means to overcome passive disinterest among staff and, in some cases, active dislike of evaluation. For instance, EE's emphasis on self-reflection and self-evaluation is also inherent in the discipline of pastoral care. All ministers in the program keep personal diaries to record parishioners' stories and their own experiences on the streets, as well as to process challenging emotions provoked by their work. Such creative freedom to identify and solve problems and the autonomy it implies is one organizational pathway to empowerment (Foster-Fishman, Salem, Chibnall, Legler, & Yapchai, 1998).

Egalitarianism and collaboration are two additional values intrinsic to both the Outreach Health Ministry program and the EE approach. These values are consistent with collectivist and strength-based organizational characteristics identified by Maton and Salem (1995) as empowering. For example, OHM uses storytelling as a way for ministers and parishioners to share themselves with one another and to level perceived inequities in relationships. Personal disclosure is encouraged and considered an essential technique to blur the boundary between personal and professional. Parishioners collaborate with the staff by providing volunteer services on the bus. Volunteers counseled, nurses ministered, and ministers served coffee. The staff displayed a strong sense of community, approaching most aspects of the program as a collective.

Both EE and the Night Ministry strive to encourage social justice, a feature of empowering organizations (Maton & Salem, 1995). The Night Ministry is founded on the principle that justice belongs to all and has challenged other congregations, local citizens, and government representatives to advocate for the rights of homeless, mentally ill, and other individuals who are socially disenfranchised. For example, the Night Ministry established a policy advocacy coalition of providers to bring the needs and concerns of homeless and runaway youth, who are not wards of the state, to the attention of local and state government officials.

Selecting Appropriate Evaluation Strategies

The ultimate challenge faced by the evaluation team was to develop an evaluation strategy that could capture the quality of interactions with the diversity of nighttime community members, the longitudinal nature of relationship development, and the variety of desired outcomes, while simultaneously helping the staff learn to develop their own evaluation tools, collect data, and use

---

[2]As funding agencies become more knowledgeable of EE and the benefits of this approach, they are more likely to be flexible and supportive of the methods and timelines necessary to build capacity and implement an empowerment evaluation (W. K. Kellogg Foundation, 1999).

evaluation results to inform program changes. To accomplish these aims, the evaluation team first had to develop a rich description of what actually happened in the program. This understanding was necessary before they could help the organization develop useful evaluation tools, determine the most important evaluation questions, and assess the extent to which evaluation was already part of the fabric of organizational life.

Another task was to create a framework by which tools could be developed in collaboration with the staff so that evaluation skills were cultivated within the organization and so that the logic or small theory of the program was evident. The team wanted to capitalize on the reflexivity of staff (i.e., ability to be reflective), both in the process of transmitting skills and in building a system for long-term evaluation of the program.

In accomplishing all tasks, the evaluation team sought to work in ways that did not disrupt or violate the relationships with the parishioners that the organization had worked so long and hard to develop. Many of the parishioners are highly mistrustful of formal institutions, given their association with illegal activities (e.g., prostitution, drugs) and their marginalized position in society. The university-based evaluation team avoided procedures that community members might associate with the formal institutions that they fear and dislike. An organizational ethnographic approach was used to understand the meaning of the program. The ethnographic paradigm was well-suited to the goals of the evaluation team because its naturalistic research strategies enabled researchers to gain experiential knowledge of a phenomenon and close understanding of what objects, activities, events, and relationships mean to people. The ethnographic paradigm is reflexive in ways that paralleled the program's style. For instance, descriptive accounts of places and events simultaneously give rise to those phenomena and are shaped by those phenomena. Participant observation was the primary means of data collection, supplemented by interviews and document reviews. Participant observations were seen as least disruptive to the operation of the program. This method also allowed the evaluation team to understand the various roles within the ministry while portraying the longitudinal nature of relationships within the program. The entire evaluation team functioned in the dual roles of participant and observer from April 1996 to June 1998. Each team member was responsible for volunteering on a particular night of the week with the bus and documenting the interactions among the staff, volunteers, and community members. By systematically covering each night of the week, the evaluation team was able to observe the different shifts and program participants and gain a complete picture of program operations as they unfolded over time. By having a consistent schedule, each team member also had the opportunity to build relationships with community members at the various stops on that night's itinerary.

While on the bus, team members served coffee and cookies, distributed condoms and clothing, counseled parishioners, and worked alongside the staff. Team members also shadowed ministers on walks through their parishes. These activities provided the team with direct access to the program and insight into the challenges of measuring it. It also led staff to perceive the evaluation team members as standing alongside them on a journey toward transformation, much like staff hoped to be perceived by parishioners.

Initial Observations

The evaluation team's initial observations and informal interviews provided important insights about the program's operation and how its philosophy of practice was enacted. Some initial observations had particular bearing on the evaluators' subsequent actions. One was that program decision making was handled democratically. This was evident at staff meetings and during program implementation. Student interns, volunteers, nurses, and ministers were vested with equal responsibility and authority for program operations. All staff shared in creating a sense of community on the streets each evening. Decisions were based on everyone's experiences, rather than only favoring the perspectives of program management. As a result, staff members shared a sense of ownership of the program.

There were, however, drawbacks of the democratic and nonhierarchical process. First, the value placed on group decision making and full consensus made it difficult to make more than small changes to the program. Second, because everyone was allowed to put forth their views so freely, over time the attitudes and beliefs of some individuals came to characterize those of the group, whether those beliefs were valid or not. Some of the collective myths observed among staff included the belief that the program could not be evaluated because of its spiritual base and that evaluation findings suggesting program failure were a result of a misunderstanding of the program. Such myths served as armor to protect the staff from accountability demands. Through these myths, the staff had found a way to accept an operating program model that departed from the desired program model. Freidman (2001) referred to this phenomenon, in which groups develop defensive routines, as designed blindness. Thus, the democratic culture had serious implications for evaluation, including defining who the evaluation stakeholders were, what was believed to merit evaluative scrutiny, and how evaluation data were to be processed by staff.

Another important observation made by the evaluation team was that many factors beyond the staff's control heavily affected (or interfered with) the staff's ability to implement the program as intended on a day-to-day basis. These factors included the presence and timing of police sweeps; the burdens on the shelter and drug treatment systems, as well as the restrictions imposed on those systems by regulatory agencies; the time of the month in relation to the distribution of government support payments; the impact on traffic and public behavior caused by events such as the Bulls winning an NBA championship; and the weather. Recognition of these factors highlighted the importance of viewing the program as a series of interactions that unfolded over time, rather than as a discrete interaction between a parishioner and the program. Indeed, the reason that the evaluation team earned trust where other evaluators had failed was because staff believed that they would not be judged for implementation barriers that were outside of their control.

Another crucial observation was that staff had difficulty describing the purpose of the program, how they wanted the program to function, and how specific program activities led to particular outcomes. Indeed, staff rarely talked about outcomes. When asked to describe a success, staff would describe the same case that they had just offered moments before as a failure. This conceptual muddiness was related to the underlying pastoral philosophy of the program. Pastoral aims, such as spiritual transformation and enlightenment, were not obviously connected to secular aims such as using a condom, kicking a habit, or seeking employment. The staff saw an individual's willingness to change his or her behavior as intricately linked to the spiritual self, a perspective that many funding institutions do not necessarily share. In OHM, trusting relationships were seen as both a means and an end, such that obtaining the means but not the ends could be seen as a success and a failure simultaneously. Getting someone to come back and hang out four or five times over the course of a few months was a success, even if they seldom spoke or were never sober on any of those occasions. Staff members were not driven by a rigid set of outcomes that were invariant across individuals. Achievements were grounded in relationship achievements and in the ebb and flow of the various dyadic exchanges in which parishioners and the Night Ministry personnel engaged.

Building an Improvement-Oriented Culture

After 6 months of observation and participation in program activities, the evaluation team developed a simple logic model of the theory underlying the Outreach Health Ministry program. During a group exercise, the model was presented to the OHM staff for group reflection and feedback. After lengthy discussion, the group agreed that the model accurately represented the intended goals and strategies of the program.

Next, the OHM staff identified the practices associated with each of the model's components. Staff worked in small groups to describe the required activities in each area of the model, creating program templates (Scheirer, 1996) for the logic model. For example, the logic model contained an element titled "build quality relationships." Staff identified behaviors that were necessary to develop a relationship with a parishioner, such as using open body language, being nonjudgmental, remembering personal information about people, and engaging in active listening. The model provided the theoretical guide for the evaluation team's evolving participant observations and served as the initial template for decision making regarding how the program was to be evaluated.

The staff used the logic model and program templates as the basis for generating key questions about program implementation. Staff teams worked together over a period of several months to develop evaluation tools for documenting program processes related to the evaluation questions, each of which loosely correspond to the domains of the logic model. Each small team included a nurse, at least one minister, and a student evaluator. Some teams also included ministerial interns. Teams regularly presented their ideas to the other teams for feedback. Each team ultimately produced at least one measure that was pilot-tested by the staff. Staff then worked through a series of revisions to the measures and procedures for collecting the data. These measures included forms to document the characteristics of the parishes in which the work was carried out, services provided by the bus, and interactions with parishioners in each of the parishes.

Using Results to Build Capacity in the
Spirit of Continuous Improvement

During this same period, the evaluation team regularly presented information about what they had learned. For example, the team developed a flow chart that described how interactions between parishioners and staff are initiated and the sequence of interactions that typically follow them. Data revealed that parishioners initiated conversations with staff more often than staff initiated conversations with parishioners and that staff avoided some approaches. Staff was curious to understand the reasons for these findings, resulting in new evaluation questions. The presentations also proved to be a vehicle to promote critical evaluative thought among program staff. It was through the presentations of ethnographic data that staff was best able to stand outside themselves and get a new perspective into the program operations, program assumptions, and the inconsistencies between program practice and program design.

EE pushed the organization to confront its own myths. One example of this occurred at a staff meeting in which the evaluation team reviewed the data that staff had collected during street interactions over a two-month period. The data indicated that the staff had more contacts (i.e., superficial/basic interactions) with women and African Americans/Blacks than with men and Caucasians/Whites. However, inconsistent with the number of contacts, data revealed that a higher proportion of substantive conversations (or more in-depth relationships) occurred with men and Caucasian/White persons. In this same meeting, staff also learned that, despite the perception that they talked about AIDS frequently, only one HIV risk-reduction counseling interaction had been recorded during the two-month period. These two findings, from the EE process, provided staff with surprising revelations about their work and reinforced the importance of collecting evaluation data.

Staff generated multiple hypotheses about the surprising findings. One hypothesis was that they had not collected data thoroughly enough. A second was that they had not adequately trained the staff (who were primarily White and male) to address the more in-depth concerns of women and people of color. The hypotheses they developed were testable, suggested clear action, and created opportunities to challenge the program status quo. The data created a forum for women to talk about how the program might include their voices and perspectives and for the ministers to talk about how reporting the content of their interactions with parishioners clashed with their training about the privacy of the pastoral relationship. The ethnographic data suggested clear areas for program improvement. More recent data suggest that the proportion of substantive encounters by gender and race now closely mirrors the proportion of superficial contacts. Contacts with women have increased modestly.

Staff members continue to use the measures that evolved out of the evaluation to inform organizational changes, to make the program more inclusive, and to keep the program from becoming an agent of the status quo. In addition, staff developed—on their own—a way to monitor client outcomes after their formal relationship with the evaluation team had ended, a sign of increased skill. The Night Ministry continues to include the OHM logic model in their grants and uses the model to articulate their vision of ministry to other outside entities. The Night Ministry honored the evaluation team with a Living the Mission Award in recognition of its success in putting the values of the organization into action. The Night Ministry also asked the evaluation team to remain involved in the organization to assist them in establishing a long-range plan for a training institute, creating a five-year strategic plan, and continuing their empowerment EE efforts.

In an attempt to reflect on the successes and challenges of this particular EE, Revs. Thomas Behrens and Barbara Bolsun of the Night Ministry graded the efforts of the evaluation team based on its adherence to each of the 10 principles of EE. Table 8.2 presents the results of this informal exercise. As the grades indicate, the weakest areas of performance were in increasing capacity (Principle 6) and institutionalizing an evaluation culture (Principle 10), though the grades were still high. Relatively lower grades in these areas can be attributed to nearly 100% turnover rate of OHM staff in 1999 and, simultaneously, to all research at the University of Illinois at Chicago being suspended for 8 months by the U.S. Office for Human Research Protections beginning in August 1999. Overall, however, the evaluation team did well in adhering to the principles (this is especially impressive because the principles were proposed after the project was completed). Because the team took the time to fully understand the program, the staff, and the context in which it operated, the team was perceived by staff to be "clueful" rather than "clueless," placing it in a strong position to demystify evaluation (Principle 4) and collaborate with stakeholders (Principle 5). The evaluation team's thorough understanding of the program, acquired through long-term collaboration, was key to the staff's acceptance of the UIC evaluation team and the team's ability to work effectively with staff. The evaluation team was viewed as part of the program culture. The small-group process was empowering to staff and helped staff articulate a framework for what they do. They used this framework to enrich their own understanding of their work, communicate with others, and develop more rigorous ways of self-examination (Principle 2). Staff acquired the sense that they could describe and measure what they did, so they did not have to rely on the myth that it was not measurable (Principle 4). Staff came to understand the value of data as a tool for planning (Principles 8 and 9) and program improvement (Principles 1 and 7).

Conclusion

Community psychology advocates collaboration, partnership, sharing, and parity among researchers, evaluators, community members, and organizations. This ideal, however, seems especially challenging to achieve within the realm of program evaluation. This is likely because of the perpetuation of the belief that only the "experts" (i.e., those with formal training) can serve in the role of evaluator. Indeed, program evaluation does involve knowledge and use of research designs, methods, and statistical analyses. However, if experts remain the sole designers of evaluation methods and the primary interpreters of evaluation findings, the potential utility and impact of the evaluation process would be limited. EE shifts the power of evaluation into the hands of stakeholders.

Table 8.2. Informal Grade Report of the Evaluation Team's Adherence to the Principles of Empowerment Evaluation as Reported by Night Ministry Staff

Category	Principle	Grade
Core values	Empowerment evaluation aims to influence the quality of programs	A
	Power and responsibility for the evaluation lies with the program stakeholders	A
	Empowerment evaluation adheres to the evaluation standards	Pass
Improvement-oriented culture	Empowerment evaluators demystify evaluation	A+
	Empowerment evaluators emphasize collaboration with program stakeholders	A
	Empowerment evaluators build stakeholders' capacity to conduct evaluation and use results effectively	B–
	Empowerment evaluators use evaluation results in the spirit of continuous improvement	A–
Developmental process	Empowerment evaluation is helpful at any stage of program development	A
	Empowerment evaluation influences program planning	A
	Empowerment evaluation institutionalizes self-evaluation	B

Another roadblock to community participation in evaluation emerges as many promising and intuitively meaningful programs often fall short of documented effects when submitted to the scrutiny of evaluation. This is known by evaluators and community stakeholders alike. This awareness leads to some degree of wariness on the part of stakeholders as to whether the evaluation process is really in their best interests. At the same time, funders are increasingly insisting that community organizations and programs provide documentation of program implementation and evidence of program outcomes. Such requirements can lead to half-hearted participation of community stakeholders in the evaluation process. As a result, stakeholders can become saboteurs of the process. EE offers a means to avoid this common pitfall of program evaluation.

Parallel to the issue of community participation in research endeavors, there is an ongoing debate within the evaluation community regarding the relative usefulness of "inside" evaluation (conducted by internal people in the program) versus "outside" evaluation (conducted by external professional evaluators). Inside evaluators are criticized because of their potential biases that might influence their evaluation reports, given that they have a direct investment in the program. On the other hand, who could know better the intricacies of a program than those who administer and deliver the program on a routine basis? Alternatively, outside evaluators are heralded as objective and well-suited to the task of accurately documenting the effects of a program. On the down side, it is questionable how well external evaluators, given their limited exposure to the daily operations of the program, can design an appropriate evaluation protocol that serves the needs of the program. Historically, the nod has gone to the outside evaluator, believing that formal research training was most important to the evaluation process. Alternatively, EE strives to establish evaluation methodologies that draw on the strengths of both internal and external perspectives and minimize the weaknesses of each.

The principles of EE propose that evaluation can be both consistent with the ideals of community psychology and results-oriented. EE, at the aspirational level, achieves the ideals of true community collaboration and embodies the belief and expectation that community stakeholders are equal contributors to the social construction of knowledge. The balance of power that characterizes EE allows community stakeholders to become invested and share the responsibility for the integrity of the process. Thus, community stakeholders are less likely to sabotage evaluation and more likely to defend and protect the evaluation process. Because EE establishes a culture that welcomes and is ready for evaluation, the evaluation process can be sustained, even when those with formal evaluation training have exited the process. Ultimately, this results in a greater likelihood of achieving desired results.

The principles of EE presented in this chapter are intended to enhance the clarity with which EE is defined, understood, and implemented. Furthermore, the Night Ministry case example is offered as one illustration of the proposed benefits of using EE. Specifically, EE is a promising approach for building capacity, fostering self-determination instead of dependency, and helping programs improve their performance. Finally, this chapter reveals the common values shared by EE and participatory research theory and methods. We look to others in the field to assist us in testing the EE framework to produce a research base regarding the effectiveness of EE. Future work will be instrumental in revealing the conditions under which EE produces desired outcomes for programs.

References

Bicknell, Y., & Telfair, J. (1999). The process of selling a community evaluation to a community: Cumberland County's experience. *New Directions in Program Evaluation, 83,* 87–93.

Chelimsky, E. (1997). The coming transformation in evaluation. In E. Chilemsky & W. Shadish (Eds.), *Evaluation for the 21st century: A handbook.* Thousand Oaks, CA: Sage.

Cousins, J. B., & Whitmore, E. (1998). Framing participatory evaluation. *New Directions for Evaluation, 80,* 5–23.

Fetterman, D. M. (1994). Empowerment evaluation. *Evaluation Practice, 15,* 1–15.

Fetterman, D. M. (1996). Empowerment evaluation: An introduction to theory and practice. In D. M. Fetterman, S. J. Kaftarian, & A. Wandersman (Eds.), *Empowerment evaluation: Knowledge and tools for self-assessment and accountability* (pp. 3–46). Newbury Park, CA: Sage.

Fetterman, D. M. (2001). *Foundations of empowerment evaluation.* Thousand Oaks, CA: Sage.

Fetterman, D. M., & Eiler, M. (2001). *Empowerment evaluation and organizational learning: A path towards mainstreaming evaluation.* Paper presented at the 2001 meeting of the American Evaluation Association, St. Louis, Missouri.

Fetterman, D. M., Kaftarian, S. J., & Wandersman, A. (1996). *Empowerment evaluation: Knowledge and tools for self-assessment and accountability.* London: Sage.

Foster-Fishman, P. G., Salem, D. A., Chibnall, S., Legler, R., & Yapchai, D. (1998). Empirical support for critical assumptions of empowerment theory. *American Journal of Community Psychology, 26,* 507–536.

Freidman, V. J. (2001). Designed blindness: An action science perspective on program theory evaluation. *American Journal of Evaluation, 22,* 161–181.

Joint Committee on Standards for Educational Evaluation. (1994). *The program evaluation standards.* Thousand Oaks, CA: Sage.

Linney, J. A., & Wandersman, A. (1991). *Prevention Plus III: Assessing alcohol and other drug prevention programs at the school and community level: A four-step guide to useful program assessment.* Rockville, MD: U.S. Department of Health and Human Services.

Maton, K. I., & Salem, D. (1995). Organizational characteristics of empowering community settings: A multiple case study approach. *American Journal of Community Psychology, 23,* 631–656.

Northwest Regional Educational Laboratory (National Mentoring Center). (1999). *Making the case: Measuring the impact of your mentoring program.* Retrieved Sept. 22, 2003, at http://www.nwrel.org/mentoring/pdf/makingcase.pdf

Patton, M. Q. (1997). *Utilization-focused evaluation* (3rd ed.). Thousand Oaks, CA: Sage.

Rossi, P. H., Freeman, H. E., & Lipsey, M. W. (1999). *Evaluation: A systematic approach* (6th ed.). London: Sage.

Scheirer, M. A. (Ed.). (1996). A user's guide to program templates: A new tool for evaluating program content. [Special issue]. *New Directions for Evaluation, 72.*

Snell-Johns, J., & Keener, D. (2000, Nov.). *The past and current evaluation capacity of two community initiatives.* Paper presented at the 2000 meeting of the American Evaluation Association, Waikiki, Hawaii.

Vanderplaat, M. (1995). Beyond technique: Issues in evaluating for empowerment. *Evaluation, 1,* 81–96.

Wandersman, A. (1999). Framing the evaluation of health and human service programs in community settings: Assessing progress. *New Directions for Evaluation, 83,* 95–102.

Wandersman, A., Flaspohler, P., Ace, A., Ford, L., Imm, P., et al. (2001, Nov.). *Mainstreaming evaluation and accountability in each program in every county of a state-wide school readiness initiative.* Paper presented at the 2001 annual meeting of the American Evaluation Association, St. Louis, Missouri.

Wandersman, A., Imm, P., Chinman, M., & Kaftarian, S. (2000). Getting to outcomes: A results-based approach to accountability. *Evaluation and Program Planning, 23*(3), 389–395.

W. K. Kellogg Foundation. (1999). *Empowerment evaluation and foundations: A matter of perspectives.* Unpublished report, Battle Creek, MI.

Yost, J., & Wandersman, A. (1998, Nov.). *Results-oriented grantmaking / grant-implementation: Mary Black Foundation's experience.* Presented at the 1998 annual meeting of the American Evaluation Association, Chicago.

Part IV

Culture and Gender

9

Feminist Perspectives: Empowerment Behind Bars

Doreen D. Salina, Jean L. Hill, Andrea L. Solarz, Linda Lesondak, Lisa Razzano, and Dorenda Dixon

The difficulty in providing a feminist perspective on participatory action research (PAR) is to derive a point of view that can be considered uniquely feminist. It is tempting to refer to the "feminist movement," as though feminism encompasses one, unified school of thought. When we speak of liberal feminism, radical feminism, socialist feminism, and womanism, however, we are discussing very different views of how knowledge is constructed and very different prescriptions for how to achieve social change. Similarly, it is also difficult to identify sharp lines of demarcation between feminist ideas and the ideas of other fields because feminism often shares a common discourse with Marxism, postmodernism, and racial analyses of society. In addition to these shared discussions, feminism shares with many fields an emphasis on the elimination of oppression.

Nonetheless, there are several broad themes that can be seen as connecting feminist perspectives to community psychology in general, and to PAR more specifically (Bond, Hill, Mulvey, & Terenzio, 2000; Hill, Bond, Mulvey, & Terenzio, 2000). These include the following:

1. *Integrating contextualized understandings:* There is an emphasis on situating the analyses of social problems in an understanding of their social context (e.g., the gendered nature of power differentials, economic and political forces, structures and values of communities, etc.).
2. *Addressing issues of diversity:* Respecting the cultural influences that shape people's lives, as well as attending to issues of differential access to power and privilege that are rooted in histories of oppression and biased societal practices toward groups (e.g., based on gender, culture, race, ethnicity, sexual orientation, disability, economic status, etc.).
3. *Including the perspective of oppressed groups:* Understanding that positions in society (e.g., based on gender, race, class, sexual orientation, etc., shape interpretations of reality and that an individual's experiences of events are central to understanding social phenomena.

4. *Adopting collaborative approaches:* The concept that research should be a partnership between the researcher and participants and that the perspective of all relevant parties should be represented and integrated at multiple stages of the research process. This includes research design and implementation to ensure the most valid understanding of the issues under study.

5. *Using multilevel, multimethod analyses:* These techniques allow researchers to better understand complex phenomena. Research beyond the individual level is essential for understanding the role of social structures, communities, and societies on human behavior, and the use of multiple methods both reduces bias associated with the use of any particular method and provides a richer picture of the phenomenon under study.

6. *Reflexivity:* This practice of examining ways that personal values, histories, and social and political positions influence one's research and how it is interpreted allows researchers to acknowledge and neutralize their own biases and to seek out other perspectives to place the issues examined in a larger social context.

7. *Taking activist orientations:* Using research in ways that have a positive impact on the political, social, or health issues under examination; reflects a goal of promoting social change and influencing decision makers.

In the following section we present a theoretical framework for understanding feminist approaches to research and the challenges presented by participatory research, and we propose the two forces of passion and pragmatics as motivation for overcoming those hurdles. Next, a project is described that illustrates how feminist principles can be applied effectively in PAR projects. Finally, we close with a brief discussion that reflects on how the described project was guided by feminist principles and present some of the more salient challenges.

Feminist Theory and Participatory Action Research

Early in the current wave of feminist thought, activists became aware early on that science and scientific knowledge were frequently used as a means to justify and support the oppression of women and other groups, leading to a more critical discussion about the basic nature of science and traditional forms of research (Collins, 1987; Fonow & Cook, 1991; Harding, 1987; Harstock, 1998; Mies, 1983; Nielson, 1990; Reinharz, 1992; Stanley & Wise, 1983). These forms of traditional research embrace the positivistic ideology that has predominated science since the end of the Middle Ages (e.g., Descartes, 1641/1960). According to this ideology, the goal of science is to seek the truth, of which there is only one version. This goal is best achieved by an individual, working alone, setting aside all emotions and personal values. If the discovered is eventually found to be flawed, one does not blame the methods, but rather the application of the methods. Truth should be sought for its own value, and any attempt to apply that knowledge is a lesser form of endeavor and probably useless. These concepts are based on clear dichotomies between individual versus collaborative work, objective versus subjective positions, truth versus opinion, intellect versus emotion, basic inquiry versus applied work, and facts versus values. These ideas form the basis of the positivistic approach to science. Not coincidentally, these ideas are in almost direct opposition to the themes presented at the beginning of this chapter.

Challenging a Positivist Ideology

Serious challenges to specific aspects of positivism arose in the 19th century. During this time, the concept of praxis, which asserts that knowledge has no value unless it is applied to solve human problems, was put forth as an alternative to positivism. Essential to praxis is the understanding that the application of knowledge requires an intense, personal, and subjective engagement on the part of the researcher—an engagement that results in change in the person of the researcher just as it results in change in the problems addressed. Supporters of praxis also strongly challenged the notion of an objective reality with its insistence that social reality is constructed to support specific distributions of wealth and power. Feminism joined this critique through the 19th-century work and writings of such women as Harriet Martineau, Ida B. Wells, and Frances Wright (Reinharz, 1992). These women demonstrated that much of society's construction of gender was designed to support power differentials and that, far from being objective, much of scientific research was conducted in such a way as to affirm these constructions. Similarly, racial critiques of the 19th century, fueled by the imperative need to address the issue of slavery, added support to the idea that notions of race—rather than reflecting some objective reality—were instead socially constructed to support existing distributions of power and wealth. Once again, it was demonstrated that the findings of positivistic scientists were not objective but used to support the social oppression.

During the 20th century these social forces converged to fuel a full-fledged philosophical challenge to positivism. Postmodernistic philosophy is based on the idea that there is no one true reality, that reality is socially constructed (Seidman, 1994). Because reality is socially constructed, and human observers develop in the context of that construction, it is not possible for one to be an objective observer. These concepts have had a deep impact on the philosophy of science because they have challenged both our ideas of what "knowledge" is and our understanding of the relationship between the researcher and the knowledge gained from that research.

In this view, knowledge is not uncovered but constructed in the context of specific cultures, relationships, and conversations. Knowledge comes not just through observation and description of a phenomenon but through deconstructing that phenomenon to clarify the structures and relationships that imparted meaning to the event. This strongly supports the view that observers have an intimate impact on the event they are observing. If reality is socially constructed, and knowledge comes through the deconstruction of the structures and relationships that support that reality, then knowledge is inherently relational in nature. This realization brings the relationship between the observer and the observed—between the researcher and the participant—into sharp and prominent focus.

Although these postmodern ideas have been widely accepted, at least in the social sciences, positivistic approaches to scientific research are still the dominant paradigm accepted by funding sources, academic institutions, and publishing outlets. The widespread critique of these approaches, and the acknowledgment of the need to change scientific practice based on that critique, have in fact resulted in little observable change, with most changes seeming largely cosmetic. For example, although many funding agencies, including the various offices of the federal government, identify the need for collaboration with participants in research, many research projects involve participants in minimal or symbolic ways (Tandon, Kelly, & Mock, 2001, p. 202).

Costs and Rewards of Participatory Action Research

The failure of the critique of positivism to result in real change is based on several factors related to the increased personal costs and decreased rewards associated with PAR projects as compared to traditional forms of research. For example, the structure of academic research limits rewards for those engaged in PAR projects; scholarly reinforcers (e.g., grants, publications, and promotions) are still heavily linked to positivistic assumptions of what constitutes "good" science. In addition, the personal costs of PAR projects are higher for both researchers and participants. PAR is time-consuming, messy, often frustrating, and difficult. These projects take a large amount of personal investment, and in most instances a great deal of self-reflection and self-criticism on the part of both researchers and participants. Although all research requires a major investment in terms of time, resources, and energy, participatory research may be unique in the demands that it places on one's sense of self. The nature of this personal investment can be seen in many descriptions of participatory research. Deborah Tolman, for example, wrote that, "after my interview with sixteen-year-old Isabel, I feel like I need to come up for air" (2001, p. 133). Brinton Lykes wrote about being "repositioned and challenged" by her PAR with Mayan women in Guatemala (2001, p. 186), and Cynthia Chataway highlighted the "vulnerability that comes with full participation in multiple layers of social complexity" (2001, p. 240).

Although these quotes are all from *researchers* engaging in PAR projects, the demands on *participants* are just as great, if not greater in some respects. PAR projects are typically conducted with people who are dealing with significant obstacles in their lives and their communities—obstacles such as poverty, discrimination, health issues, and serious trauma such as sexual abuse or war refugee status. In many, if not most cases, their personal resources are already severely overwhelmed by the day-to-day tasks of their lives. The costs of diverting scarce personal and community resources to a PAR project can have serious ramifications for such groups and individuals (Roy & Cain, 2001).

Although difficult to accomplish, the structural forces that limit rewards for engaging in PAR projects *can* be changed (books such as this one will contribute toward that goal). It is doubtful, however, that the increased personal costs of PAR projects compared to traditional research can be eliminated. This is because, for all sets of collaborators, there is a personal struggle involved in setting aside the belief in one "true" reality, coupled with a reluctance to proactively engage in the conflicts that arise from this struggle.

Connected to the attraction of one "true" reality is our fundamental distrust in the notion of relativism as it is related to social construction. If all realities are socially constructed, then what basis do we have for assigning value to those constructions? On a general level those of us involved in feminist and community work can point to our espoused values of eliminating oppression and fostering social change as a basis for evaluating the "worth" of competing constructions. But this general basis often gives little guidance in the day-to-day work of participatory research. An increase in the number of collaborators inevitably results in an increase in the number of different opinions—opinions regarding the goals of the research, appropriate methods, appropriate analyses, appropriate interpretations, and appropriate use of results. As individuals, it is difficult, if not impossible, to accept that all those differing opinions are of equal value, and this belief that one viewpoint is inherently more valuable than another is an emotional barrier to negotiating participatory research. In addition, social forces such as sexism, racism, and heterosexism potentiate these individual biases and often function as significant obstacles for collaborative, feminist endeavors (Salina & Lesondak, 2002).

The differences between researcher and participants in knowledge of the research process dictate a difference in power and in the value assigned to competing opinions. Grundy wrote, "Power in emancipatory action research resides wholly within the group" (Grundy, 1982, p. 363). But how can this occur when there are real differences in the knowledge and power held by individual group members, and when those differences have an impact on the value assigned to competing opinions?

When opinions compete, the task is to decide on the "best" or perhaps "most useful" viewpoint and move on; the emphasis is on the product of the collaboration, not the collaboration itself. If, on the other hand, knowledge is viewed as relational in nature, then the relationships become much more important, and the process becomes the focus of the project. Differences in opinion become something to explore and learn from, not just resolve.

These are the primary reasons why engaging in PAR is so personally taxing for researchers. Researchers must be constantly on guard against their own emotional tendencies to believe there is one true answer, to which their viewpoint is privileged, and that others must accept the desired end product. Turning to feminism, we can clearly see that stating that our intellectual positions have changed, without taking into account the emotional ramifications of those changes, results in a situation in which we ignore real and important areas of conflict. And when one ignores important areas of conflict in any relationship one is, in fact, ignoring the needs and contributions of at least one member of that relationship—generally the member with the least power. The most common resolution to this situation is that the member who feels ignored leaves the relationship, leaving the more powerful member wondering what went wrong.

There is no easy way to resolve this dilemma. Acknowledging our biases, values, privilege, and power means acknowledging areas of conflict. Most of us have been strongly socialized to avoid conflict, but the presence of conflict and the need to confront it, although personally challenging and emotionally draining, is also a source of growth. As bell hooks said of the feminist movement, "When women come together, rather than pretend union, we would acknowledge that we are divided and must develop strategies to overcome fears, prejudices, resentments, competitiveness, etc" (hooks, 1984, p. 63). PAR also requires this acknowledgment—and these strategies—if it is to be effective.

Motivations for Participatory Action Research: Passion and Pragmatics

Although the intellectual rejection of the positivistic approach to science may seem sufficient justification for the adoption of PAR, it actually does little to keep researchers motivated through the time-consuming, personally demanding, conflict-ridden process of participatory research. Intellectual arguments may be necessary, but they certainly are not sufficient as motivators; strong emotional reasons are needed for engaging in PAR. These strong emotional motivators fall under the two headings of *passion* and *pragmatics*.

Feminism supplies strong, passionate reasons for engaging in PAR. Feminist analyses of research and history demonstrate conclusively the damage done in the name of objective, value-free, positivistic science. The result has been socially constructed notions of gender that generally go unchallenged, that support power differentials based on gender, and that result in the oppression of women.

A passion for the expression of voice has become central to much of modern feminist writing (Belenky, Clinchy, Goldberger, & Tarule, 1986; Chodorow, 1989), and this passion supplies a strong motivating force for engaging in PAR, even with all the increased costs and decreased rewards. One of the central findings of feminist research has been that alternative voices, particularly those of oppressed groups, are often silenced in mainstream constructions of reality. This is graphically illustrated by the fact that a significant amount of social science research that was used to form our theories of how "humans" develop and interact was based on work with largely male populations. Prominent examples include research on moral reasoning (Gilligan, 1987), criminal behavior (Mann, 1984), and theories of social change (Kelly-Gadol, 1987). Feminist historians and literary critics have also documented a long-standing deficit of female voices in those fields that in some cases continues today (Mankiller, Mink, Navarro, Smith, & Steinem, 1998). This silencing of voices is not just a matter for theoretical discussion. It is a matter of passionate interest for the members of the silenced groups, and for those who believe that all of humankind benefits from diversity. This passion arises from the deep-seated belief that to silence a group is akin to annihilating a group.

Assuming that all voices have value is not the same thing as accepting that they all are *equally* valid or useful. It is possible to reconcile this passionate belief that silenced voices must be heard with our distrust of the relativistic argument that all voices have equal value. From this position, we have a moral and passionate obligation to include diverse views in our research and an intellectual and pragmatic obligation to deconstruct and evaluate those viewpoints. In a broad sense, this is what the process of PAR is all about—the elucidation, inclusion, and consideration of all positions, followed by the systematic critique of those positions in light of the goal of the project. To make matters more complicated, the collaborative nature of PAR requires that deconstruction and evaluation must occur within the context of the relationship between the researcher and the participants, and must include an analysis of the researcher's own viewpoint.

Although feminist researchers may have clear theoretical and passionate motivations for engaging in PAR, these may not apply, or may not be sufficient, for individuals who do not identify themselves with movements dedicated to social change. For many researchers—perhaps most who use PAR—their motivation seems to come not from intellectual or passionate beliefs (or at least not solely from those sources) but rather from a concern with pragmatics.

In general, PAR has been adopted in those disciplines that are most concerned with the application of research findings and that have documented the least success in translating traditional research into positive action. Since the 1970s, for example, educational researchers have documented the failure of university-generated research to stimulate meaningful change in public schools (Cohen & Garet, 1975; Dial, 1994; House, 1972). Likewise, the field of evaluation is filled with accounts of evaluation results left to gather dust on shelves, while organizations continue with established and often less than maximally effective practices (Weiss, 1972; Wholey, Scanlon, Duffy, Fukumotu, & Vogt, 1970; Williams & Evans, 1969).

These fields have adopted PAR methods not as much for theoretical formulations of "best practice" in research but rather from the pragmatic and pressing need to change research practice to produce results that are meaningful, useful, and amenable to adoption by the communities of interest. This point is perhaps most obvious in the field of health, where researchers were generating a knowledge base that they believed to be critical to the communities involved, only to see their research results underused if not completely ignored in practice.

Comparisons of the relative efficacy of traditional research versus PAR in their ability to translate to measurable change are lacking in the published literature. However, there is a strong assumption that PAR projects are more effective than traditional research programs in resulting in real change. Because PAR projects generally include the step of reflection, which then leads to a new cycle of planning and acting, reports of these projects usually incorporate a discussion of the process of the research, including observed results. But these descriptions of change in individual PAR projects do not serve the same purpose as an overall evaluation of the success of the method as a whole. Currently, many researchers still trust the method. However, we need to trust the method to challenge ourselves and the participants to make the significant investments required by PAR. It is the significant magnitude of these investments that makes it an ethical imperative that at some point distrust and critique enters the project. At some point in the near future, we are going to have to document that those investments are more than justified by the results.

The Women's Health, Empowerment, and STD/HIV Prevention Project

PAR requires that one challenges assumptions that one's own views are privileged in any way essential to the project. It requires that one remains on guard against emotional attachment to one, true answer to a problem and to product over process. It requires that one remains suspicious of easy answers, and instead look for and engage in potential areas of conflict. By addressing these areas of conflict we can develop new understanding and useful, innovative answers to the social problems we wish to change.

These themes and ideas are illustrated in a PAR project implemented by the first author and her colleagues. The Women's Health, Empowerment, and STD/HIV Prevention Project was developed within a feminist framework to provide a comprehensive STD/HIV prevention and empowerment program to incarcerated women in a large urban jail.[1] Both feminist and community psychology approaches emphasize giving voice to oppressed groups, and incarcerated women represent one of the most disempowered groups in U.S. society. Although many women have difficulty negotiating safer sex strategies with their sexual partners and often engage in HIV risk behaviors (Salina, Razzano, & Lesondak, 2000), incarcerated women face additional challenges. Affected by multiple forms of oppression and denied access to key resources, this group has high rates of substance abuse, poverty, homelessness, and STDs. These combined conditions of extreme levels of oppression and increased vulnerability to a life-threatening illness provided a passionate motivation for engaging in this project.

The incidence of STD/HIV/AIDS within the criminal justice system is a significant health concern facing women detainees. The 1999 rate of confirmed cases of AIDS in incarcerated individuals nationwide was five times that of the general population, with 1.7% of inmates in local jails identified as STD/HIV positive (Bureau of Justice Statistics, 2001). In Chicago, the proportion of AIDS cases affecting women has tripled from 7% in 1988 to 22% in 1997. However, although AIDS is currently the second leading cause of death for female offenders (Bureau of Justice Statistics, 2001), little is known about the specific relationships between risk behaviors and other public health problems.

In the Women's Health, Empowerment, and STD/HIV Prevention Project, incarcerated women learned to identify their own risk factors for contracting or transmitting STD/HIV and to use behavioral skills and strategies to reduce their risk. It is a tenet of the program that the development and reinforcement

[1]This project was made possible by a grant from the Chicago Department of Public Health. A special thanks to Terrie McDermott, Jennifer Black from the Department of Women Justice Services, and the women themselves for their valuable input into this project.

of appropriate help-seeking behaviors will empower women to take control over social influences and environmental barriers that often have an impact on their ability to accept control over their own health needs. The program also provides behavioral skills and social support within an empowerment agenda. Women in the program, many of whom are disenfranchised from mainstream health efforts, learn how to recognize specific situations that may interfere with engaging in health-positive behaviors and that affect their ability to avoid STD/HIV exposure. They are provided with linkages and referrals for other problems of living and, through empowerment activities, increase their ability to alter social barriers to health and to better care for themselves and their children's health and well-being.

Overcoming the Challenges of Conducting Participatory Action Research

Conducting PAR, or for that matter, any research, within a correctional setting presents unique challenges usually not present in other settings. For example, an action agenda can cause a number of ethical and political conflicts (Fonow & Cook, 1991), because correctional programs generally have a function and philosophy that are counter to empowerment activities. The traditional institutional view of the function of the correctional system is to detain and punish offenders, regardless of social factors that may have influenced incarceration. Research, which is often viewed as politically dangerous, is not typically well-received, and additional understanding of the incarcerated individual is generally considered valuable only as it relates to reducing recidivism. Early efforts to evaluate this project were met with suspicion by correctional administrators and direct staff, and initially the research team was denied access to the population. Although project staff were initially welcomed to provide health promotion activities, data collection activities were forbidden, presenting an obvious problem for assessing the effectiveness of the intervention.

These structural aspects of access to the population provided a clear pragmatic rationale for engaging in the collaborative approach that is central to PAR and is espoused by both feminist and community psychology ideologies. Fundamentally, unless every group touched by this project believed that their concerns were heard and addressed, the project simply would not work. Early in the program development phase, the research team had to decide about the various stakeholders and how to handle their sometimes divergent needs and perspectives. We recognized that the women in treatment were the major stakeholders in this project and that we had much to learn from them before we could design the most appropriate and effective prevention program. The research team also recognized that the support of the systems in which incarcerated and postrelease women would be found would be extremely important for a successful outcome.

To engage system stakeholders early on, a collaboration was established with two national substance abuse treatment programs in Chicago that serve large numbers of formerly incarcerated women. In return for access to their clients, the Women's Health, Empowerment, and STD/HIV Prevention Project delivered the prevention intervention, which counted toward state-mandated hours of health education, to the women. The research team also engaged the women in treatment from the beginning of the research process. All measures were reviewed by a group of formerly incarcerated women, and the prevention curriculum was refined based on feedback from informal focus groups and participants in pilot tests.

The research team developed a pre- and postintervention quantitative design to measure both important demographics about the women and outcomes from the intervention, thus blending qualitative and quantitative methods. Although the quantitative data collected in the treatment centers indicated that incarceration history was the primary predictor of HIV risk behaviors, the stories told by the women themselves yielded a far richer understanding of the context in which these behaviors occurred. The research team spent many hours discussing the women's stories while examining the quantitative data and discovered that these two forms of data were not always consistent. For example, although many women reported high levels of self-efficacy regarding obtaining condoms and knowing how to negotiate safer sex with their partner(s), many also admitted not using them. The research team openly discussed their own thoughts about the puzzling results as well as their responses to the women's stories in an effort to integrate both the women participants' perspectives and those of the researchers (Rappaport, 1993). Researcher reflexivity was central to this process. The researchers began to understand the deep level of distrust present within the women and how some of the initial assumptions generated by the research team did not reflect the full scope of the women's experiences. Many incarcerated women have been through the criminal justice system repeatedly and have learned that the system has little to offer and that it can be difficult to trust those who offer help (Hobfoll, 1998). As a result of this team reflexivity, the researchers were better able to modify the program based on what the women discussed about their own life experiences. They were also able to inform the treatment centers about the reported needs of the women so they could use this information to develop other health activities.

As the researchers continually refined their understanding of HIV risk reduction programming for incarcerated women, they also decided that formal collaboration with key systems was an important way to address needed services and stretch scarce resources. They thus applied for and received funding for the project through the Chicago Department of Public Health (CDPH). The proposed project included a formal collaboration with the director of Corrections at CDPH and her staff, such that STD/HIV counseling and testing services would be provided through the CDPH in the correctional setting itself, with appropriate follow-up, treatment, and linkages. The CDPH was identified as an integral partner in the program; by providing needed in-kind services, this allowed for a comprehensive empowerment program focused on HIV risk reduction. The scope of services would have been significantly reduced without these formal collaborations and partnerships.

An effective prevention program with incarcerated women must take into account the many real factors and barriers to health promotion activities. Rappaport wrote about "giving voice to the participants' definition of reality"

(Rappaport, 1990, 1993) and determined that empowerment programs need to emphasize existing strengths in the group of concern rather than its deficits (Rappaport, 1990). To identify and understand these strengths, researchers are required to bring a contextualized understanding to their work by analyzing the specific meanings of behaviors in the participants' lives. Although the researchers had spent the requisite time reviewing the literature and engaging in many philosophical discussions about the best methods of using prevention science to address STD/HIV risk with incarcerated women, they still needed to hear directly from the women. By encouraging the women to speak for themselves about their experiences, the researchers came to have a better understanding of the complexities of the problems being addressed. For example, incarcerated women often engage in behaviors that allow them to survive in hostile environments and settings, and behaviors labeled as maladaptive by others can be critically adaptive in acquiring basic commodities such as food and shelter for these women and their children.

We recognized that an impartial, scientific stance was not effective or desirable because we were, as feminist researchers, attempting to identify the social context of the harsh realities of the incarcerated women's lives. We understood that for some women, engaging in HIV risk behaviors represented access to important commodities such as intimacy, power, and control. By developing a trusting and collaborative relationship with the women themselves, they began to reveal how they viewed unprotected sex, which often had nothing to do with disempowerment and everything to do with maintaining control over their intimate lives and physical bodies. Many women who engage in sex work for income believe that they are able to have a degree of intimacy with their intimate partner that is not present or desired by their sex clients. This understanding could not have been possible without the women being willing to share these intimate details. By recognizing that incarcerated women actively cope and interact within an oppressive and hostile environment, we do not view the women as powerless and helpless but rather as survivors of the oppressive forces of sexism, racism, and classism.

Finding a New Niche

As a result of the successful collaboration with the CDPH and the focus on empowerment of women, the research team was invited to provide the program as part of the comprehensive health services to incarcerated women in the same facility (but a different division) to which they had previously been denied access. The Department of Women's Justice Services (DWJS) was established in December 1999 as a result of a National Institute of Corrections Project in which policy makers focused on the alarming increase in the number of women in the correctional system. It supervises several programs that focus on the needs of nonviolent, incarcerated women, with an emphasis on facilitating change through treatment and empowerment. The vision of the DWJS is to develop an effective community alternative to jail for nonviolent women detainees; its mission is to empower women to make changes in their lives that focus on healing, empowerment, and long-term support. To break the intergenerational cycle within the criminal justice system, services are designed to be comprehensive, accessible, supportive, and sensitive to the multitude of barriers with which the women struggle.

One of the critical changes DWJS implemented was creating gender-responsive requirements for treatment programs for incarcerated women under their jurisdiction. The gender-responsive treatment approach is based on new theories related to gender that include an understanding of the additional barriers present for women because of their gender—recognizing the social context in which maladaptive, illegal, or risk behaviors occur allows for a better understanding of the unique challenges that women face. To address these programmatic challenges, the DWJS created the Sheriff's Female Furlough Program (SFFP), a diversion program for nonviolent women offenders, most of whom are incarcerated for or struggle with substance abuse issues. In this program, participants report to the jail during the day but return home to their communities in the evening. The SFFP creates a woman-supportive environment through staff training, program development, content, and materials that reflects an understanding of the realities of women's lives, and are responsive to the issues of the women participants. The integrated, comprehensive program uses approaches based on theories that fit the psychological, social, and cultural needs of women by focusing on existing strengths within each woman and her community. All programs must use a strength- or asset-based approach to treatment and skill building and include cognitive, affective, and behavioral approaches. DWJS staff attempt to develop a safe, supportive, and nurturing women-centered environment that encourages trust, bonding, and connection within a correctional setting.

Finding a segment of the correctional system that was focused on gender-responsive programs for incarcerated women was an ideal fit for the goals of the Women's Health, Empowerment, and STD/HIV Prevention Project. The research team began to meet regularly with the DWJS to better understand what they were trying to develop and to ascertain how their skills and the program would best fit into such an endeavor. Rappaport (1990) described this as a mutual influence process, which allows collaborative partners to actively listen and comprehend the other's perspective. This process generally facilitates learning and greater understanding of a particular social problem, allowing for the deconstruction of the ideological assumptions embedded within each person within the collaboration (Riger, 1992). This process encouraged mutual sharing and trust and yielded greater innovation in framing the gendered context of the research (Fonow & Cook, 1991).

To further strengthen the collaborative process, the researchers asked DWJS staff for input on the quantitative questionnaire. To be sensitive to any political implications, they also allowed the department's legal counsel to examine and approve the measure, which included detailed questions about sexual behavior (appropriate institutional review board approval had already been obtained for the project). Formerly incarcerated women also examined it and assisted the researchers in modifying the wording and the types of questions asked. This yielded a questionnaire that was inclusive of all the stakeholders' perspectives. The DWJS staff had questions themselves about other non-

HIV related needs, and so a section was added to the questionnaire that would allow SFFP to better develop additional programs.

Over time, it became apparent that the women participants had many unmet needs. Women revealed in focus groups, on questionnaires, and in conversation with the researchers that even though HIV is a life-threatening illness, it was of lower concern to them than was obtaining housing, health care, and substance abuse treatment. Because of this, an individual component was added at the end of the program to give the participants the opportunity to speak with staff about these concerns and needs. Through these individual sessions, which flowed from the underlying empowerment agenda of the STD/HIV program, women began to identify what barriers they believed stood in their way to a more health-positive life. Staff and student volunteers were trained to assist the women, and SFFP staff agreed to allow the women to use the phone to connect with appropriate community agencies (an almost unheard-of event within a correctional setting but reflective of the gender-responsive nature of this program).

The DWJS has developed an extensive array of collaborative relationships of community-based agencies and individuals with expertise in working with incarcerated women. These agencies, which include employment agencies, treatment centers, churches, and the like, have a common focus on addressing the complex needs of women detainees. Many of the staff at these agencies are formerly incarcerated women themselves and can represent both their community-based organization (CBO) and the perspective of women detainees. All partners are expected to take a gendered-responsive approach in service delivery.

Future Directions

The Women's Health, Empowerment, and STD/HIV Prevention Project, having reached hundreds of women and having heard their personal stories, is being revised to include this greater breadth of knowledge. The researchers are planning to present the findings to the women themselves in small group format to engage in a respectful and inclusive dialogue about what the results mean. The original name of the project has been dropped and the women themselves have been asked to rename it. The empowerment agenda is being expanded to include collaborating with other agencies where women need services. Furthermore, project findings are being disseminated to Chicago-based task forces and health coalitions so they can apply this knowledge in an effective and empowering manner.

By using multiple methods of inquiry, the researchers were better able to understand the lived experiences of the women (Riger, 1992) and gained knowledge at the same time they imparted it. Mies (1991) wrote that different forms of knowledge, not simply scientific, are necessary to fully understand the social construction of gendered issues. Although it would have been desirable to expand further the use of qualitative research techniques in the evaluation of the intervention, funding constraints unfortunately did not make it possible to use both qualitative and quantitative methodologies in a formal manner. In addition, because one of the goals of the researchers is to obtain additional funding to expand activities, we are mindful of the practical constraints of applying for funding with only qualitative data—quantitative or positivistic methodologies are still the primary or preferred methodology approved by federal funders.

Currently, the researchers are analyzing the results of both the data collection and related focus groups as well as engaging in "think tank" sessions with all project staff so they can better understand the social context of the results. The project is being altered and restructured as a result of these multiple sources of information obtained about HIV risk. DWJS staff, the research team, and these community-based agencies have developed solid collaborative working relationships and have begun to meet monthly to assist in the continued development of a comprehensive coalition of services that can be implemented for detained women. Finally, as a result of the participatory relationship among the stakeholders, a collaboratively developed PAR grant was submitted to federal funding sources.

Conclusion

In this chapter, we have outlined some of the characteristics shared by feminist approaches to research and PAR, presented theoretical underpinnings of the feminist perspective, and described a PAR project that engenders a feminist approach. As was noted in the beginning of the chapter, it is difficult to pinpoint ideas that are uniquely feminist. However, it is indeed possible to describe a gestalt that can be identified as a feminist approach—an approach that in many ways reflects a focus on the *process* of research and a set of *values* as much as on the *techniques* of research.

The Women's Health, Empowerment, and STD/HIV Prevention Project considered by Salina and Lesondak presents a good example of how researchers (both male and female) can apply feminist principles to the design and implementation of PAR. Clearly, the researchers in this case experienced the dual motivators of passion and pragmatics identified in the theoretical section of this chapter. Their initial passion for working with an oppressed group was fueled by the personal stories of adversity and strength told by the women. The researchers maintained their commitment to a PAR process, even in the face of such adversities as being locked out of the correctional facility when data collection activities were discussed. In addition, the complex and widely differing viewpoints of the many stakeholders pragmatically dictated PAR as the most viable approach for developing an effective HIV intervention in a jail because it gave voice and recognition to all collaborators (including the recipients of the intervention).

The broad common themes that connect feminist perspectives to community psychology—and in turn to PAR—are reflected throughout the Women's Health, Empowerment, and STD/HIV Prevention Project. The researchers integrated contextualized understandings of both the program participants and the system stakeholders throughout the process, consistent with the tenets of

PAR and feminism. This is reflected, for example, in their efforts to understand how the context of the women's lives dictated their priorities and options, as well as in understanding the political factors influencing the correctional settings. Rather than searching for one, true, overarching reality, the researchers instead focused on many, small, contextualized realities that were collaboratively developed during the course of the project. Attention to issues of diversity was also a key characteristic. In particular, there was a focus on understanding issues of differential access to power and privilege for the participants, including the context of the correctional setting. The researchers understood the importance of speaking from the standpoints of oppressed groups. This is reflected, for example, in the extent to which the researchers took care to get input and feedback from the women participants in many different contexts (e.g., by having the participants review data collection measures and the design of the implementation). The study is characterized by its collaborative approach, with both stakeholders and potential participants of the intervention being involved at multiple stages of the process, including in the initial design of the intervention. The project also used multilevel, multimethod analyses. Although the researchers had hoped to include a stronger formal focus on qualitative methods, substantial qualitative data were collected and used to reflect on and better interpret the quantitative data. In addition, information was gathered to document the impact of the intervention not just on the women participants but on the systems in which the programs are nested. The researchers regularly engaged in reflexivity throughout the project. For example, this practice allowed them to recognize their own biases about the high priority they expected STD/HIV prevention to be for the incarcerated women and to recognize the importance of collecting additional information to inform the development of programs to address the other needs the women identified. Finally, this project illustrates several ways to take an activist orientation to research. In addition to conducting research that focuses on important policy-relevant issues, the researchers engaged policy makers (e.g., the CDPH) in the implementation of the intervention and engaged in a regular process of reporting findings to programmatic policy makers to inform the development and delivery of services.

Translating theory to applied settings is almost always a challenge for community-based researchers. Multiple barriers exist, and agendas are often varied and covert. However, by using a feminist framework and principles of collaboration, sharing power, and recognizing their own biases, these researchers were able to develop and participate in an effective working group within a correctional setting. This collaboration developed a forum where information is more easily exchanged, where different perspectives are welcome, and where the detained women themselves are valued for their contributions and for surviving their environments.

This project represents just one example of how PAR conceptualized within a feminist framework can be used to empower participants from oppressed groups, provide important health services and linkages, and create systemic change. It remains a challenge for the field to examine and question the extent to which the feminist principles described are regularly integrated into the practice of community-based PAR, to ensure that training programs are adequately preparing students to conduct this exciting, challenging form of research and to challenge institutional norms that devalue approaches that do not follow the traditional positivist ideology.

References

Belenky, M., Clinchy, B., Goldberger, N., & Tarule, J. (1986). *Women's ways of knowing: The development of self, voice and mind.* New York: Basic Books.

Bond, M. A., Hill, J., Mulvey, A., & Terenzio, M. (2000). Weaving feminism and community psychology: An introduction to a special issue. *American Journal of Community Psychology, 28,* 585–597.

Bureau of Justice Statistics (BJS). (2001). *HIV in prisons and jails, 1999 (NCJ 187456).* Washington, DC: U.S. Department of Justice.

Chataway, C. (2001). Negotiating the observer–observed relationship. In D. Tolman & M. Brydon-Miller (Eds.), *From subjects to subjectivities: A handbook of interpretive and participatory methods* (pp. 239–255). New York: New York University Press.

Chodorow, N. (1989). *Feminism and psychoanalytic theory.* New Haven, CT: Yale University Press.

Cohen, D., & Garet, M. (1975). Reforming educational policy with applied social research. *Harvard Educational Review, 45,* 17–41.

Collins, P. H. (1987). *Black feminist thought: Knowledge, consciousness, and the politics of empowerment.* New York: Routledge.

Descartes, R. (1960). *Meditations on first philosophy.* Indianapolis, IN: Bobbs-Merrill Comp. (Original published 1641)

Dial, M. (1994). The misuse of evaluation in educational programs. In C. Stevens & M. Dial (Eds.), *Preventing the misuse of evaluation* (pp. 61–68). San Francisco: Jossey-Bass.

Fonow, M. M., & Cook, J. A. (Eds.). (1991). *Beyond methodology: Feminist scholarship as lived research.* Bloomington: Indiana University Press.

Gilligan, C. (1987). Woman's place in man's life cycle. In S. Harding (Ed.), *Feminism and methodology* (pp. 57–73). Indianapolis: Indiana University Press.

Grundy, S. (1982). Three modes of action research. *Curriculum Perspectives, 2*(3), 23–34.

Harding, S. (1987). *Feminism and methodology.* Bloomington: Indiana University Press.

Harstock, N. (1998). *Feminist standpoint revisited and other essays.* Boulder, CO: Westview Press.

Hill, J., Bond, M., Mulvey, A., & Terenzio, M. (2000). Methodological issues and challenges for a feminist community psychology issue. *American Journal of Community Psychology, 28,* 759–772.

Hobfoll, S. E. (1998). *Stress, culture and community: The psychology and philosophy of stress.* New York: Plenum Press.

House, E. (1972). The conscience of educational evaluation. *Teachers College Record, 73,* 405–414.

hooks, b. (1984). *Feminist theory: From margin to center.* Boston: South End Press.

Kelly-Gadol, J. (1987). The social relation of the sexes: Methodological implications of women's history. In S. Harding (Ed.), *Feminism and methodology* (pp. 15–28). Indianapolis: Indiana University Press.

Lykes, M. B. (2001). Activist participatory research and the arts with rural Mayan women. In D. Tolman & M. Brydon-Miller (Eds.), *From subjects to subjectivities: A handbook of interpretive and participatory methods* (pp. 183–199). New York: New York University Press.

Mankiller, W., Mink, G., Navarro, M., Smith, B., & Steinem, G. (Eds.). (1998). *The readers companion to U.S. women's history.* New York: Houghton Mifflin.

Mann, C. R. (1984). *Female crime and delinquency.* Tuscaloosa: University of Alabama Press.

Mies, M. (1983). Toward a methodology for feminist research. In G. Bowles & R. Duelli Klein (Eds.), *Theories of women's studies* (pp. 117–139). London: Routledge & Kegan Paul.

Mies, M. (1991). Women's research or feminist research? The debate surrounding feminist science and methodology. In M. M. Fonow & J. Cook (Eds.), *Beyond methodology: Feminist scholarship as lived research* (pp. 60–84). Bloomington: Indiana University Press.

Nielson, J. M. (Ed.). (1990). *Feminist research methods: Exemplary readings in the social sciences* (pp. 69–93). Boulder, CO: Westview Press.

Rappaport, J. (1990). Research methods and the empowerment agenda. In P. Tolan, C. Keys, F. Chertok, & L. Jason (Eds.), *Researching community psychology: Issues of theory and methods* (pp. 51–63). Washington, DC: American Psychological Association.

Rappaport, J. (1993). Narrative studies, personal stories and identity transformation in the mutual help context. *Journal of Applied Behavioral Science, 29,* 239–256.

Reinharz, S. (1992). *Feminist methods in social research.* New York: Oxford University Press.

Riger, S. (1992). Epistemological debates, feminist voices. *American Psychologist, 47,* 730–740.

Roy, C., & Cain, R. (2001). The involvement of people living with HIV/AIDS in community-based organizations: Contributions and constraints. *AIDS Care, 13,* 421–432.

Salina, D., & Lesondak, L. (2002). Racist, sexist and heterosexist behaviors. In L. Jason & D. Glenwick (Eds.), *Innovative strategies for promoting health and mental health across the life span* (pp. 301–323). New York: Springer.

Salina, D., & Lesondak, L. (2003). *Women's Health, Empowerment, STD/HIV Prevention Project.* Unpublished manuscript.

Salina, D., Razzano, L., & Lesondak, L. (2000). Women and sexual behavior: Taking control in the age of AIDS. *Journal of Prevention and Intervention in the Community, 19*(1), 41–54.

Seidman, S. (1994). *Contested knowledge: Social theory in the postmodern era.* Malden, MA: Blackwell.

Stanley, L., & Wise, S. (1983). *Breaking out: Feminist consciousness and feminist research.* London: Routledge & Kegan Paul.

Tandon, S. D., Kelly, J., & Mock, L. (2001). Developing African American community leadership. In D. Tolman & M. Brydon-Miller (Eds.), *From subjects to subjectivities: A handbook of interpretive and participatory methods* (pp. 200–217). New York: New York University Press.

Tolman, D. (2001). Echoes of sexual objectification. In D. Tolman & M. Brydon-Miller (Eds.), *From subjects to subjectivities: A handbook of interpretive and participatory methods* (pp. 130–144). New York: New York University Press.

Weiss, C. (Ed.). (1972). *Evaluating action programs.* Boston: Allyn & Bacon.

Wholey, J., Scanlon, J., Duff, H., Fukumotu, J., & Vogt, L. (1970). *Federal evaluation policy: Analyzing the effects of public programs.* Washington, DC: Urban Institute.

Williams, W., & Evans, J. (1969). The politics of evaluation: The case of Head Start. *Annals of the American Academy of Political and Social Science, 385,* 118–132.

10

Culturally Anchored Research: Quandaries, Guidelines, and Exemplars for Community Psychology

Christopher B. Keys, Susan McMahon,
Bernadette Sánchez, Lorna London,
and Jaleel Abdul-Adil

Community psychologists have long been interested in studying phenomena in diverse cultural groups, whether they are defined by differences such as ethnicity, socioeconomic status, sexual orientation, disabilities, or combinations of these and other characteristics. The meanings of culture are multiple; Rohner (1984) has identified four elements common to all cultures as conceptualized by anthropologists and cross-cultural psychologists. First, human beings develop in a cultural context, and thus their behavior is mediated and formed by culture. Second, socialization processes transmit values, norms, and behaviors of a culture from one generation to the next through social processes. Third, many aspects of culture cannot be overtly described or measured, such as "a way of life" and "heritage." These aspects are transmitted to individuals as they are socialized. Fourth, the last element common to all cultures is that one can find evidence of cultures in patterns and social regularities among members of a given culture.

Overall, these elements suggest that culture is not simply a characteristic such as ethnic background. It is also the context in which individuals live or work and their shared interpretations of that context. The cultural context and interpretation of the context influence individuals' behaviors and values. There are dimensions of culture that are more salient than others depending on an individual's context. Given these cultural elements, Hughes, Seidman, and Williams (1993) suggested that culture has a pervasive influence in the research process. In community psychology, the guiding principle that has been used in developing culturally anchored methodology is that culture provides

The order of the first three authors is alphabetical; each contributed equally to this manuscript. We appreciate the contributions of Fabricio Balcazar, Jean Bartruel, Pennie G. Foster-Fishman, and David Henry to the ideas presented in this chapter.

a context for and is infused throughout the research process. Hughes and colleagues discussed in depth how culture influences each step of the process, from problem formulation to interpretation of results. They offered guidelines for researchers who are committed to being sensitive to cultural nuances. For example, they suggested including multiple stakeholders when formulating the research questions and design of a study and using within-group designs to capture the diversity of a particular group.

Sasao and Sue (1993) developed the cube model as a culturally anchored ecological framework for conducting research in ethnic–cultural communities. This model includes three interacting elements to consider: (a) three different types of research questions: descriptive, explanatory, and prevention/treatment; (b) a range of quantitative and qualitative methods; and (3) the cultural complexity of the ethnic–cultural community of interest. The framework and guidelines offered by Hughes et al. (1993) and Sasao and Sue (1993) are the only two approaches articulated in the community psychology literature to date for conducting culturally anchored research.

In this chapter, we develop another framework for anchoring research in the culture of participants. This framework builds on and goes beyond past approaches by using Boykin's triple quandary theory as a guide. Using this theory, we illustrate how researchers may conduct culturally anchored research with persons from marginalized communities. The basis for conducting culturally anchored research is to understand the important challenges faced by these communities.

Boykin (1986) developed a triple-quandary framework to describe the African American experience in the United States. Quandaries are major dilemmas, challenges, or conditions that people face in the process of developing their cultural identities. This theory takes into account the experiences of African Americans and includes three quandaries: negotiating mainstream U.S. society, being a member of an oppressed group, and identifying with one's African heritage. Coming to terms with the conflict and competition within and among these quandaries consumes considerable time and energy and can affect the success of African Americans in both marginalized and mainstream societies. Boykin proposed that how one addresses these quandaries influences the development of one's cultural identity.

We have adapted and extended Boykin's framework to provide a guide for engaging in culturally anchored research with marginalized populations. We drew on Boykin's framework and the concept of a quandary as a basis to think about the challenges that people from various cultural backgrounds face; yet our framework was not developed to be analogous to Boykin's. Our focus is to explicate an approach to anchoring research in the culture of marginalized groups, not to provide a framework for understanding the identity development of African Americans or other groups.

Moreover, our framework was created to illustrate how examining quandaries can foster the development of guidelines for community research at multiple levels, including the societal, interpersonal, and individual levels. A societal-level quandary, such as the societal oppression of marginalized groups, involves the institutionalized use of power and influence. Societal oppression limits opportunities for people from different cultures. It often blinds members of the majority culture to their complicity in creating and sustaining inequity. An interpersonal-level quandary, such as being in controlling relationships, involves interpersonal prejudice and discrimination that characterizes hierarchical relationships between people in power and members of marginalized groups. These first two examples on the societal and the interpersonal levels involve power and control. These levels can be difficult to distinguish because they influence and interact with one another. However, we have pulled them apart to illustrate the various processes that can influence people from marginalized groups. A third quandary, coming to terms with one's identity, is presented as an example of an individual-level quandary even as it is also shaped in part by societal and interpersonal influences. It is inherently different from the other two quandaries in that it recognizes and calls attention to the beneficial outcomes that can result from positively identifying with one's cultural group.

All three quandaries specify major areas that the research community needs to address with significant energy, creativity, and resources over time to anchor research in the culture of marginalized groups. It is important for social scientists to think about the impacts of each of these quandaries for members of marginalized and mainstream groups, as well as their implications for research. This effort includes, yet goes beyond, the specifics of research methods for one study or one research program. It also requires attention to the social structures that support research as well as the topics selected for study. Community psychology principles can help in making advances in the field and can lead to specific guidelines for conducting culturally anchored research. Finally, we can learn from exemplars that illustrate these research guidelines. See Table 10.1 for a summary of this theoretical quandary framework.

This quandary framework has multiple applications for conducting culturally anchored research. It is primarily intended to be relevant for research with people who have experienced historical and societal oppression, specifically in terms of race, ethnicity, class, gender, religion, sexual orientation, or disability. The discussion of each quandary tends to focus on the issues in a theoretical manner, with empirical examples of research used to illustrate the major concepts. Various groups are used in the examples to demonstrate how this model for culturally anchored research is applicable to multiple cultures. Also, guidelines are provided in each quandary for conducting culturally anchored research. However, the research strategies that might be used for one study with a cultural group might not necessarily work for another, because there are differences across and within various marginalized groups. This framework for engaging in culturally anchored research provides one lens to examine the many complex issues involved in working with people from various backgrounds. Of course, there are a variety of other lenses that can be helpful in research with these populations.

Societal Oppression of Marginalized Groups

The first quandary that members of marginalized groups face is oppression by mainstream society. Societal oppression refers to the use of power and influence

Table 10.1. Overview of Cultural Quandaries: Impact, Implications, Guidelines, and Exemplars

Quandary	Major impacts	Research implications	Community psychology values	Research guidelines	Exemplars[a]
Societal level Societal oppression of marginalized groups	Prejudice toward marginalized groups Discrimination and exclusion in society's actions toward marginalized groups Greater negativity in attitude and action by group members	Lack of researchers from marginalized groups Lack of research on societal oppression	Systemic change Social justice	Build the research infrastructure to support the intellectual and career development of members of marginalized groups Conduct more research on societal oppression and its antidotes	NIDRR's policies, programs & incentives to support the inclusion of people with disabilities SCRA strategies to advance new ideas through special issues of newsletter & journal, conference symposia, and listservs
Interpersonal level Being in controlling relationships	Lack of voice and influence over life choices.	Lack of cooperation with researchers Lack of researcher access to cultural perspective	Collaboration Human diversity Adventuresome research methods	Develop more egalitarian relationships Develop methods that capture the culture of participants	Exploration before data collection Member checking Qualitative research Grounded theory
Individual level Coming to terms with one's identity	Positive impact of strengths Negative impact of rejecting cultural identity	Need for more research assessing strengths & accomplishments Need for more empirical research that examines identity among members of marginalized groups	Identify competencies rather than dwell on deficits Consider the relationship of the individual and the environment	Identify cultural identity as an important content area Develop methods to assess cultural identity using a strengths-based approach	Incorporate ethnic/racial identity into assessment Consider contextual factors in choosing methods Integrate methods Consider & address own identity issues

[a]Exemplars suggest ways to pursue the research guidelines. Adventuresome researchers are encouraged to follow community psychology perspectives and the resulting guidelines presented to develop and adapt methods suited to their own research situations.

over time in systematic and institutional ways to significantly limit the opportunities for growth and development of group members. Societal oppression manifests itself in prejudicial attitudes and discriminatory actions toward groups thus marginalized and their members. For example, a prejudiced view that people with disabilities and members of other marginalized groups are not capable of contributing to society and are best excluded from it could be considered oppressive in intent.

The impact of such prejudice is evident in the segregation of persons with disabilities and members of other marginalized groups from mainstream society in schooling, working, and residential living opportunities (Braddock, Emerson, Felce, & Stancliffe, 2001). Such discrimination limits opportunities for people with disabilities and others at the margins, reducing the likelihood that they can have access to needed resources, become fully included in contemporary society, and use their talents constructively. Over time, discriminatory acts of mainstream society may contribute to increased negative behavior among group members.

Prejudicial societal attitudes may also be internalized by some members of marginalized groups with negative results. For example, Steele and Aronson (1995) have identified the powerful phenomenon of stereotype threat. Stereotype threat occurs when subtle, contextual references to a negative stereotype about a marginalized group held by mainstream society leads members of that group to enact those negative qualities. Thus, when African American students are asked to write their race as well as their name on an academic test, their race may become more salient and activate a negative stereotype concerning the lower academic achievement of African Americans. Some African American students perform worse on the examination than those not asked to write their race on their test forms. In a parallel manner, over time discriminatory acts of mainstream society may contribute to increased negative behavior, including intragroup aggression among group members. As these examples suggest, the impact of societal oppression may be felt in direct and subtle ways by members of different marginalized groups.

What is the impact of societal oppression on scientific research? First, such oppression devalues members of marginalized groups and reduces opportunities for them to develop their research competencies. For example, although 20% of the U.S. population has a disability, the resources supporting college students with disabilities are generally inadequate (Feldman, 2001). Such resources are even less capable of supporting scholars with disabilities as they pursue intensive graduate study. As a consequence, the number of faculty members with visible disabilities is minuscule.

Another impact of societal oppression is a lack of research on societal oppression, its mechanisms, and its effects. Although considerable theoretical work has been done on oppression in general and oppression of persons with disabilities in particular, there has been insufficient empirical attention to societal oppression and its effects. Psychological researchers from the mainstream tend to focus on members of marginalized groups as individuals. They pay less attention to the cultural and contextual factors that contribute to systematic institutionalized oppression (Sampson, 1993). There are, for example, few studies to date on the barriers faced by disabled members of ethnic minority groups as they seek to rebuild their lives after a spinal cord injury (Hernandez, Hayes, Balcazar, & Keys, 2001).

The community psychology values of social justice and systemic change can be resources for researchers in addressing the quandary of societal oppression. Social justice is a commitment to equal opportunity and rights for all members of society. It is codified to some extent in law and legal precedent and involves taking affirmative steps to include members of underrepresented groups in the full round of life in society including the research enterprise. Systemic change refers to the importance of analyzing and addressing problems at appropriate supraindividual levels that, in this instance, have some degree of societal impact. Simply considering an individual person or research study is an insufficient response to a societal pattern of arrangements and action. Changes in those larger patterns of arrangements and action are necessary.

Research Guideline 1: Build the Research Infrastructure to Support the Intellectual and Career Development of Members of Marginalized Groups

One of the most effective ways to address the exclusionary impact of prejudice and discrimination is to actively include members of marginalized groups fully in research. One means to ensure that the research roles of members of marginalized groups are those of substance, power, and dignity is to affirmatively develop researchers from those groups. How better to anchor research in the culture of marginalized groups than to develop researchers who identify as members of these groups?

One exemplar in this regard is the National Institute of Disability and Rehabilitation Research (NIDRR), which supports the professional development of researchers with disabilities. NIDRR is a federal center in the U.S. Department of Education with the mission of providing national leadership in research on disabilities and rehabilitation. NIDRR leaders make it a priority to hire organizational leaders and professional grant program staff who have disabilities. They provide incentives to research grant applicants who have disabilities, a track record of hiring research staff with disabilities, and cogent plans to recruit and train grant staff and students with disabilities. They provide fellowships for the development of disability researchers and favor talented persons with disabilities in that competition. They include persons with disabilities in most grant review panels. NIDRR leaders consult with the disability community as they prepare new strategic plans and requests for proposals. NIDRR has championed the use of multiple methods in research, such as participatory action research, to understand disability issues. As a result of these activities, over the past two decades NIDRR has made important progress in legitimizing and valuing the role researchers with disabilities play in understanding disability and rehabilitation. In many disciplines more researchers with disabilities are now available to apply for grants, to be employed as faculty in new disability studies programs at colleges and universities, to serve on journal editorial boards, and contribute to disability research that is anchored in disability culture and awareness of societal oppression.

Research Guideline 2: Create the Intellectual Context for Empirically Exploring Societal Oppression and Its Impact

Societal oppression can become accepted as members of the mainstream may be unaware of its operation and negative impacts, and members of marginalized groups might become inured to them. As a consequence, to develop and sustain the critical perspective necessary to analyze and assess oppression and its effects, researchers need to create an intellectual climate that is supportive of critical analysis. Creating such a climate is a challenge in the United States in the early 21st century given the strong centrist tendencies in public discourse that mitigate against taking a strong critical stance. Moreover, although community psychology has examined a number of important constructs over the last four decades (e.g., prevention, social support, ecology, empowerment), none of them has generally involved the sharp critique of society, its power arrangements, and their disparate impact on those at the margins. Creating and protecting a robust intellectual climate for considering societal oppression and liberation is thus a meaningful challenge. Addressing this challenge is expected to generate greater controversy and perhaps less funding from government sources than many other topics of community psychology research.

A good place to begin is to consider methods used successfully to develop other constructs in community research. These include conducting research on the topic, developing symposia and conferences, editing books and special issues of community psychology journals and newsletters, teaching seminars, encouraging and supporting graduate students to conduct research, and developing a Society for Community Research and Action (SCRA) interest group and perhaps a dedicated listserv. Jay Haley once said that it takes 20 years for an idea to gain entry to a university. If so, then it may take an intellectual infrastructure, consisting of many of the elements mentioned, to create and sustain the intellectual climate necessary to pursue an understanding of societal oppression and liberation over time. Such an endeavor is worthwhile because it elucidates the fundamental power relationships in society. Thus it better enables us to understand how these power relationships can compromise our attempts to create a more just society and how they can affect our ability to conduct research with members of marginalized groups.

Being in Controlling Relationships: An Interpersonal Quandary

The second quandary faced by individuals from marginalized populations is being in controlling relationships. Controlling relationships refer to interpersonal associations in which one member has power over another and thus the ability to greatly influence and even determine the activities of another. The relationship is not mutual or reciprocal Rather it is characterized by one-way communication and influence by the powerful over the powerless. Members of marginalized groups have hierarchical relationships with those in positions of power because of their status in society. Individuals in positions of power tend to have a degree of control over those in marginalized positions. For example, professionals and parents control many aspects of the daily routine of people with developmental disabilities (Heller & Factor, 1991). Lesbian, gay, bisexual, and transgendered (LGBT) youth might experience being in controlling relationships as well in the form of bullying, harassment, and physical abuse by peers, parents, and teachers (Rivers & D'Augelli, 2001).

A major impact of the control over individuals from marginalized groups is their lack of voice and influence over life choices. Their relationships with those in power are characterized by a low degree of control, which results in the voices of marginalized members being lost. They have an unequal say in what happens in their lives and are limited by the decisions that others make for them and their lack of freedom in relationships.

This quandary of being in controlling relationships has implications for research methods. An implication is that marginalized members distrust researchers who approach their communities. For example, many African Americans distrust institutions and individuals in positions of authority because of their negative experiences in controlling relationships. The Tuskegee study is a historical example of the abuse and control experienced by African Americans. In this study researchers identified and observed African Americans with syphilis and did not intervene, although effective treatments were available. In part because of the unprincipled, interpersonal control these and other researchers exercised over participants and its negative and sometimes fatal consequences, many African Americans today still are wary of cooperating with scientists (Jordan, Bogat, & Smith, 2001).

In addition, another implication that controlling relationships might have for research methods is that the perspective of individuals from marginalized groups is not fully captured. For instance, Angelique and Culley (2000) found that community psychologists have used their power as researchers to make women research participants less visible. Community investigators have omitted women from the title or abstract and used gender-neutral language in studies that primarily targeted women. The scarcity of research on marginalized groups, real and apparent, is a result in significant measure to the control of individuals in positions of power.

The field of community psychology embraces many values that can assist researchers in helping them obtain the cooperation, trust, and cultural perspectives of community members. Values for collaboration, human diversity, and innovative techniques should guide one's work in conducting culturally anchored research (Dalton, Elias, & Wandersman, 2001). The value for collaboration dictates that researchers enter communities with the intention of creating a relationship such that community members believe that they can contribute their knowledge and resources. Human diversity prescribes that individuals and communities should be respected along various diversity dimensions, such as gender, race–ethnicity, sexual orientation, religion, socioeconomic status, and ability–disability. Finally, community psychologists value adventuresome research methods, using alternative methods and techniques, to conduct culturally anchored research (Hughes et al., 1993). Incorporating these values in research may provide individuals from marginalized groups a voice in the research process, and thus a basis for trusting and cooperating with researchers.

Guideline 3: Develop More Egalitarian Relationships With Research Participants

Researchers should develop egalitarian relationships with participants to minimize the control typically found in research relationships (Bond, 1990; Serrano-Garcia, 1990). Egalitarian relationships are characterized as more supportive and reciprocal than the typical researcher–participant relationship, which could facilitate the development of culturally anchored research.

One way to develop egalitarian relationships is to engage in a period of exploration before formal data collection. In Sánchez's qualitative study (2002) of mentorship among Mexican American adolescents, a number of steps were taken to get to know participants' culture and develop egalitarian relationships, including reading ethnographies about U.S. Mexican communities, developing relationships with Mexican Americans, and attending meetings of a Mexican student organization on the campus in which the research occurred. In addition, the researcher participated in social activities to develop rapport with potential participants before the interview process began.

Another way to develop egalitarian relationships is for researchers to share more personal information about themselves than they would usually reveal in the research process. Community psychologists and feminist researchers have noted that the information revealed in the research process can be a source of power differences between researchers and participants (Campbell & Wasco, 2000; Serrano-Garcia, 1990). Typically, researchers share information that is far less personal and intimate than the information shared by participants, promoting the hierarchy between researchers and the researched (Campbell & Wasco, 2000). Sánchez (2002) revealed personal information about herself to participants to gain their trust and make them feel comfortable. Specifically, before interviewing participants, the researcher stated her personal reasons for pursuing a doctoral degree, studying the topic of mentorship, and her interest in the education of Latinos. Also, during the interviews, Sánchez shared experiences about her family and mentoring relationships where appropriate. These steps helped the researcher gain participants' trust, and thus, obtain culturally anchored information.

Also, in psychological research, the researcher typically reveals the true purpose of the study at the debriefing, after data collection, so that participants' responses are not biased. However, not knowing the aim of the study might reinforce the hierarchical relationship between a researcher and participant (Campbell & Wasco, 2000). Participants might feel uncomfortable revealing personal information when they do not have an understanding of the research aim. In Sánchez's study (2002), some mentee participants had an understanding of the researcher's intent because the true nature of the study was revealed before data collection. These participants seemed more invested in the study because they were more willing to allow her to interview their mentors compared to participants who did not know the aim of the study beforehand.

Another technique that can be used to develop egalitarian relationships is member checking, which involves sharing findings with members of the population from which data were collected and requesting their feedback regarding its accuracy and completeness (Lincoln & Guba, 1985). Member checking can give participants an active role in the research process and allow their voices to be heard. An example is Sánchez's study (2002) where she met with nine participants to discuss some of her findings and to hear participants' opinions on what she found. This process allowed Sánchez to confirm her interpretation of participants' words with how they viewed their experiences. Member checks increase the likelihood that findings are culturally anchored.

Guideline 4: Researchers Develop and Adapt
Methods of Data Collection and Analysis
That Capture the Perspective of Participants

In the spirit of adventuresome research methods, community psychologists should consider using innovative methodology and data analytical techniques. For instance, researchers have used narratives (e.g., Mulvey et al., 2000) and in-depth interviews (Sánchez, 2002) to capture the perspectives of marginalized groups. The aim of such qualitative methods is to capture the interpretations of research participants in a manner that is culturally anchored in their worldviews (Patton, 1987). Using qualitative methods can assist researchers in minimizing controlling relationships with participants, and thus obtain culturally anchored data.

Another innovative data collection technique that can be used to minimize controlling relationships is the use of art. Psychologists are accustomed to collecting and presenting data in written text form. Some theses and dissertations (e.g., Parks, 2002) have collected data in the form of pictures, where participants took pictures of various aspects of their own lives. Using photography gave participants more control in the research process than is normally given.

In addition to innovative data collection methods, researchers may use data analytical techniques that minimize controlling relationships between researchers and participants and thus capture the cultural perspective of participants. For example, Sánchez (2002) used grounded theory to analyze data, a technique that allows one to develop theory based on participants' perspectives and words (Strauss & Corbin, 1998). Rather than the researcher developing codes a priori based on her knowledge and the literature, the researcher developed codes based on participant interviews. It is important that researchers consider alternative techniques in data analysis to ensure that the experiences of participants are revealed in an accurate manner, thus making the research culturally anchored. Finally, it is important that researchers note the presence of members of marginalized groups in the titles, abstracts, and language of their research articles.

Coming to Terms With One's Identity:
An Individual Quandary

The third major quandary faced by persons from marginalized groups is coming to terms with identity issues. This quandary differs from the other two quandaries in that it is inherently positive. If we only attend to the negatives, as represented in the quandaries of societal oppression and controlling relation-ships, we may miss some of the positives, particularly the contributions of culture. This quandary recognizes the positive and complex role that identity can play for all people, particularly for those from marginalized groups. Consis-tent with Boykin's triple quandary framework, this quandary is influenced by the quandaries of societal oppression and interpersonal control that can contribute to doubts about one's competence in particular areas (Watts, Griffith, & Abdul-Adil, 1999). The quandary of coming to terms with one's identity involves becoming aware of one's psychological and other connections to a particular group. It underscores the importance of self-identification, involve-ment in activities with one's group, participation in cultural traditions, and feelings toward one's group (Phinney, 1992). The process of developing a secure sense of self varies with development, experience, and context (Atkinson, Morten, & Sue, 1993; Cross, 1978).

Frable (1997) suggested there is a need to assess people's many social identities (gender, racial, ethnic, sexual, and class) and explore the various functions of identity. Theoretical developments have evolved regarding various aspects of identity. For example, Olney and Kim (2001) suggested that the process of integrating the experience of disability with a positive self-perception is one that involves defining challenges in coping with limitations, managing one's identity, and embracing one's difference. For LGBT people, the coming-out process typically moves from guilt and shame to positive self-esteem (D'Augelli, 2003). For the purpose of illustrating this quandary, the following discussion will focus on ethnic and racial identity as one example in conducting culturally anchored research.

A primary impact of this quandary is that cultural identity can serve a positive and protective function for people from a wide variety of cultural backgrounds. For example, ethnic identity has been found to be positively associated with self-worth and self-esteem (Roberts et al., 1999) and effective problem-solving strategies (Dubow, Pargament, Boxer, & Tarakeshwar, 2000). A second impact of this quandary is that there can be negative consequences for people who do not feel connected to their cultural group. For example, "racelessness" attitudes (separation from one's culture of origin) can lead to greater risk for psychological distress (Arroyo & Zigler, 1995).

This quandary has two important implications for research. The first impli-cation is that there is a need for more research that focuses on strengths and accomplishments. Although strengths-based research in psychology has increased over the past decade, there continues to be a greater emphasis on deficits (Cowen, 2000). A second implication of this quandary is a need for more empirical research that examines various types of identity among members of marginalized groups. Over the past three decades many have theorized that ethnic identity is an important developmental factor for ethnic minority group members (Atkinson et al., 1993; Cross, 1978), yet the theoretical literature far surpasses empirical research (Phinney, 1990), and few studies incorporate social context when examining identity issues (Yeh & Huang, 1996).

It can be instructive to consider the relationship between the individual and the environment in terms of its impact on identity. Cultural values, histo-ries, and traditions play a crucial role in one's ecology and context. Personal, familial, and community factors have been found to influence racial identity development, and cultural factors within the home and community may conflict with the values represented within schools (Bass & Coleman, 1997). For example, the mainstream educational system often conflicts with the sociocultural realities of African American youth (Boykin, 1986; Ghee, Walker, & Younger, 1997), and this lack of person–environment fit may contribute to lower academic achievement among some African American students (Bass & Coleman, 1997). Incorporating cultural identity into the educational process has improved academic motivation, knowledge of Black history, frequency of academic behaviors, and self-esteem (Ghee et al., 1997).

Research Guideline 5: Include Cultural Identity as an Important Content Area When Engaging in Culturally Anchored Research

Phinney's (1990) multigroup research on ethnic identity has underscored the importance of ethnic identity for all adolescents, as well as the positive role in the development of the self. Yet the influence of culture, at the individual and person–environment levels, may be particularly important for marginalized people, given the previously discussed quandaries. Positive cultural identities may serve a more powerful protective function for people of marginalized backgrounds compared to those in the mainstream who do not experience such societal oppression and interpersonal control. Mainstream theories of psychological development, typically developed in relation to privileged groups, do not incorporate culture explicitly (e.g., Erikson, 1968). Moreover, most studies examining adjustment do not include an assessment of ethnic identity, and most interventions to promote adjustment do not include goals of enhancing ethnic identity. Given the centrality of identity issues in culturally anchored research, ignoring these issues limits our understanding of (a) diversity; (b) experiences of people from marginalized groups; (c) the dynamic interplay between context, individual differences, and health-related outcomes; and (d) possibilities to build on strengths that culture embodies.

One example of a strengths-based approach is to examine how identity relates to competencies and protects individuals from negative outcomes. Although there is a growing empirical literature on resiliency, identity is just beginning to be examined as a protective factor. In a study of urban African American youth, McMahon and Watts (2002) found that global self-worth and ethnic identity were related to competency and adjustment. Although there was overlap between global self-worth and ethnic identity, they each appeared to make unique contributions to various outcomes assessed. These findings support the literature that describes them as separate constructs, with self-esteem focusing more on individual aspects of competence (Phinney, Cantu, & Kurtz, 1997) and ethnic identity focusing more on connections to one's ethnic group (Helms, 1990; Phinney, 1992). A strong positive sense of ethnic identity was associated with more active coping, fewer beliefs supporting aggression, and fewer aggressive behaviors. Given that these youth reside in an entirely African American community, the assessment of aggression was essentially in relation to other African American people. Thus, it is possible that identifying with one's ethnic group inhibits violence against "one's own," as Wilson (1991) hypothesized. These findings are encouraging and suggest that there is a need to advance our developmental understanding of ethnic identity as a protective factor for members of marginalized groups.

Research Guideline 6: Develop Methods to Assess Cultural Identity as a Strengths-Based Approach

A variety of approaches have evolved to assess identity, yet there continues to be a gap between theory and method in identity research. Given the complexity of assessing cultural identity, culturally anchored research can benefit from both etic (understanding culture through researchers' perspectives) and emic approaches (understanding a particular group's culture through participants' perspectives; Creswell, 1998; Hughes et al., 1993; Roosa & Gonzales, 2000). Phinney (1990) has developed a quantitative framework for understanding general aspects of group identity, including self-identification as a group member, a sense of belonging, and attitudes toward one's group. This approach has advanced the field in examining the importance of ethnic–racial identity for people across a wide variety of ethnic and racial backgrounds. It is, however, only a beginning, in that it does not account for the unique histories, traditions, and values that each group may espouse, which may be assessed more appropriately through emic and qualitative approaches.

To assess and support strong positive identities, researchers need to first understand and address their own identity issues. Sanford (1982) suggested that researchers spend more time learning about themselves in a developmental context and talking with the people they want to learn about. Researchers would also benefit from considering the extent to which they match their participant population, in terms of background, language, and value systems (Hughes et al., 1993). For example, given that McMahon is a Caucasian female, she took several steps before engaging in research with African American youth, including (a) partnering with an African American male who had a great deal of experience with this population; (b) spending time talking with people at all levels from the target population and school settings; (c) reflecting on how her own background influenced her identity development, as well as how it differed from the population with which she intended to work; and (d) conducting pilot study research that included observation, focus groups, and assessment of measures. These steps helped McMahon to learn about the community in which she was working, to identify the economic and sociopolitical barriers the population faced, and to assess the potential risk and protective factors, including ethnic identity, with which youth in this community struggle. Assessment of identity issues informs our action strategies, enabling us to take a holistic, strengths-based approach to understanding and promoting positive development among peoples' many social identities in culturally anchored research.

In thinking about the need to culturally anchor our research, it is important to consider the aforementioned quandaries that occur on societal, interpersonal, and individual levels. The section that follows outlines a community-based intervention that illustrates a way in which a prevention program can benefit from considering the multilevel quandaries of different cultural groups and thus move toward research and intervention that are culturally anchored.

Kids' College: A Kaleidoscope of Cultures

Kids' College: A Kaleidoscope of Cultures is a multicultural intervention program that teaches children about people of other cultures through culturally specific activities (London & Linney, 1995; London, Tierney, Buhin, Greco, & Cooper, 2002). The goals and objectives of the program are fourfold: (a) to reduce prejudice and stereotyping attitudes, (b) to increase knowledge about different cultures, (c) to increase cross-race friendships, and (d) to increase children's self-esteem and own ethnic pride and identity.

The Kids' College program is made up of six components based on contact theory (Allport, 1954; Miller, 1990) and cooperative learning theory (Cosden & Haring, 1992; London et al., 2002). The six components include (a) games from around the world, involving an interactive cultural game to establish close contact among the participants in a fun and friendly, noncompetitive atmosphere; (b) My World Through My Eyes, introducing a guest speaker to guide the participants through their culture; (c) Cultural Cuisine, more commonly referred to as lunchtime, as a time for children to sample foods representing the different countries being studied; (d) Classroom Creativity, involving a variety of group activities that give children an opportunity for cooperative interaction designed to achieve a particular goal; (e) KC Rap Session, encouraging children to talk openly about personal experiences regarding prejudice and discrimination in an accepting and nonthreatening atmosphere; and (f) Community Exploration, allowing children an opportunity to take field trips and see the diversity of culture that exists in our communities.

Societal Oppression of Marginalized Groups

The issue of racism and prejudice has long been a focus of concern for marginalized groups, and serves as the basis for the Kids' College intervention. Prejudice is often a result of societal oppression that comes from lack of knowledge and misinformation and embraces an attitude that is tied to an overgeneralized belief. Knowledge and contact alone are insufficient to change attitudes and behaviors and reduce prejudice (Allport, 1954; Byrnes & Kiger, 1990). For this reason, Kids' College moves beyond just providing children with information and opportunities for casual contact with racially and ethnically diverse children. Kids' College gives children multicultural experiences and sustained cooperative contact in a friendly, noncompetitive atmosphere. Diversity was represented among Kids' College staff, who modeled positive relationships, as well as those that emerged among the participants. Staff training involved discussion and activities that facilitated self-exploration about their own prejudices and stereotypes before their work with the children. During program implementation, children participated in similar activities and discussions during their rap sessions. Given that staff had been through this process, they could empathize and appreciate the challenges facing some children from marginalized groups.

When adults are culturally anchored, we believe that they can more readily promote conditions to positively impact the next generation. In so doing, these adults help children expand their potential to develop more positive cultural identities and attitudes and embrace a greater respect for people from all cultural backgrounds. Research examining Kids' College participants' behaviors and attitudes revealed a decrease in prejudicial attitudes (London et al., 2002). This decrease suggests that a culturally anchored intervention based in culturally anchored research may be a promising, developmentally appropriate way to address the prejudicial attitudes that foster societal oppression.

Being in Controlling Relationships

In following recommendations made by Dalton, Elias, and Wandersman (2001), Kids' College works to use collaboration as a way to effect positive change. Instead of program staff making unilateral decisions about what a community needed with reference to a bias-reduction intervention, Kids' College staff invited representatives from the community, schools, and universities to participate in the design and implementation of the program. In the design of Kids' College, all stakeholders were involved in decision making, including the children who would participate in the program, their families, school teachers and administrators, and community psychologists. In so doing, each person brought a unique perspective to the discussion and had a voice in the process of the intervention and research. This approach took away a hierarchical perspective that can often serve to alienate members of marginalized groups and instead provided a sense of control over an intervention that directly benefited them. We found that this approach both led to a greater acceptance and ownership of the program and its evolution and also allowed trusting relationships to develop.

Ridley (1989) noted that racism often leads to tangible benefits for the dominant group, such as social privilege, economic status, and political power. During discussions with children, it was important to explore the historical context of racism and take the focus off blaming the victim. By showing a willingness to discuss difficult and uncomfortable topics such as prejudice, power, and oppression, staff encouraged participants in Kids' College to take control, share their feelings, trust others, and build more equal relationships.

Finding ways to share the results of Kids' College research with community members and have them help make sense of it is another way of disrupting the hierarchy that often exists in research. Research findings belong not only in professional journals but also in forums community members use. Kids' College newsletters discuss the results of our work with parents, and can serve to inform programs even after we are no longer in their community.

Being authentic and genuine goes a long way in forging egalitarian relationships, and appropriate self-disclosure often strengthens the bond between researchers and community members. Removing some of the hierarchical barriers and letting the participants see that we are real people, with real feelings, lends to our credibility and the development of trust. Sharing some of our own experiences with racism and prejudice often served to validate fears and surface concerns that the children previously had chosen not to share. Children were able to observe a culturally diverse group of facilitators model healthy discussions of difficult topics, which led to more in-depth interactions among themselves. These in-depth interactions seemed to validate the children's experience and self-esteem (London et al., 2002).

Coming to Terms With One's Identity

Models of minority identity development, as noted by researchers such as Phinney (1990); Marcia (1980); and Atkinson, Morten, and Sue (1993), underline the important challenge facing children and adolescents of coming to terms with a bicultural value system, which can influence their sense of identity. This bicultural system includes values from both ones' own culture and the culture of the mainstream. Research on cultural attitude acquisition often points to the important relationship between identity, self-esteem, and reduction of prejudicial attitudes. In essence, the more secure an individual feels with his or her own sense of identity, the fewer prejudicial attitudes he or she espouses (Claney & Parker, 1989; Ponterotto & Pedersen, 1993). As a way to address ethnic identity in the Kids' College program, children are encouraged to share information about their cultural heritage with their classmates. By embracing their culture and focusing on the strengths of their heritage, these children verbally express sentiments reflecting positive aspects of their lives. In many situations, these children have previously found themselves criticized or marginalized because of their cultural background. By providing an opportunity to showcase their cultural strengths, children's identities are acknowledged and respected. Indeed, our research indicated that ethnic pride increased following participation in Kids' College (London et al., 2002).

If our intervention and research can move beyond cultural sensitivity and toward a culturally anchored approach, we can advance the field of community psychology. Programs such as Kids' College serve to uplift marginalized groups by addressing systemic problems of oppression, racism, and prejudice (at a societal level). They reduce the hierarchical levels seen in controlling relationships by inviting all stakeholders to participate in all aspects of the research (at an interpersonal level). They embrace cultural identity issues as a source of strength and buffer against the formation of prejudicial attitudes (at an individual level). By including people from marginalized groups in the design, implementation, and assessment of the program, we move away from a hierarchical structure that perpetuates division. By discussing issues that are often challenging and emotionally charged in an environment that is safe, people are encouraged to explore and resolve these feelings. In addition, by using a research methodology that incorporates quantitative and qualitative methodologies, the voice of the participants can be heard. Kids' College demonstrates how a program anchored in the cultures of individual participants helps them both become more anchored in their own cultures and also value the cultures of others. This program is but one illustration of the importance of culturally anchored methods for addressing some of the quandaries facing members of marginalized groups.

Culturally Anchored Research Guidelines: From Platitudes to Practice

Culturally anchored research that effectively integrates accurate cultural knowledge with rigorous research methodology remains an aspirational goal more honored in the breach than the observance by community researchers. Despite some sincere efforts, the effective implementation of culturally anchored research continues to present numerous challenges for researchers. As a consequence, practitioners who seek to advance the field must be courageous in challenging community researchers to move beyond the existing platitudes for cultural sensitivity to the successful practice of culturally anchored research that effectively serves marginalized groups.

In seeking successful practice, community scientists can begin by engaging in creative discourse about the current state of their efforts with culturally anchored research. Key questions that can be used to spark open and honest exchanges include:

Does culturally anchored research actually increase understanding of important societal issues and lead to improved lives for members of marginalized groups? More specifically, what are the unique contributions of culturally anchored research with regard to community participation and research outcomes? We anticipate several contributions from more culturally anchored research. The guidelines provided in this chapter are a framework for grounding research in the culture of participants. Such an approach may increase the likelihood that scientists will create knowledge that both does justice to the perspective of group members and also makes that perspective more widely available to others outside the group itself. It may increase the likelihood that research with members of marginalized groups will recognize the fluid, multidimensional nature of culture and within-group differences. As a consequence, more voices may be shared and heard in the ongoing intellectual conversation that is scientific research. Culturally anchored research also is expected to reduce the likelihood that research that ignores or exploits members of low-power groups will occur or be given prolonged, serious attention. However, given the nascent quality of the development of culturally anchored research, these benefits have only been realized in a handful of studies to date.

What are the challenges of conducting culturally anchored research? A basic initial challenge is whether we researchers are too anchored in our own culture of scientific tradition to also anchor our work in the culture of marginalized groups. This additional anchoring may involve thinking "outside the box" of accepted epistemologies, methods, and practices to bring methods from other disciplines and the perspectives of members of marginalized groups "inside the box" of community research, thereby making it more multidisciplinary and collaborative. A second and related challenge is approaching community collaboration in good faith. The temptation is to seek the community's rubber stamp of approval for our own plans rather than including the voices of previously marginalized community constituencies in a more egalitarian research process. A third challenge is maintaining a balance of emphasis on social justice and science. If we focus much more on social change than on science, then we risk losing the value added over time by a growing base of credible knowledge. If we overemphasize science over social justice, we risk that science will become irrelevant to the inequities that motivate our inquiry.

A related challenge is whether community scientists who typically benefit to a significant extent from the status quo are too comfortable to advance a social critique of oppression and the need for liberation in contemporary society. Being both beneficiaries of stability and advocates for changes can be a precarious perch. For example, some members of urban marginalized groups in the 1960s even coined the term "poverty pimps" to refer to those researchers who exploited the psychosocial problems of impoverished groups for professional publications and tenure-track promotions.

Finally, as social change efforts gain momentum, what are the risks of success and their effects? As more members of marginalized groups become community scientists, are there fewer opportunities for mainstream researchers? On the other hand, as members of previously marginalized groups become more numerous and prominent in other important sectors of society, does science risk losing societal relevance and support if it resists resolutely and remains highly mainstream in its membership?

In addition, community researchers who have addressed their own challenges also must contend with those challenges facing community members and the research community at large. For many members of marginalized groups, research participation is not a top priority. Their research experience has often been nonexistent or negative, as the Tuskegee example starkly shows. Their major concerns often revolve around immediate life issues and have little to do with someone else's scientific agenda. Also, existing scientific organizations may be reluctant to support culturally anchored research. They may not recognize the value of the guidelines recommended and may rely solely on traditional criteria rather than focusing on the strengths of culturally anchored work, such as constituent validity (Keys & Frank, 1987).

What are the best practices of culturally anchored research that facilitate community participation and research outcomes? The examples offered in this chapter provide a starting point for cataloging the best practices of culturally anchored research. Over time we anticipate that community researchers will develop an evidence base that demonstrates which methods have the greatest utility.

What are the implications of community participation for training future generations of community psychologists in conceptual and applied research models? Few researchers and members of marginalized groups have had much training in culturally anchored methods. A handful of graduate students have had experience in research and intervention projects that model state-of-the-art approaches to culturally anchored work. However, there has been little systematic attention paid to issues of culture even in the curricula of graduate community psychology programs, a place where such coursework would be particularly likely to occur. Such a lack of inclusion of diversity issues in the graduate research curriculum four decades after the relevance of such issues began to be discussed may suggest one major reason why students from outside the mainstream often find becoming researchers an intimidating proposition.

Conclusion

Although these questions and challenges they contain may be daunting, we believe the pursuit of excellence in culturally anchored research is more than worth the effort. Contemporary psychology and community research does not do justice to the complexity of the multicultural landscape and to issues of diversity more broadly. Approaches and methods that highlight the value of and the procedures for anchoring science in cultures other than the mainstream are needed. As U.S. society rapidly becomes more diverse, as a growing number of heretofore silenced groups find their voices, and as advances in technology increase our capacity to work globally, culturally anchored approaches will grow in relevance and importance. Science needs approaches that underscore the benefits of identifying the issues of greatest importance to members of marginalized groups. The research community needs approaches that point the way to developing an infrastructure that develops the research talent of members of marginalized groups and enhances our understanding of societal oppression and liberation. Science and society need the new knowledge that will become accessible from research based on more egalitarian relationships between researchers and participants that considers issues of strengths, individual–environment interaction, and identity development.

Culturally anchored research draws on the substance of community psychology and the realities that confront members of marginalized groups. We consider culturally anchored research a developing approach that is an open system. We encourage other researchers to address this challenge and consider using the approach outlined in at least two ways. First, consider using it as stated to implement research that is anchored in the culture of a marginalized group. Second, based on that or other experiences and knowledge, use the framework as a heuristic to identify other quandaries that are most appropriate for particular marginalized groups of interest. We hope other scientists will add to the diverse activities—administrative, political, conceptual, and methodological—that can be used to develop more research that is grounded in the cultures of those who participate in it.

References

Allport, G. W. (1954). *The nature of prejudice*. Reading, MA: Addison-Wesley.

Angelique, H. L., & Culley, M. R. (2000). Searching for feminism: An analysis of community psychology literature relevant to women's concerns. *American Journal of Community Psychology, 28*(6), 793–813.

Arroyo, C. G., & Zigler, E. (1995). Racial identity, academic achievement, and the psychological well-being of economically disadvantaged adolescents. *Journal of Personality and Social Psychology, 69*(5), 903–914.

Atkinson, D., Morten, G., & Sue, D. (1993). *Counseling American minorities: A cross-cultural perspective*. Dubuque, IA: Wm. C. Brown.

Bass, C. K., & Coleman, H. L. K. (1997). Enhancing the cultural identity of early adolescent male African Americans. *Professional School Counseling, 1,* 48–51.

Bond, M. (1990). Defining the research relationship: Maximizing participation in an unequal world. In P. Tolan, C. Keys, F. Chertok, & L. Jason (Eds.), *Researching community psychology: Issues of theory and methods* (pp. 183–186). Washington DC: American Psychological Association.

Boykin, W. A. (1986). The triple quandary and the schooling of Afro-American children. In U. Neisser (Ed.), *The school achievement of minority children* (pp. 57–89). Mawah, NJ: Erlbaum.

Braddock, D., Emerson, E., Felce, D., & Stancliffe, R. J. (2001). Living with circumstances of children and adults with mental retardation or developmental disabilities in the United States, Canada, England, and Wales. *Mental Retardation & Developmental Disabilities Research Reviews, 7*(2), 115–121.

Byrnes, D., & Kiger, G. (1990). *Ethical and pedagogical issues in the use of simulation activities in the classroom: Evaluating the "blue eyes-brown eyes" prejudice-reduction simulation.* Utah State University (ERIC Document Reproduction Service No. ED 300 491).

Campbell, R., & Wasco, S. M. (2000). Feminist approaches to social science: Epistemological and methodological tenets. *American Journal of Community Psychology, 28*(6), 773–791.

Claney, D., & Parker, W. M. (1989). Assessing White racial consciousness and perceived comfort with Black individuals: A preliminary study. *Journal of Counseling and Development, 67,* 449–451.

Cosden, M. A., & Haring, T. G. (1992). Cooperative learning in the classroom: Contingencies, group interactions, and students with special needs. *Journal of Behavioral Education, 2*(1), 53–71.

Cowen, E. L. (2000). Community psychology and routes to psychological wellness. In J. Rappaport & S. Seidman (Eds.), *Handbook of community psychology* (pp. 79–99). New York: Kluwer Academic/Plenum Press.

Creswell, J. W. (1998). *Qualitative inquiry and research design: Choosing among five traditions.* Thousand Oaks, CA: Sage.

Cross, W. (1978). The Thomas and Cross models of psychological nigrescence: A literature review. *Journal of Black Psychology, 4,* 13–31.

Dalton, J. H., Elias, M. J., & Wandersman, A. (2001). *Community psychology: Linking individuals and communities.* Stamford, CT: Wadsworth.

D'Augelli, A. R. (2003). Coming out in community psychology: Personal narrative and disciplinary change. *American Journal of Community Psychology, 31,* 343–354.

Dubow, E. F., Pargament, K. I., Boxer, P., & Tarakeshwar, N. (2000). Initial investigation of Jewish early adolescents' ethnic identity, stress, and coping. *Journal of Early Adolescence, 20*(4), 418–441.

Erikson, E. (1968). *Identity: Youth and crisis.* New York: Norton.

Feldman, S. (2001). *Studying blind: The access barriers to graduate education for individuals with visual impairments.* Unpublished doctoral dissertation proposal, University of Illinois at Chicago.

Frable, D. E. S. (1997). Gender, racial, ethnic, sexual, and class identities. *Annual Review of Psychology, 48,* 139–162.

Ghee, K. L., Walker, J., & Younger, A. C. (1997). The RAAMUS Academy: Evaluation of an educultural intervention for young African-American Males. In R. J. Watts & R. J. Jagers (Eds.), *Manhood development in urban African-American communities* (pp. 87–102). New York: Hawthorn Press.

Heller, T., & Factor, A. (1991). Permanency planning for adults with mental retardation living with family caregivers. *American Journal of Mental Retardation, 96,* 163–176.

Helms, J. (1990). *Black and White racial identity: Theory, research, and practice.* New York: Greenwood.

Hernandez, B., Hayes, E., Balcazar, F., & Keys, C. (2001). Responding to the needs of the underserved: A peer-mentor approach. *Psychosocial Process, 14,* 142–149.

Hughes, D., Siedman, E., & Williams, N. (1993). Cultural phenomena and the research enterprise: Toward a culturally anchored methodology. *American Journal of Community Psychology, 21,* 687–703.

Jordan, L. C., Bogat, G. A., & Smith, G. (2001). Collaborating for social change: The Black psychologists and the Black community. *American Journal of Community Psychology, 29*(4), 599–620.

Keys, C. B., & Frank, S. (1987). Community psychology and the study of organizations: A reciprocal relationship. *American Journal of Community Psychology, 15*(3), 239–251.

Lincoln, Y. S., & Guba, E. G. (1985). *Naturalistic inquiry.* Newbury Park, CA: Sage.

London, L. H., & Linney, J. A. (1995). *Kids' College: An intervention to decrease prejudice in children.* Unpublished manuscript, University of South Carolina.

London, L. H., Tierney, G., Buhin, L., Greco, D. M., & Cooper, C. J. (2002). Kids' College: Enhancing children's appreciation and acceptance of cultural diversity. *Journal of Prevention and Intervention in the Community 24,* 63–78.

Marcia, J. (1980). Identity in adolescence. In J. Adelson (Ed.), *Handbook of adolescent psychology* (pp. 159–187). New York: John Wiley.

McMahon, S. D., & Watts, R. J. (2002). Ethnic identity in Urban African American Youth: Exploring links with self-worth, aggression and other psychosocial variables. *Journal of Community Psychology, 30*(4), 411–431.

Miller, R. L. (1990). Beyond contact theory: The impact of community affluence on integration efforts in five suburban high schools. *Youth and Society, 22*(1), 12–34.

Mulvey, A., Terenzio, M., Hill, J., Bond, M. A., Huygens, I., et al. (2000). Stories of relative privilege: Power and social change in feminist community psychology. *American Journal of Community Psychology, 28*(6), 883–911.

Olney, M. F., & Kim, A. (2001). Beyond adjustment: Integration of cognitive disability into identity. *Disability & Society, 16*(4), 563–583.

Parks, M. (2002). *Photoethnographic methods of neighborhood assessment: Seeing the context through the child's perspective.* Unpublished doctoral dissertation, DePaul University.

Patton, M. Q. (1987). *How to use qualitative methods in evaluation.* Newbury Park, CA: Sage.

Phinney, J. S. (1990). Ethnic identity in adolescents and adults: A review of research. *Psychological Bulletin, 108,* 499–514.

Phinney, J. S. (1992). The Multigroup Ethnic Identity Measure: A new scale for use with diverse groups. *Journal of Adolescent Research, 7*(2), 156–176.

Phinney, J. S., Cantu, C. L., & Kurtz, D. A. (1997). Ethnic and American identity as predictors of self-esteem among African American, Latino, and White Adolescents. *Journal of Youth and Adolescence, 26*(2), 165–185.

Ponterotto, J. G., & Pedersen, P. B. (1993). *Preventing prejudice: A guide for counselors and educators.* Newbury Park, CA: Sage.

Ridley, C. R. (1989). Racism in counseling as an adverse behavioral process. In P. B. Pedersen, J. G. Draguns, W. J. Lonner, & J. E. Trimble (Eds.), *Counseling across cultures* (pp. 55–77). Honolulu: University of Hawaii Press.

Rivers, I., & D'Augelli, A. R. (2001). The victimization of lesbian, gay, and bisexual youths. In A. R. D'Augelli & C. J. Patterson (Eds.), *Lesbian, gay, and bisexual identities and youth: Psychological perspectives* (pp. 199–223). New York: Oxford.

Roberts, R. E., Phinney, J. S., Masse, L. C., Chen, Y. R., Roberts, C. R., et al. (1999). The structure of ethnic identity of young adolescents from diverse ethnocultural groups. *Journal of Early Adolescence, 19*(3), 301–322.

Rohner, R. (1984). Toward a conception of culture for cross-cultural psychology. *Journal of Cross-Cultural Psychology, 15*(2), 111–138.

Roosa, M. W., & Gonzales, N. A. (2000). Minority issues in prevention: Introduction to the special issue. *American Journal of Community Psychology, 28,* 145–148.

Sánchez, B. (2002). *Mentorship of Latino older adolescents: An alternative definition and its role in academic achievement.* Unpublished doctoral dissertation, University of Illinois at Chicago.

Sampson, E. E. (1993). Identity politics: Challenges to psychology's understanding. *American Psychologist, 48*(12), 1219–1230.

Sanford, N. (1982). Social psychology: Its place in personology. *American Psychologist, 37,* 896–903.

Sasao, T., & Sue, S. (1993). Toward a culturally anchored ecological framework of research in ethnic–cultural communities. *American Journal of Community Psychology, 21,* 705–727.

Serrano-Garcia, I. (1990). Implementing research: Putting our values to work. In P. Tolan, C. Keys, F. Chertok, & L. Jason (Eds.), *Researching community psychology: Issues of theory and methods* (pp. 171–182). Washington DC: American Psychological Association.

Steele, C., & Aronson, J. (1995). Stereotype threat and the intellectual test performance of African Americans. *Journal of Personality and Social Psychology, 69,* 797–811.

Strauss, A., & Corbin, J. (1998). *Basics of qualitative research: Techniques and procedures for developing grounded theory* (2nd ed.). London: Sage.

Watts, R., Griffith, D., & Abdul-Adil, J. (1999). Socio-political development as an antidote for oppression-theory and action. *American Journal of Community Psychology, 27*(2), 255–272.

Wilson, A. (1991). *Understanding Black adolescent male violence: Its prevention and remediation* (pp. 5–20, 32–45). New York: Afrikan World InfoSystems.

Ye, C. J., & Huang, K. (1996). The collectivistic nature of ethnic identity development among Asian-American college students. *Adolescence, 31*(123), 645–661.

11

Community Narratives: The Use of Narrative Ethnography in Participatory Community Research

Gary W. Harper, Cécile Lardon, Julian Rappaport, Audrey K. Bangi, Richard Contreras, and Ana Pedraza

Sustained citizen participation in social, organizational, and civic life is a passionate experience. Those who engage in it do not do so as disinterested parties, neutral about outcomes or distant from their experiences. Participants have a story to tell. They will tell it to those who are willing (and sometimes even to those who are not willing) to listen. Indeed, one might argue that the very point of citizen participation is to tell one's story—to make one's views known, efforts felt, values actualized, and passions realized. We have a lot to learn from listening to the stories people tell.

This chapter briefly outlines a conceptual framework for a narrative ethnographic approach to research and evaluation that incorporates citizen participation and community collaboration. We then illustrate ways in which this methodology can be applied in community settings with a description of a collaborative participatory action project aimed at improving the sexual health of Mexican American female adolescents. We close the chapter by discussing some practical implications of using narrative ethnography in community settings.

Stories, Narratives, Meaning, and Identity

Modern cognitive psychology and social cognition tell us that stories create memory, emotion, meaning, and personal and collective identity (see, e.g., Bower & Clark, 1969; Bruner, 1986, 1990; Schank, 1990; Wyer, 1995). The term *narrative* is used in a variety of ways in social science. Sometimes

---

The research reported in this chapter was supported in part by grants from the AIDS Foundation of Chicago and the Illinois Campus Compact.

narrative refers to a *method* for data collection, sometimes it refers to the way in which data are *analyzed,* and sometimes it refers to a psychological *theory.* Here (following Mankowski & Rappaport 1995, 2000; and Rappaport, 1995, 2000) we use the term *story* to refer to personal stories and *narrative* to refer to a shared or common story. This use of the term narrative, then, necessarily links individuals and communities. This is an important theoretical point: By definition, narratives are shared stories.

It is also theoretically useful to distinguish between dominant cultural narratives and community or setting narratives. Dominant cultural narratives are shared stories that are communicated in media and popular symbols to describe a particular group of people in a stereotyped fashion (e.g., "the dangerous black man" or "housing project residents"), referents that conjure up over-learned stories of violence, teenage pregnancy, and drug use (Rappaport, 1998; Salzer, 1998, 2000). Community narratives are the shared stories told by community members about themselves. Dominant cultural narratives about people with few material resources tend to be negative and often these negative narratives are accepted into the personal stories (and identities) of the people who are their target. However, because there is a reciprocal relationship between narratives and personal stories, identity development and change (conversion experiences) may be understood in terms of the appropriation of shared narratives into one's personal life story on the one hand and the creation of new narratives or modification of existing narratives (social change) on the other (Mankowski & Rappaport, 1995). This means that personal identity (and ultimately behavior) may be susceptible to change through encounter with the new community narratives we experience when trying to make sense out of our lives. The possibility of new community narratives serves as a potential point of intervention for those who are willing to work collaboratively with the people of concern.

Bringing Narrative Ethnography to the Study of Citizen Participation

The topic of citizen participation, so central to community psychology, is ideally suited to a narrative and to an ethnographic psychology. The idea is simple: We will know about citizen participation by watching and listening and working *with* people who do it. They will tell us who they are, what they want from their participation (or *non*participation), and *how* they are experiencing it. Underlying such a statement is a theoretical point of view rooted in both epistemology and in the understanding that the *methods themselves are relational* (and empowering) and thus require the researcher to develop more than a superficial relationship with the people of concern. In the case of citizen participation, the methods are congruent with the content—they ask us to participate with the participators.

One may use a narrative data collection method (e.g., ask people in interviews to tell stories) without doing ethnography and without ascribing to a narrative psychological theory. However, adding ethnographic data to the ways in which stories are collected is a means to strengthen the findings by use of multiple methods—triangulation in the traditional research paradigm—and narrative theory is a useful heuristic for organizing our thoughts about the relationship between individuals and their communities. Narrative is a concept that spans levels of analysis, because individual stories are viewed as a function of group membership (see, e.g., Cain, 1991; Kitchell, Hannan & Kempton, 2000; Kloos, 1999).

Not all stories are told verbally. Narratives may be communicated by the social regularities of ritual, performance, or artistic displays. The narrative method, applied to interview techniques, focus groups, ethnographic observations, or other forms of data collection, is based on preservation of the whole— the beginning, middle, and end—the point or the "moral" of the story. These methods are designed to capture the lived experience of participants, in their own voices. Systematic participant observation is one powerful method for collection of such data. Joining with citizen groups as a participant (who keeps systematic field notes) is a way for a researcher or evaluator to both assist and to understand the people of concern. Naturally occurring stories will both guide the participation and inform the research and the intervention.

Engagement (or failure to engage) in acts of citizen participation is a deeply personal experience filled with implications for meaning and identity. It is inevitable that people who participate in collective activities will find meaning in those activities. Meaning making and identity are best understood through the actual voices of the people of concern, unfiltered by categorical classification or arithmetic transformation. Although the content of their passions may vary, the motives of the participants differ, and the strategies and tactics for engagement change as a function of opportunities and organizational and temperamental factors. The constant is *passion*—an emotional commitment to *something larger than one's self, yet to which the self is closely aligned.* This is the ground on which psychology and social action meet. It is here that real people live their lives as individual members of collectives. The stories they tell are the doorways to understanding their lives. Common stories, shared among people (i.e., narratives) mark a psychological sense of community.

Beyond the level of the individual, stories of meaning and identity also function as *motivators*. Citizen groups and organizations share a community narrative that explains to themselves, and to others, who they are, what they are doing, and why. These community narratives function as motivators. People are motivated by a story, an understanding of what they are working for, and of who they can become—now, and in the future. Stories can be historical, cultural (e.g., the Exodus story; the story of the American Civil rights movement; the story of Rosa Parks told as it really was—with her less of an individual hero and more a part of a collective struggle), contemporary (e.g., they can show why we need national health care; prescription coverage for elderly individuals), or future (e.g., possible selves; immigrant stories of success). Because narratives are resources, people need communities to uncover, create, and sustain narratives for meaning, identity, and personal and social change. We can both learn from and assist people in the pursuit of these tasks. We can help to uncover both tales of terror and of joy, and help give voice to hidden narratives. We can also assist in the cocreation of new narratives. What follows is a description of one such effort.

Improving the Sexual Health of Mexican American Female Adolescents

The collaborative partnership detailed in this chapter was developed between Project VIDA, a Latino-focused community-based HIV/AIDS service organization in Chicago, and a faculty member and students at DePaul University to conduct a comprehensive process evaluation of the SHERO'S HIV prevention program. The SHERO'S program was developed out of a recognized community need for culturally and developmentally appropriate HIV prevention and other sexual risk-reduction services. The empowerment and self–care-oriented curriculum of the intervention introduces Mexican American female adolescents between the ages of 12 to 21 to information and coping skills to help them manage the unique environmental, interpersonal, and individual-level stressors that place them at risk for negative sexual health outcomes (e.g., HIV, sexually transmitted infections [STIs], unplanned pregnancies). It includes various activities and exercises that assist the young women in recognizing the range of community and cultural narratives that serve as barriers to self-protection (e.g., gender-specific stereotypes and norms related to dating and sexual activity) and that increase their likelihood of engaging in health-protective behaviors.

This partnership used a narrative ethnographic approach based on narrative theory as it has been applied to community narratives (Mankowski & Rappaport, 2000; Rappaport, 1995, 2000) and was guided by elements of empowerment evaluation (Fetterman, 1996). Narrative theory guided the manner in which the collaborative team worked together to reveal the various narratives and stories that were present in the individuals, agency, and community through the process evaluation activities. The collaborative team was then able to use this information to help youth in the community modify existing narratives and create new narratives through the agency's revised prevention intervention (Rappaport, 1995, 2000). Empowerment evaluation theory supported the formation of a collaborative partnership whereby community members became active participants in all phases of the evaluation.

Throughout the collaboration between the DePaul evaluators and Project VIDA, narratives and stories were used to describe and document the characteristics of the SHERO's program; describe the range of clients being served by the program; detail the various cultural, social, environmental, relational, and individual factors that influence both sexual risk and sexual health practices of young women from the community; improve the delivery of HIV prevention services by modifying SHERO's current program; gain insight into future funding; and improve the agency's organizational structure related to service delivery. This information was integrated into clear and coherent conceptual themes with subsequent action plans. During this process, community members received training throughout to develop the skills and abilities to conduct this process of self-evaluation on their own (Fetterman, 1996). In addition, the collaborative team was able to tell the community agency's stories and narratives in ways that were accessible to a larger audience (Mankowski & Rappaport, 2000). This took the form of presentations for program funders; presentations at local, regional, and national academic and community conferences;

newsletter articles; standardized program implementation materials (e.g., program manuals); and grant applications for future funding. This is an example of stories/narratives as resources that can bring about positive social change and awareness (Rappaport, 2000). The following three sections illustrate the multiple ways in which narrative ethnographic work explores and reveals the richness and complexity of community narratives.

Narratives as a Form of Learning About the Culture, Community, and People

Because narratives can be viewed as a way that individuals and communities build cohesion and create a collective sense of identity (Mankowski & Rappaport, 2000), the evaluators sought to learn about and understand several levels of narratives to become better acquainted with the community, the agency, and the youth being served. These included a range of dominant cultural narratives related to Mexican American culture, community narratives related to both the physical agency itself (Project VIDA) as well as the neighborhood within which Project VIDA exists (Little Village in Chicago), and personal stories of the staff, agency clients, and community members. The methods that were used to explore these narratives were based in an ecological theoretical framework, were diverse in their focus, and assessed multiple levels of influence. They involved active participation in the agency and the surrounding community—involvement that exposes one to narratives that occur naturally in the environment (Mankowski & Rappaport, 2000).

Written Text as a Narrative

In addition to actively listening to and recording the narratives of community members, it is helpful to learn about historical narratives in the form of written text and archival information as another way to analyze and interpret people's experiences (Stuber, 2000). The evaluation team learned about dominant cultural and community narratives through reading literature related to the lives of Mexican Americans, academic articles and books related to Mexican American cultural factors (e.g., sexual silence, *machismo, marianismo, familismo*), neighborhood- and Latino-specific newspapers, and popular press magazines such as *Latina* and *Latingirl*. Community narratives about the agency itself were revealed by reading archival data sources related to the history and activities of the agency, including annual reports, previous grant applications, and progress reports.

Physical Spaces and Structures as Narratives

The evaluators learned a great deal about the dominant cultural narratives, as well as the community narratives of both the Little Village neighborhood and Project VIDA by touring the community and spending time observing the physical space both within Project VIDA and around the surrounding

Figure 11.1. Decorative gateway welcoming visitors to the Little Village community (photograph courtesy of Grace Frantilla).

neighborhood. Little Village is a working-class community whose residents are predominately Mexican American and Mexican immigrants, and the neighborhood's pride in its cultural heritage is quite evident in its public buildings and spaces. The community is marked on one end by two Spanish-style towers with a connecting arch that welcomes visitors with the phrase *"Bienvenidos A Little Village"* across the bridge (see Figure 11.1). Murals also grace the walls of several buildings with images of proud Mexican men and women (see Figure 11.2). Even the physical structure of some of the buildings reflect the Mexican heritage, because they are adorned with architectural facades and structures that resemble Aztec pyramids and temples. The physical space of Project VIDA is a quiet house in a residential neighborhood, with only a small sign in the window identifying it as Project VIDA. Its unassuming structure blends into the neighborhood and reflects the cultural value of keeping matters of sexuality quiet and private.

Members of the evaluation team learned more about the narratives of the agency staff and clients by exploring the surrounding neighborhood on foot and by using public transportation to travel from the university to the agency. In addition, they spent time learning about the neighborhood residents by eating in local restaurants, buying foods from local street vendors, shopping in retail stores, and generally interacting with residents of the neighborhood. These activities were invaluable, because they offered the evaluators useful information about the daily lives of the young women who would be participat-

Figure 11.2. Mural of historical Mexican/Mexican American figures on a building in the Little Village community (photograph courtesy of Grace Frantilla).

ing in the prevention efforts and about the neighborhood context within which they would be using their new skills and rewriting old stories.

Rituals as Narratives

Another way in which community narratives can be shared is through rituals (Rappaport, 2000). Rituals can take many forms and they may involve varying degrees of structure and function. Often they convey information about the immediate setting in which they are practiced and may have their roots in larger cultural narratives. For instance, early in the establishment of the collaborative relationship it was clear that one example of a VIDA ritual was the sharing of food and personal stories before meetings. All of the initial meetings were held at the agency, and when the evaluators arrived they were greeted with fresh sweet breads from a local Mexican bakery. This process seemed to set the tone for the meeting and was a time for the agency staff and evaluators to learn more about their newfound partners. There was some hesitation by members to talk openly about their personal and professional activities during this "checking in" period, but as people became better acquainted with each other there was a greater sense of comfort during these sessions.

Thus, it became quite evident that the sharing of food and personal stories was a part of the culture of the agency, which was strongly influenced by Mexican culture. If the evaluators would have refused the food and not engaged in the premeeting checking in and socializing, this could have been perceived by the agency staff as a sign of distrust or lack of engagement by the evaluators. The staff at the agency saw this sharing of food with the evaluators as a token of their appreciation for the evaluators' contributions to the agency and as a way to welcome them into their home. By recognizing and participating in this ritual, the evaluators also were able to better understand the agency's connection to the larger Mexican culture as well as to the Little Village neighborhood. In addition, understanding the importance of such rituals was helpful in working with the intervention that was developed, as the theme of sharing food and personal stories was also carried over into the preventive intervention that was evaluated.

Fundraising and Cultural Events as Narratives

Another way for narratives to be revealed is through social interactions and performances (Rappaport, 2000). In the world of nonprofit agencies where there is a continual search for more funds to keep programs running, these social interactions and performances may occur in the form of fundraising events. At the beginning of this collaborative relationship, Project VIDA was a relatively small community-based organization that depended on fundraising events to keep the agency afloat. Because fundraising activities were ongoing throughout the year and required the involvement of all agency staff, it was important for the evaluators to better understand this aspect of the agency. In addition, because the agency has strong connections to its surrounding community, many of the fundraisers also included a cultural or community component.

One fundraising function that the evaluators and staff attended early in the relationship was a cultural celebration fundraiser for Project VIDA and other Latino-focused agencies in the city. The event was held at a local Latino dance club, and throughout the night the evaluators and staff joined together as they ate, danced, and socialized. This was an excellent opportunity to build rapport in a social setting and to share different individual life stories and larger narratives. The agency staff had the opportunity to view the evaluators not as "experts" in a work environment but rather as individuals who were sharing in a common cause and enjoying a festive evening. Participation in this cultural fundraiser helped agency staff to see that the evaluators shared in the concerns of the agency and were there to support the continued actions of the agency. It also gave the evaluators additional information regarding the incorporation of dominant Mexican cultural narratives into various aspects of the agency's functioning, as well as the lives of many of the staff.

In addition to this particular function, the evaluators joined to raise money and increase awareness of the agency's activities through other fundraisers and cultural events such as the annual AIDS Walk, car washes, raffles, AIDS Quilt display, and the Latino Film Festival. For instance, the Latino Film Festival offered a deeper understanding of Latino culture and narratives through the visual representations provided by talented Latino artists and conversations with agency staff, and the AIDS Walk revealed information about the agency's connection to the larger HIV prevention community and culture. Participating in large-scale events such as the AIDS Walk fundraiser and the display of the AIDS Quilt revealed new narratives about the larger HIV/AIDS epidemic and often led to the sharing of personal stories by the staff and evaluators regarding their commitment to improving the sexual health of Latina adolescents. The evaluators' involvement in these activities and learning of multiple cultural and community narratives demonstrated to Project VIDA their genuine commitment to the agency and their true interest in improving prevention services for Mexican American female adolescents.

Agency Programs and Activities as Narratives

Becoming active participants in a community exposes one to narratives that occur naturally in the environment (Mankowski & Rappaport, 2000). In working with a nonprofit agency, one level of the community is the setting or agency itself and the programs and activities that are conducted within it. Attending program activities helped the evaluators to gain a better understanding of the work that the agency staff members were conducting and revealed both cultural and community narratives that were evident in the program activities and interactions. It also helped to humanize the evaluators and break down the hierarchical view of the evaluators. For example, conducting street-based outreach with the agency staff members offered invaluable information about the interactions that occur between staff members and clients, and the evaluators were able to witness the exchange of cultural narratives that were communicated in the form of conversational language and stereotypes (e.g., sexually promiscuous females being called "ho's" or "players"). Spending time in the setting engaging in informal conversation, casual observations, and participating in day-to-day agency activities (e.g., filling the water cooler) all revealed a range of personal stories, community narratives, and cultural narratives. Through this process the evaluators learned about the multiple roles that staff members play, the relationships among and between various staff members, and the dynamics within these relationships. Informal conversations and interactions with staff members also revealed their connection to larger community and cultural narratives in the form of interactional styles, dress, language, and personal stereotypes.

Narratives as a Way to Give Voice to the Experiences of the Agency and the People

The agency and evaluators worked collaboratively on the development of the process evaluation plan for several months to create a set of methods that would reveal relevant stories and narratives within the community, agency, staff, and participants that could eventually assist in the modification of the SHERO's program. The evaluation plan included a range of techniques and methods that were created with the cultural, environmental, and developmental needs of the youth and the agency in mind. We attempted to use a diverse range of ethnographic and evaluation methods for recording and analyzing stories and narratives and to ensure that these methods were tapping into multiple levels of influence experienced by the young women. Various combinations of agency staff and evaluators implemented the evaluation strategies, and training was conducted along the way to improve the skills of those involved in the evaluation.

Individual In-Depth Interviews

Individual interviews were conducted with past program participants to explore their reflections on the applied utility of the SHERO's program. These interviews also served to record personal stories that could offer additional information about unique stressors that currently face young women in the community. These stories offered valuable insight regarding the ways in which cultural and community narratives strongly influenced the dating and sexual scripts of these young women, as well as how these narratives have influenced their conceptualization of self with regard to sexuality. Although individual stories reflect the personal experiences of only one individual and thus may be seen by some as idiosyncratic in nature, they are shaped by the community and cultural narratives that prevail within the individuals' various communities of membership (Rappaport, 2000). Thus by learning about the experiences of different young women who live in the community where the SHERO's program was being implemented we were able to learn about individual- and community-level factors that affect sexual activity. By revealing the elements of the current stories and narratives that increased the participants' likelihood of participating in sexual risk behaviors, the collaborative team hoped to modify elements of the SHERO's program so that it would assist the participants in creating new empowering narratives that would increase their likelihood of engaging in health-protective behaviors.

The interviews were conducted by the program coordinator of the SHERO's program and by a senior member of the evaluation team. The young women who participated in these interviews shared a range of personal stories that revealed a great deal about the community and cultural narratives that have influenced their sexual health practices. For example, one past program participant talked about how the cultural norm of "sexual silence" had restricted her from asking questions and talking about sex-related matters for fear that others would think that she is a "whore" for addressing topics related to sexuality. This tension had kept her from ever talking with others about her discomfort in having sexual activity with males who were sexually coercive until she attended the SHERO's program.

Another common theme that emerged was that several young women talked about sexual relationships with older men. Careful examination of the interview transcripts illustrated that in these situations the young women often reported being coerced into not using condoms because of power differentials related to status, age, and gender. Acknowledgment that such sexual unions were relatively common in the community and that they presented a potential avenue for HIV/STI infections and unplanned pregnancies prompted the collaborative team to add a component to the program to address this particular issue. The collaborative team's increased knowledge of this phenomenon resulted in the desire to share this narrative in ways that were accessible to a larger audience by making the legal, medical, and other professional communities more aware of the HIV-related risks associated with young women engaging in sexual activity with older men (Harper, Bangi, Contreras, & Pedraza, 2001; Harper, Doll, Bangi, & Contreras, 2002). Through the dissemination of this information, the team was able to elaborate on such risks to a wider audience of colleagues, policy makers, community leaders, and health educators.

Focus Groups

Focus groups allowed for the telling of both individual stories and collective narratives by young women who had experienced the full intervention. These groups provided participants with the opportunity to offer insight into aspects of the program that were not meeting their needs. By giving these young women a venue to tell their stories and to share them with other participants, we provided the participants with an empowering experience whereby they were able to have a role in the shaping and creation of new stories that would be told in the subsequent prevention programs. The young women who participated in the groups often talked about their concern with the array of negative influences in their community and expressed their desire to help others who may be at risk for negative health outcomes such as HIV infection. They shared that by participating in the process evaluation they felt empowered because the information they offered was being used to make the program more effective for other young women.

Based on this information and the team discussions, the structure and content of the sessions was continually modified and reassessed. For example, some community guest speakers were changed and some of the topics covered in the sessions were modified to more accurately address the community and cultural narratives that were affecting the young women's participation in sexual risk behaviors. Participants also shared that they preferred sessions that incorporated group discussions and interactive exercises when conveying information or revealing new stories and narratives that the youth could incorporate into their lives. This information was used to make appropriate modifications to improve the program for future participants. One positive unintended consequence of these focus groups was that through the sharing of personal stories, rival gang members realized that they had similar life experiences and that they were part of shared narratives.

Narratives as a Form of Action and Empowerment

The development of empowering narratives is critical to bringing about social change, because many narratives that have damaging effects often become so common through the development of stereotypes and habitual behaviors that individuals do not even realize their impact (Rappaport, 2000). Many young Mexican American women, like members of other numerous minority groups, perceive that their range of empowering stories or narratives are limited and thus have not explored potential new pathways or options that would lead to increased sexual health. Because empowering narratives serve as potential resources that are not evenly distributed across groups of people with varying degrees of power and voice in society (Rappaport, 2000), the collaborative team worked together to provide young women with an increased choice of stories to incorporate into their own personal life stories. Thus, this new repertoire of stories was designed to increase the young women's awareness of alternative ways to view themselves and to increase their options for future life directions.

In attempting to promote empowerment and sexual health, some of these new stories required critical examinations of cultural norms and beliefs related to heterosexual interactions and sexuality. Thus, the intervention could be viewed by some as a way of "subverting culture" (Ortiz-Torres, Serrano-Garcia, & Torres-Burgos, 2000). Instead of idealizing existing cultural norms, the program challenges gender-based inequalities and double standards and promotes changes in social norms and normative beliefs that promote HIV-risk behaviors. The collaborative team concurs with Ortiz-Torres et al. (2000) in their assertion that HIV risk reduction interventions for Latina women must include a critical examination of the aspects of culture that both promote and impede HIV prevention efforts. In addition, we agree that culture should not be used as a vehicle for the additional oppression of women and other groups of people in society. Instead culture should be "a space where respect for diversity and participation in the development of new values leads all of us closer to health, dignity, and freedom" (p. 877).

Sexual/Reproductive Health

Because Latina females receive the cultural message that they are to be inexperienced in sexual matters and should suppress desires to be sexual, discussions within families about the physical maturation of their bodies and the emergence of sexual feelings as a normal part of their development are either nonexistent or fairly limited (Holland, Ramazanoglu, Sharpe, & Thomson, 1994). Given the components of this old story, the intervention integrated greater understanding of one's sexual and reproductive body parts and functions to maintain health. This was a distinct departure from an intervention that focused strictly on disease prevention because new messages acknowledged that knowing about one's body was not shameful but instead signaled the importance of caring about health. By discussing messages related to sexual health, youth were able to acknowledge the various changes in their bodies and take ownership for decisions regarding their physical health and well-being. Through a more positive and honest account of sexuality, the information in this session functions as a resource for enhancing the youths' likelihood to make healthy choices.

Sexual Pleasure

The old story of sexual pleasure is influenced by how cultures dictate gender roles. For instance, there is greater latitude for the sexual behavior of males (e.g., promiscuity), whereas females are expected to be monogamous and suppress their own sexual desires (Gomez & Marin, 1996). The new story acknowledged the limitations of the traditional gender roles and was enhanced to include an awareness of young women's sexuality. To encourage consistent condom use and instill a sense of pride and responsibility for their actions, participants were asked to brainstorm ways to introduce condoms to a sexual partner that would not be looked on as "ruining the mood" (e.g., hiding condom on body and asking partner to find it, wrapping condoms as a present and giving them after a romantic dinner) and increase the likelihood that condoms will be accessible when they decide to have sex.

Discussions built on the notion that sexuality can be a mutually positive experience in which females can derive enjoyment from sexual expression. Sex did not solely have to fulfill a male partner's sexual desires or be used manipulatively to stay in a relationship. Through this account, participants were able to associate sex with the physical expression of love and realize that they could exercise a choice in its expression.

Role of Religion

Gender expectations regarding sexual decisions and behaviors were also influenced by an old story that incorporated themes consistent with Catholicism, whose religious teachings affect the vast majority of participants in this program. Stemming from the symbolism embodied by the Virgin of Guadalupe, females receive mixed messages regarding sexual practices—motherhood is held in high esteem because it promotes new life but chastity is regarded as honorable (Rodriguez, 1994). The intervention incorporated the sharing of personal stories and common beliefs held about youth who were affected by pregnancy or STIs. The consideration of childbearing as a solution to a young woman's problems at home or attempt to secure a long-term relationship with her male partner was discussed in light of the financial and emotional responsibilities of teenage motherhood as well as on future goals (e.g., educational, professional, personal). Discussions also extended to the complexities of caring for a child who may be infected with HIV or may be born with parent(s) infected with HIV. This new narrative reinforced the idea that knowledge about and use of condoms is an expression of caring about personal health and the health of others.

Sexual Assertiveness and Communication

Young Latina females' comfort discussing sexual issues with their male partners were affected by an old story regarding sexual silence (Marin, Gomez, & Hearst, 1993). For instance, reluctance to initiate discussions about safer sex was affected by fears of possible rejection by male partners. Given the perceived costs of asserting personal desires to engage in safer sex practices, the intervention featured a problem-solving method for talking with male partners about safer sex. Pictures of Mexican American couples that were taken in Little Village helped facilitate discussions about possible communication difficulties experienced by couples in their own community. New narratives were created as participants evaluated the role each partner played in a relationship (e.g., providing emotional support, maintaining physical health) and brainstormed ways in which young women can convey their needs (e.g., commitment, responsibility) in a relationship. Thus, participants were able to assert positive qualities of womanhood (e.g., strength, determination).

Gang Culture/Membership

Themes regarding gang culture were closely tied to the environment within which many of the program participants live. Gang lines clearly mark boundaries of the surrounding neighborhoods and represent limitations on young women's selection of potential sexual partners and in general on their futures. The old story regarding membership in a gang involves an elevated status associated with being affiliated with a gang, either as a gang member or as a dating/sexual partner of a gang member. To bring to light the realities of gang culture, the intervention included a session discussing the risks associated with being a gang member, as well as in being in a romantic relationship with a gang member. Facilitators shared the HIV risks associated with gang fights where exposure to blood was common, thus presenting the potential for HIV transmission through contaminated blood. Other stories shared with participants included the dangers of gang initiation rituals, which often involve great risk to personal safety and sexual health.

Living With HIV

The old story about individuals living with HIV hinders adolescents from considering their personal vulnerabilities to HIV infection. Based on comments that many participants made during group activities, it appeared that they distanced themselves from those living with HIV based on three dimensions: group identity/membership, sexual behavior patterns, and physical appearance. Community narratives indicated that those living with HIV were gay men, drug users, or prostitutes. With regard to sexual behavior, the young women perceived that those infected with HIV had numerous sexual partners and labeled them with such terms as "sluts," "ho's," and "freaks." They also expressed beliefs that those affected by HIV are emaciated and have skin discoloration.

Thus, for participants to realize their personal susceptibility to HIV infection, the last session of the intervention consisted of a young Mexican American woman who shared personal experiences of being HIV-positive. Because the speaker mirrored many of the value systems and beliefs that participants held, the myths and stereotypes participants had of HIV-positive individuals were debunked. Agency staff also shared stories regarding the loss of friends who had died from complications related to AIDS. The new story that emerged as a result of the retelling of these experiences provided a way for participants to evaluate their personal risks of infection and realize that HIV testing is the most accurate way to determine HIV status.

Discussion: Applying Narrative Ethnography in Community Settings

Just as with other methodologies in community psychology research and evaluation, there is no "one way" to conduct narrative ethnography. Rather, a variety of methods and activities should be combined in such a way to discover and understand a community's narratives. Following are some pragmatic considerations in working toward this goal.

Relationships Between Researchers, Community-Based Organizations, and Communities

As many in the field of community psychology have pointed out, community research relies on the relationships between the researchers and members of the participating communities (for example, Chataway, 1997; Kelly, Mock, & Tandon, 2001; Mohatt, 1989; Rappaport, 1990). When using a narrative ethnographic approach, the development of a mutually beneficial and trusting relationship between the researcher or evaluator and the community will enable the collaborative team to incorporate multiple perspectives, share different narratives, challenge old narratives that may be damaging, and create new ones *together*. In narrative ethnography, therefore, attention to these relationships is especially important for at least two reasons. First, it requires community members to trust and have faith in the researcher's willingness and ability to understand the narratives in their proper social, political, cultural, and economic contexts. This concern is not specific to narrative ethnography but does play a crucial role. When researchers and evaluators are engaged in narrative ethnographic activities, community members need to have enough trust to talk about the complex and often sensitive issues and experiences concerning their community and to provide access to other sources of information.

Similarly, researchers and evaluators need to be able to trust their informants to provide truthful information. Researchers need to know that the pieces of information they are exposed to via a variety of means are genuine and authentic. This can only be achieved in a working relationship in which all participants feel comfortable with each other, have taken the time to build mutual trust and respect, and are committed to the common goal.

Second, narratives include themes about relationships between researchers–evaluators and the community, as well as between CBOs and the larger community. These narratives might include themes of social status, experience with social change, perceived power, and exploitation. For example, in a community there may be narratives about what a researcher or evaluator is and what research or evaluation can do for the community. University researchers–evaluators may be seen as experts on a particular topic, but they may also be seen as "outsiders" without any real understanding of the community. Some communities have had negative experiences with researchers that have become narratives of exploitation. One striking example is the Barrow Alcohol Study conducted in an Alaska Native community that had quite damaging consequences for the participating community (Foulks, 1987, 1989) because of the researchers' lack of knowledge of the local culture and the absence of collaboration between the researchers and the community.

In addition to the relationship between researchers and communities, CBOs also have particular relationships with the community in which they are located and the communities they serve—and these may not necessarily be the same communities. There may be important narratives concerning these relationships that should be included in the research.

Learning About the Community

To build a trusting relationship with a community, researchers need to become familiar with their hosts and partners. This is crucial to narrative ethnography because narratives do not exist in a social, political, or cultural vacuum. Stories and narratives have meaning only in relation to each other and to the settings out of which they grow. Therefore, one cannot understand, nor possibly even recognize, the web of narratives in a community without developing a deeper understanding of that community. As the project described in this chapter demonstrates, this can be done in a variety of ways, including reading informational materials about the community and spending time on its streets and in its shops and restaurants. Most important, researchers need to become participants in a variety of community organizations, functions, and activities to gain an experience-based knowledge of the host setting. This, of course, cannot be accomplished in one visit, or even several visits. Rather, continued participation over a longer period of time may be required. In some cases (see, e.g., Kelly, Mock, & Tandon, 2001; Kelly et al., in press) this process can take several years. Community psychologists need to be willing to make this investment of time and resources when using a narrative ethnographic approach, as it will bear great fruit in the form of improved relationships, evidence of authenticity, and truly meaningful narratives.

Considering Narratives as Multidimensional Constructs

One of the advantages of narrative ethnography is its ability to uncover complex and subtle themes in a community's narratives. However, one would lose this advantage if the narratives were treated as self-contained entities with clear beginnings and endings. Rather, researchers and evaluators should engage with the community and its members in placing the stories and narratives in their proper contexts, including the social, political, cultural, and economic contexts that exist in any social setting. For example, the narratives about female adolescents' sexuality in this community occurred within a Mexican

American culture situated in a low-income urban neighborhood in a major Midwestern city. Narratives about sexuality, abstinence, and relationships take on a particular meaning within each context. Mainstream U.S. urban narratives about female sexuality are different from traditional Mexican narratives, yet in this setting they are blended in specific ways to form the narratives communicated to the participants and project evaluators.

One might picture this collection of narratives as a multidimensional web. The narratives are the nodes in the web and are connected to each other in multiple ways. Some are connected directly, and others only have indirect connections through other narratives. This web metaphor is also expressed in postmodern theories of organizations (e.g., Martin, 1992) that acknowledge the many different ways in which members of an organization may be linked to each other, creating a loosely linked organizational whole out of these ever-shifting relationships. In essence, it is the narrative ethnographer's job to work closely with members of the community to collaboratively reconstruct this web for a particular moment in time—much like a snapshot that can be used to facilitate a critical analysis that leads to action (Friere, 1993).

In addition to understanding the current contexts it is also crucial to consider the historical context for these narratives. It is no coincident that these particular stories are told in this particular way at this particular time. Twenty years earlier, the narratives about women's roles in intimate partnerships and about sexuality would undoubtedly have been quite different. However, these earlier narratives have shaped, and still influence, current ones.

Conclusion

As described in this chapter, information about community narratives can come from multiple sources, including written text, oral histories, physical spaces and structures, pieces of art displayed in public and private, songs, poems, food, rituals, merchandise in stores, media outlets, places of worship, services, political organizations, local cookbooks, journals, public commentaries (e.g., newspapers, graffiti), ways of conducting business, and many more. Obviously, not all sources will be necessary or appropriate for any particular study. A collaborative and trusting relationship with the community can help researchers determine which sources will be most critical to examine.

Methods for accessing these sources of information also can, and should, be varied. They may include individual and group interviews, participant and nonparticipant observation, archival research, content analysis of speeches and publications, journaling, and others. Again, the usefulness and appropriateness of any of these methods needs to be discussed with members of the community. Some communities may not have many written materials, whereas other communities may restrict access to certain places or events. Also, some methods may limit the sources of information to those deemed culturally appropriate.

Narrative ethnography provides a flexible and context-specific way to conduct community-based research. In its basic principles and assumptions it is quite compatible with other research methodologies and concepts in community psychology, such as participatory action research, empowerment evaluation, ecological theory, empowerment theory, and health promotion. Furthermore, narrative ethnography is useful in conducting basic research studies within communities, as well as different types of action research initiatives, such as those involving program evaluation or the facilitation of community change.

References

Bower, G. H., & Clark, M. C. (1969). Narrative stories as mediators for serial learning. *Psychonomic Science, 14,* 181–182.

Bruner, J. (1986). *Actual minds, possible worlds.* Cambridge, MA: Harvard University Press.

Bruner, J. (1990). *Acts of meaning.* Cambridge, MA: Harvard University Press.

Cain, C. (1991). Personal stories: Identity acquisition and self-understanding in Alcoholics Anonymous. *Ethos, 19,* 210–253.

Chataway, C. (1997). An examination of the constraints on mutual inquiry in a participatory action research project. *Journal of Social Issues, 53,* 747–766.

Fetterman, D. M. (1996). Empowerment evaluation: An introduction to theory and practice. In D. M. Fetterman, S. J. Kaftarian, & A. Wandersman (Eds.), *Empowerment evaluation: Knowledge and tools for self-assessment and accountability* (pp. 3–48). Thousand Oaks, CA: Sage.

Foulks, E. F. (1987). Social stratification and alcohol use in North Alaska. *Journal of Community Psychology, 15,* 349–356.

Foulks, E. F. (1989). Misalliances in the Barrow Alcohol Study. *American Indian and Alaska Native Health Research, 2,* 7–17.

Freire, P. (1993). *Pedagogy of the oppressed* (Rev. ed.). New York: Continuum. (Original work published 1970)

Gomez, C. A., & Marin, B. V. O. (1996). Gender, culture, and power: Barriers to HIV prevention strategies for women. *Journal of Sex Research, 33,* 355–362.

Harper, G. W., Bangi, A. K., Contreras, R., & Pedraza, A. (2001). Age matters for adolescent females: Sexual relationships with older men presents risks for HIV. *Psychology & AIDS Exchange, 29,* 1–13.

Harper, G. W., Doll, M., Bangi, A. K., & Contreras, R. (2002). Female adolescents and older male sex partners: HIV associated risk. *Journal of Adolescent Health, 19,* 1–2.

Holland, J., Ramazanoglu, C., Sharpe, S., & Thomson, R. (1994). Achieving masculine sexuality: Young men's strategies for managing vulnerability. In L. Doyal, J. Naidoo, & T. Wilton (Eds.), *AIDS: Setting a feminist agenda* (pp. 122–148). London: Taylor & Francis.

Kelly, J. G., Azelton, L. S., Lardon, C. L., Mock, L. O., Tandon, S. D., et al. (in press). On community leadership: Stories about collaboration in action research. *American Journal of Community Psychology.*

Kelly, J. G., Mock, L. O., & Tandon, S. D. (2001). Collaborative inquiry with African American community leaders: Comments on a participatory action research process. In P. Reason & H. Bradbury (Eds.), *Handbook of action research: Participative inquiry and practice* (pp. 348–355). Thousand Oaks, CA: Sage.

Kitchell, A., Hannan, E., & Kempton, W. (2000). Identity through stories: Story structure and function in two environmental groups. *Human Organization, 59,* 96–105.

Kloos, B. (1999). *Cultivating identity: Meaning-making in the context of residential treatment settings for persons with histories of psychological disorders.* Unpublished doctoral dissertation, University of Illinois at Urbana–Champaign.

Mankowski, E., & Rappaport, J. (1995). Stories, identity and the psychological sense of community. In R. S. Wyer, Jr. (Ed.), *Advances in social cognition* (Vol. 8, pp. 211–226). Hillsdale, NJ: Erlbaum.

Mankowski, E. S., & Rappaport, J. (2000). Narrative concepts and analysis in spiritually-based communities. *Journal of Community Psychology, 28*(5), 479–493.

Marin, B., Gomez, C., & Hearst, N. (1993). Multiple heterosexual partners and condom use among Hispanics and non-Hispanic whites. *Family Planning Perspectives, 25,* 170–174.

Martin, J. (1992). *Cultures in organizations: Three perspectives*. New York: Oxford University Press.

Mohatt, G.V. (1989). The community as informant or collaborator? *American Indian and Alaska Native Health Research, 2,* 64–70.

Ortiz-Torres, B., Serrano-Garcia, I., & Torres-Burgos, N. (2000). Surbverting culture: Promoting HIV/AIDS prevention among Puerto Rican and Dominican women. *American Journal of Community Psychology, 28,* 859–881.

Rappaport, J. (1990). Research methods and the empowerment social agenda. In P. Tolan, C. Keys, F. Chertok, & L. Jason (Eds.), *Researching community psychology* (pp. 51–63). Washington, DC: American Psychological Association.

Rappaport, J. (1995). Empowerment meets narrative: Listening to stories and creating settings. *American Journal of Community Psychology, 23,* 795–807.

Rappaport, J. (1998). The art of social change: Community narratives as resources for individual and collective identity. In X. B. Arriaga & S. Oskamp (Eds.), *Addressing community problems: Psychosocial research and intervention* (pp. 225–246). Thousand Oaks, CA: Sage.

Rappaport, J. (2000). Community narratives: Tales of terror and joy. *American Journal of Community Psychology, 28*(2), 1–24.

Rodriguez, J. (1994). *Our Lady of Guadalupe: Faith and empowerment among Mexican-American women*. Austin: University of Texas Press.

Salzer, M. S. (1998). Narrative approach to assessing interactions between society, community and person. *Journal of Community Psychology, 26,* 569–580.

Salzer, M. S. (2000). Toward a narrative conceptualization of stereotypes: Contextualizing perceptions of public housing residents. *Journal of Community and Applied Social Psychology, 10,* 123–137.

Schank, R. C. (1990). *Tell me a story: A new look at real and artificial memory*. New York: Scribner.

Stuber, S. C. (2000). The interposition of personal life stories and community narratives in a Roman Catholic religious community. *Journal of Community Psychology, 28*(5), 507–515.

Wyer, R. S., Jr. (Ed.). (1995). *Advances in social cognition* (Vol. 8). Hillsdale, NJ: Erlbaum.

Part V _____

Stakeholder Perspectives

12

Community Concerns About Participatory Research

Constance W. Van der Eb, Nancy Peddle,
Mary Buntin, Daryl Holtz Isenberg, Lura Duncan,
Steven Everett, Angela Glass, Lorraine Keck,
Ricardo Millett, Lynne Mock, and Paul Molloy

This chapter represents some of the diverse voices of community agencies and self-help organizations. Our perspective has been largely absent from the literature, even from the related text by Tolan, Keys, Chertok, and Jason (1990). Therefore, our participation in this book signifies an advance in academicians' valuation of community expertise. This chapter offers a community perspective, tempered by personal and indirect experiences, of the contributions to participatory research presented in the preceding chapters. Our objective is to facilitate respectful and effective university–community collaborations for participatory community research and for program development. Several themes emerged from our considerations of the fit of participatory research methods and findings with the realities of social and economic problems, as experienced at the community level. These themes are the focus of this chapter.

Community Consensus Themes

Six themes are of great importance to us: advocacy, topic selection, language, relationships, ethics, and funding and sustainability. Together, these individual themes speak to two values—concerns crucial to individuals and community groups: (a) the assistance of academia in solving community problems is welcome when researchers are committed to valuing the individual's real-world experience and to being sensitive to cultural and personal differences and (b) research must contribute to the betterment of the participating community (i.e., the project should be meaningful to the community and provide useful information to operate and sustain program interventions).

Advocacy

Participatory research is appealing to communities because it focuses on understanding and providing solutions to community problems. We see the research project as a form of advocacy. In essence, a topic worthy of community research indicates its status as a concern warranting attention from the larger community. Participatory research offers community researchers the unique role of being both advocate and scholar, especially when community conditions–disadvantages hamper local initiatives for community improvements. Personal qualities of commitment, patience, and a sense of mission, which are found in the effective participatory researcher, help researchers to join with community researcher–participants, organizations, funders, and other citizens to change the community for the better. We believe that such broad-based collaboration leads to diverse benefits: research products that are actually implemented at the local community level—information that is useful to policy makers, local leaders, and residents as well as to the academic community—and enhancement of participants' motivation and skills for self-advocacy (see chapter 1).

The community recognizes that researchers have the expertise, credibility, and access to potential resources needed by community members. We appreciate the willingness of community psychologists to advocate the participatory research approach within their universities. Yet we urge extension of these advocacy efforts into the community to help us voice our concerns effectively, tap into resources for community improvement, and challenge the status quo, as necessary, to achieve community goals.

Topic Selection

Community participants must care about the research topic and its interventions. Is the topic important to the community? Will it suggest strategies capable of triggering needed changes, even if they challenge the practices and assumptions of organizations or people in power? We focused on these concerns along with issues of community input, prevention- versus strength-based orientation, and multidisciplinary input to research design.

We observe that much participatory research focuses on issues relating to poor and disenfranchised individuals. Opportunities to advance social change exist in other sectors of society. We would like to see community researchers pursue topics of dominance, control, and violence as perpetrated by people with power as well.

Before selection, community members—such as agency administrators, service providers, and potential service recipients—should be asked whether the topic is meaningful and appropriate. In chapter 9, Salina et al. describe how their plan to provide HIV/AIDS prevention education to incarcerated women was altered after participants identified housing and transportation problems as higher priorities. The researchers responded by changing their interventions. The community also recommends that researchers tap the expertise of colleagues in other disciplines for diverse experiences and viewpoints that may benefit research topics and design.

We concur with the observations in chapters 1 and 4 that community members are more engaged by strength-based rather than problem-oriented interventions, and we encourage the use of this model. The value of moving beyond prevention programs to programs that focus on promotion of opportunities, skills, and talents of participants resonates with those of us who have participated in community projects.

The talents of university community psychologists should be devoted to topics that will challenge existing practices and concepts and, perhaps, identify means to benefit communities "from the top down," as well as "from the bottom up." We wonder about the influence of attributes, attitudes, and actions of the leadership in governmental, corporate, financial, and other arenas on the life experiences of ordinary citizens.

Language

Effective participatory research requires ongoing, clear communication with mutually shared definitions and terms among all stakeholders. Language is a critical issue. When researchers and community members cannot understand each other's words, opportunities for rich interaction and collaboration are missed. A desirable approach to a given community results in bilingualism: "I want you to teach me your language, and I'll teach you mine."

Language is also critical because a person's words, inflections, and tone of voice are part of his or her identity and reflect community affiliations. Community participants want researchers to "keep it simple" and to "be willing to learn the community language" to promote mutual respect and shared power. The research team's sensitivity to communication modes (e.g., e-mail, phone, and in person) and style (degree of formality, frequency) further supports respectful interactions. Attention to language is fundamental to participatory research and opens the door to relationship building.

Relationships

Participatory research is built on a foundation of relationships in which all stakeholders believe they have knowledge and resources to contribute (see chapter 10). Yet many participating communities are underserved, marginalized, or are by nature vulnerable, lacking a voice as well as sufficient influence. Negative experiences in controlling relationships cause many marginalized individuals to be wary of institutions, authority figures, and outsiders (see chapters 7 and 10). Researchers should not assume relationship building will be easier among more educated or relatively advantaged populations. We have encountered instances when trust was or was perceived to have been breached or community participants felt unappreciated or even used. The community researcher's task is to diminish this reticence by making a commitment to initiate and nurture trusting relationships with community participants.

We appreciate it when researchers set the stage for partnership by spending time in the community. Informal conversations and participation in various community activities help the researcher to learn about the local culture, its history, and social realities. Our community input can enhance the appropriateness and effectiveness of programs (chapter 8).

Community–university partnerships require nurturing to thrive. Many steps may be taken to promote these relationships (see chapter 5). The following practices are especially helpful: (a) including community participants in all phases of the research process; (b) bringing the research team and community participants together on a regular basis to share information, maintain a two-way learning relationship, and assist with key decisions; (c) enjoying the benefits of diversity in background and experience while being sensitive to personal biases; (d) cooperatively deciding how to manage power differentials inherent to the interactions of research staff with community members; (e) defining roles and responsibilities early on and generating guidelines for conflict resolution; (f) sharing credit for success and using failures as opportunities to improve.

Ethics

We urge community researchers to be sensitive to the connection between participation and ethical practices. Suarez-Balcazar et al. list principles in chapter 6 that help university partnerships to avoid academic exploitation of communities and to form trusting relationships. We concur with the conclusion of Torres-Harding et al. in chapter 3 that participatory research may have the greatest implications for how research can be conducted ethically.

Participatory research offers the community one safeguard from earlier abuses such as the Tuskegee experiment.[1] However, we are concerned about harm done by researchers as well as instances of harm done to researchers by community groups (see chapter 7). For example, Rainbows (a self-help group for children of newly divorced parents) found that their researchers pirated their model and set up a competing program. Research papers have also been placed on the Internet without the requisite permission (see chapter 7). We assert that there is the same responsibility to a human participant review process in participatory research work as there is in other approaches to research.

The community strongly agrees that ethical relationships: (a) begin with building relationships; (b) are created when the researcher is open and transparent and knows his or her cultural biases; (c) can promote beneficial social change for all; and (d) take into consideration the differences in power, experience, and culture (see Appendix B).

Funding and Sustainability

In our experience, access to research funds, distribution of funds, education of funders, and development of collaborations that lead to sustainability of action components are critical issues. Although university faculties tend to have

---

[1]In the Tuskegee experiment, researchers allowed Black men to go untreated for venereal disease so that they might study the long-term effects of the disease.

greater access to research funds (via grants) than community groups, they bring financial resources to the community group for only a limited time. In addition, the pressure on academicians to publish research findings can drive the research question/topic and fundraising and take precedence over community priorities/needs. We urge researchers to locate funding sources and university systems willing to support participatory research topics, even projects that involve a challenge to those in power (i.e., corporate America, elected officials, or the housing authority).

Distribution of funds becomes an issue when funding goes only to the investigators and promotes power over the community group. Tension may exist between research needs and community needs—in other words, "research versus utility." A way to balance power and to enhance community commitment is to increase the community's resources and leadership early in the process. Community participation balances power, assists in distribution of funds, and is a key component of intervention sustainability.

We see a need to inform funders that participatory research requires sustained commitment of time, money, and effort to produce high quality scientific/utility benefits. Including funders in the earliest phases of research planning might stimulate greater appreciation of the value of participatory research methods and findings and, potentially, lead to improved financial support of participatory research projects.

Sustainability and motivation to participate seem to reach optimal levels when the project benefits the group's mission or the community as a whole. Adoption of a community empowerment and improvement perspective will guide intervention development in ecologically sound ways (see chapters 1 and 4). Participatory research has the potential to further program sustainability as: (a) community members learn new skills; (b) research is more relevant and applicable; (c) new resources are identified; and (d) community members recognize their strengths to help themselves and others. Steps contributing to sustainability are: (a) including community partners in forming mission and goals for the interventions, (b) including and paying individuals from the community in the management of the project's daily operations from its inception, (c) developing the community's capacity to locate and secure resources, and (d) sharing the findings of the research project with the community group for interpretation and implementation.

Conclusion

We are impressed and encouraged by the efforts of the researchers to engage with the community organizations to create meaningful participatory research projects. We consider six themes to be especially important to community participants of university–community collaborations: advocacy, topic selection, language, relationships, ethics, and funding and sustainability. Ongoing attention to these themes, beginning at project conceptualization, will foster citizen commitment and enrich research outcomes. We encourage continued advocacy for adoption of the participatory research approach in community research. Researchers have academic knowledge and the community has real-world experience (Jason, 1997). Together they have the resources needed to make research relevant and useful.

References

Jason, L. A. (1997). *Community building: Values for a sensible future.* Westport, CT: Praeger.

Tolan, P., Keys, C., Chertok, F., & Jason, L. A. (Eds.). (1990). *Researching community psychology: Issues of theories and methods.* Washington, DC: American Psychological Association.

13

Student Reflections on Community Research Practices and Their Implications

Michelle Bloodworth, Chisina Kapungu, John Majer, Katherine McDonald, Aparna Sharma, Judah Viola, and Bianca Wilson

As students, we often acquire an abundance of first-hand experience with various community research practices. Our training typically involves applied experiences in the areas of evaluating programs, serving as community advocates–liaisons, grant writing, recruiting participants, conducting interviews, collaborating on research teams, collecting data, and report writing. In these roles, we often spend a lot of time in direct contact with community partners and in the day-to-day operations of a research project. Thus our comments represent an important perspective that we feel will contribute to the future of participatory community research. As graduate students from three Chicago universities, we offer a diverse voice, because we vary in terms of our ethnicity, age, gender, sexual orientation, regional origin, and level of graduate training. These individual differences sparked provocative dialogue during the weeks preceding the conference and throughout the completion of this chapter. In this section, we address the roles of nonfaculty perspectives within the community research arena, the traditional conceptualization of community partners, and highlight important strategies in participatory research methods that deserve continued exploration. In addition, we explore future directions for community researchers through a discussion of the training implications of the various lessons learned about collaborative endeavors between community and academic settings.

The order of the seven authors is alphabetical; each author contributed equally to this manuscript. We are grateful for the support of Radhika Chimata in preparation of this chapter.

Expanding Perspectives in
Community Research

Among the editors of this volume are a student and a community member, although clearly the majority of editors and contributors are academic faculty. Although we appreciate the fact that students and nonacademic members were included in this volume, as they essentially were not in the first Chicago Conference on Researching Community Psychology (see Tolan, Keys, Chertok, & Jason, 1990), it is important for the field to find ways of being more inclusive of these voices originating from multiple perspectives. Although students coauthored several chapters (i.e., introduction, 1, 2, 6, 8, 11, 13, conclusion), we believe that more substantial student participation would have been a better reflection of the community of people involved in conducting participatory research. We offer a comment on this process and product because one of the core values within community psychology is stakeholder participation, which upholds that involving citizens in the process of identifying and solving problems in their own communities is more advantageous than relying on outside experts alone. Multiple perspectives toward inquiry represent a vital function for the future of our field (Kelly, 1990). In applying this conceptual framework to academic research, we view the academy as one type of community that uses conferences and publications for change and action within that community. As such, students are critical stakeholders in the process of identifying and solving the field's problems. Without including these multiple perspectives, community researchers run the risk of perpetuating a shortsighted and negative practice in the field.

Community psychologists would do better to examine and openly discuss potential shortcomings of any partnership. This includes examining the influences of various political forces, self-interests, and power hierarchies within academic structures that make up the collaborative research process. Creating a structure within which both student and community commentaries could be expressed in this volume was a step in the right direction. Although we continue to note and learn from the field's progress in diversifying perspectives throughout the scholarly process, it is important that we simultaneously articulate and strive toward these unmet goals.

Traditional Conceptualizations of Community:
Who Is the Community?

Community researchers have continued to challenge notions of the monolithic "community," highlighting that people identify themselves as being part of multiple communities along multiple dimensions (e.g., neighborhood boundaries, social identities, lived experiences). We agree with this perspective and add a second issue for consideration: that the traditional use of the phrase "the community" has been grounded in a history in which much of the research being conducted has not been with people with whom researchers identified. That is, academic community researchers have a history of conducting research with minority groups and marginalized individuals, but the researchers them-selves traditionally have not been from, or identified with, those groups. Thus, discourse around working with communities has relied heavily on a framework in which the researchers were, by their own language and description, "outsid-ers." Community psychology's trend to focus on traditionally underrepresented groups in research has been rightfully followed by the field's increased ability to attract and recruit researchers from these underrepresented groups. This evolution of researcher composition must now also encourage researchers to rethink the traditional conceptualization of community partnerships, because there are research implications unique to researchers who feel that they are members of the communities with which they work. For example, researchers who personally identify with their community(s) might struggle with the bound-aries between their dual roles as researcher and as a community member, making the traditional language used to discuss these divisions less applicable. Jordan, Bogat, and Smith (2001) discussed the complexity of the issues that arise for community researchers who are both academically and personally invested in their community research, because they must negotiate community perceptions that academia and researchers have less than good intentions while simultaneously building bridges between these settings. As the field continues to attract people who may work with specific populations and groups with which they personally identify, we believe it is imperative that researchers adapt their language for defining communities in addition to community bound-aries in ways that do not assume the historic divide that exists in university–community research.

Critical Participatory Research Strategies

Many successful strategies as well as challenges involved in the process of conducting participatory research are addressed in the previous chapters. As we processed information in preparation for this brief commentary through literature reviews, our conference involvement, and discussions among our-selves, we identified a list of strategies that could improve our understanding and practice of community research. Some examples of these strategies include, but are not limited to: conducting needs assessments, being genuine and honest with research partners, using qualitative research to capture the community members' perspectives, being accountable to both science and research part-ners, moving from prevention of negative outcomes to promotion of positive development, being graded on participatory methods by community research partners, and sharing power in multiple phases of the research process. The following are three additional strategies in community research practices that we wish to highlight as important for researchers engaged in community-based research to further explore: (a) recognizing participatory research as a continuum; (b) listening to participatory research partners; and (c) engaging in self-exploration, a complementary strategy to listening to research partners, yet addressed less so in research and practice.

Recognizing Participatory Research as a Continuum

We feel that our field should be mindful that participatory research exists along a continuum. Although many of the strategies discussed in this volume emphasize equal power sharing between all parties, some of the chapters do not. As stated in chapter 6, there are situations when an effective strategy in collaboration is to not share all the power with one group of stakeholders to protect the well-being of another group of stakeholders. Indeed, conditions vary in participatory research, and this calls for project-specific approaches to power-sharing so that the research will be mutually beneficial.

Listening to Our Partners

An important aspect of conducting participatory research emphasized in this volume is listening to the communities and groups with whom we work (see, e.g., Appendix B). If participatory methodologies should involve some degree of displacement of control, how do researchers begin to truly hear participatory partners in the quest for useful knowledge? This process would require researchers to engage community partners beginning with the initial conception of a project and to be prepared to incorporate partners' recommendations at the risk or benefit of changing the course of the research (Serrano-Garcia, 1990). Therefore, community research training should involve the development of listening and facilitation skills that prepare researchers to include multiple contributions of all involved in the participatory project while not losing the important contributions that researchers bring to the partnership.

Self-Exploration

To be successful listeners and collaborators, it is essential to spend time examining ourselves in addition to the cultural context of a community. We feel that community psychology's core value of embracing diversity should be combined with a more introspective assessment of who we are as researchers and as people. Certainly issues such as funding, the motivations for acquiring tenure and promotion, juggling course loads, bolstering vitaes, professional networking, and political favoritism within and across university settings are some real issues that affect researchers who operate from academic settings. However, it is important that community researchers explore and address the impacts of these academic–cultural forces, because they can play a role in the participatory research process.

It is equally critical that we explore and express who we are on a personal level in addition to learning about the culture of academia and science. That is, as we engage in participatory research, it is essential that we actively examine and acknowledge the multifarious nature of our roles, values, and biases. It is likely that our multilayered values and experiences as individuals, as members within a highly industrialized Western society, and as developing community psychologists from academic settings influence our ability to work collaboratively with each other in addition to our relationship with community constituents (Jason, 1991). In chapter 10, Keys et al. discuss useful tools for alleviating the effects of their biases by having informal conversations with people in their own settings and understanding differences between their perspectives. Therefore, we feel that self-exploration involves examining ourselves on various levels, and that this should be both a formal training objective and an ongoing professional practice designed to help us see into our core values.

Training Implications

The growing use and appropriateness of participatory research methodologies for community research demands that we examine our current training practices. As the science of participatory methods improves, it is important that we ensure that our graduate programs grow to include the changing nature of participatory methods and create ways to incorporate this body of knowledge into our education. We suggest that the field establish more settings where we can discuss real-world barriers to using participatory methods. Describing research processes that did not run exactly as planned provides a more representative account of community research methodology (Jason, 1991). For example, focusing on interventions that did not run smoothly would provide a legitimate report of how collaborative research efforts with communities can be categorized on a continuum of participation and action. It is rare to use the highest level of some participatory research methodologies, such as participatory action research, which requires that the degree of control, the amount of collaboration, and the degree of commitment on the part of the community remain high throughout the research (see chapter 4). Because the how, why, and when to use participatory research will vary in each collaborative project, the key to honing participatory research skills lies in the training of future community researchers in assessing the characteristics of and distinctions between different settings that require different strategies.

Conclusion

Our participation in this volume as student reflectors directed our attention toward a number of important considerations for future endeavors—among which were the expansion of perspective of nonacademic persons in the process and products of community research discussions, reconceptualizing the boundaries of who is part of the community, and complementing the processes for understanding the cultural standpoints of researched populations with exploring the cultural orientations of academia and academics. Developing our creative skills in planning research that focuses on community-identified concerns and working through existing barriers to providing settings for dialogue will ultimately facilitate our own development in better articulating and addressing the critical issues in community research. As we adjust the trajectory of community psychology, we hope the immediate future will continue to be marked by thoughtful consideration of issues concerning community researchers' training and increasing creative solutions to complex challenges.

References

Jason, L. A. (1991). Participating in social change: A fundamental value for our discipline. *American Journal of Community Psychology, 19,* 1–16.

Jordan L., Bogat, A., & Smith, G. (2001). Collaborating for social change: The Black psychologist and the Black community. *American Journal of Community Psychology, 29,* 599–620.

Kelly, J. G. (1990). Changing contexts and the field of community psychology. *American Journal of Community Psychology, 18,* 769–792.

Serrano-Garcia, I. (1990). Implementing research: Putting our values to work. In P. Tolan, C. Keys, F. Chertok, & L. A. Jason (Eds.), *Researching community psychology: Issues of theory and methods* (pp. 171–182). Washington, DC: American Psychological Association.

Tolan, P., Keys, C., Chertok, F., & Jason, L. A. (1990). *Researching community psychology: Issues of theory and methods.* Washington DC: American Psychological Association.

14

Faculty Deconstructs Participatory Research

Stephanie Riger, Olga Reyes, Roderick W. Watts,
James G. Kelly, Marybeth Shinn, Cary Cherniss,
Leonard A. Jason, and Edison Trickett

The themes in this chapter represent the voice of the faculty members who have reviewed the contributions in this book for the field of participatory community research. As readers consider the issues stimulated by the previous chapters, they are encouraged to examine participatory methods from other disciplines (see, e.g., Reason & Bradbury, 2001; Tolman & Bydon-Miller, 2001).

Themes

A recurrent theme throughout the chapters was *the complex nature of collaboration*. This very complexity deems necessary the systematic study of collaboration. One dimension worth considering is the utilitarian value of collaboration. For example, the authors of chapter 7 argued that collaboration is not inherently socially just and does not necessarily improve the quality of science.

Another important consideration is *the functional prerequisites of collaboration* for researchers and community members. What are the institutional constraints that inhibit or facilitate successful collaboration? Understanding these may be useful to parties initiating collaboration. For example, a Research 101 workshop has previously been found useful by researchers (see chapter 8). Communities have responded with curiosity about the research process, feeling enlightened about the research task and the institutional hurdles that create the circumstances participants find objectionable.

Analogously, a Community 101 workshop might be helpful to the researcher—for example, in identifying pressing community needs. Even though research may address a relevant issue, a community may face more immediately critical needs. Illustrating this point dramatically was the intervention mentioned in chapter 9 to decrease sexual risk, in which female participants lived in circumstances so dire that instruction on condom usage seemed irrelevant. Discussing the correct way to apply a condom was embarrassing even to the authors in that context.

Collaboration calls for researchers and community members to *get to know one another* well enough to allow for the trust necessary for effective collaboration. In effect, researchers and community members must *become bicultural,* achieving some degree of fluency in the other's language. The challenge is analogous to intercultural contact, where there is a cultural difference between parties, whether socioeconomic, ethnic, or otherwise. Early on, differences between researchers and community members can contribute to miscommunication, fear, and distrust. Cross-cultural concepts such as acculturation and multiculturality can be helpful (Segall, Dasen, Berry, & Poortinga, 1999). Researcher and community participants can speed progress in their collaboration by seeking out settings rich in the culture of the unknown group. Informal ethnography and lived experience with the other group can contribute to the multicultural orientation needed to establish effective cross-cultural communication and trust. Further, the melding of disparate values that is necessary for a mutually acceptable research agenda is more likely when both parties are familiar with the others' viewpoint.

Although useful, this solution to intercultural challenges is rarely so straightforward in practice. Complicating the relationship are preexisting experiences and attitudes the groups have about each other. Differences in social power because of institutional affiliations or social group memberships may also make the accommodation imbalanced. Overidentification by researchers can compromise their credibility or perspective, whereas for community members this may increase social distance and disparities in life experience between them and their constituencies. Cultural competence may be the necessary attribute for researchers. A better understanding of this unique form of acculturation would be invaluable in community research.

Inherent in building relationships, and thus in collaboration, is *conflict.* One potential source stems from the good of some research to make things better. Even if residents admit something in their community is "not good," when researchers impose such a label, they risk further widening the gulf between parties. Anticipating conflict and establishing guidelines for managing it may greatly benefit a collaboration.

What happens when things simply do not work? Success stories may offer many lessons, but so might failed efforts, as Mirvis and Berg (1977) realized in publishing a compendium of failures in organizational development. Community members who engage in such failures may have unique insight into what compromised success.

Deconstructing Terminology

The final theme, and the one that frames the rest of this chapter, concerns the need for clarifying terminology. Throughout this volume, it was evident that although different groups used similar terms—*community, research, collaboration*—often different meanings were intended. Before solutions to the complex issues raised by collaboration can be considered, relevant parties must at least share a common understanding about the language of collaboration. The purpose of this discussion is to highlight the complexities that the five field-advancing questions raise. To do so, one of the questions is closely examined: "How have collaborations between community members and researchers affected both communities and research quality?"

How?

Inevitably, when community members and researchers interact, they affect each other. Thus, rather than ask "if" or "how" these groups are affected, a more appropriate set of questions might be "under what circumstances" is impact likely to maximize benefit to both parties and "in what ways."

One possible outcome of participation is that it can have a negative impact on participants and researchers. Participation takes time and effort and may even be burdensome, especially where resources are scarce (Riger, 1999). Historically, researchers who elect to collaborate with community groups have faced institutional constraints, for example, the pressure to secure large grants and be first or sole author on publications. Realizing a collaborative style under these circumstances is a challenge for the university researcher, who, for example, may be inhibited from investing the expanded time often required in building a relationship with a community.

Collaborations

Participatory research spans a wide range of relationships, from joint planning and implementation to getting a letter of support for a grant proposal. In support of this flexible definition to participation, Bond (1990) suggested that the extent and nature of collaboration be tailored to the demands of the proposed research. This approach is designed to preserve the integrity of the research while maximizing its validity. Alternatively, Serrano-Garcia (1990) spoke to the many advantages in involving participants maximally from identification of the target social problem to the ultimate dissemination of findings. Whichever of these models one adopts, community participants must always assume a central role.

Various chapters demonstrated the essential role of community participants in research. The police detective in chapter 5 with whom the authors collaborated in a successful intervention campaign to decrease nicotine sales to minors stated that Jason's tactful review of findings and solicitation of community input on his findings helped solidify trust and the collaborative relationship. Without community input, researchers risk irrelevant outcomes.

Between

The word *between* suggests a relationship between two entities. But neither communities nor researchers are necessarily homogenous or mutually exclusive groups. Communities and researchers include a multiplicity of viewpoints.

Implications for collaboration derive from the observation that contentious groups within communities and within academia may complicate the research process. The alliance of university researchers with some community groups or even members *within* a community group may help forge such contentiousness. Consider the case of this volume, in which, despite the editors' best efforts, the community members participated are still demographically removed from that of participants that are often the target of research. Characteristically, community members who are authors of chapters in this book were closer to researchers in education and experiential background than those absent. What happens between those two groups? What happens when one segment of a community group has greater facility in communicating with researchers than another? What impact is there on the overall group's ultimate decision to work with researchers?

Community Members

Is a community member an agency, a person, or both? Who decides this? Defining *community member* and *researcher* will derive from the perspective one holds. One author of this chapter knows of a state agency that received "community outreach" credit for linking with a research institute.

Research

What constitutes *research*? These issues were extensively discussed at the First Chicago Conference on Community Research (Tolan, Keys, Chertok, & Jason, 1990). One of the authors has had experiences where community members see research and help for their community as mutually exclusive. In one instance a community member listening to the researcher's proposed intervention asked, "Do you want to help us or do you want to do research?"

Impact

The use of *affected* assumes that some transformation has occurred. How should impact be assessed? Who should assess this impact? On what level should change be assessed: the individual; the community; the larger social system? What kind of change should one look for? Over how long a time period should change be assessed? Some research on preventive interventions shows little long-lasting impact once researchers have gone. What are the markers that serve as the barometer for change?

Communities

Traditionally, *community* was defined geographically. But other forms of community are possible: Communities of interest and Internet communities are just two examples (Hunter & Riger, 1986). Research may even create communities. For example, in one study, people with chronic fatigue syndrome, pre-

viously undiagnosed, became members of that community through their participation in research (see chapter 1).

Research Quality

Whose standards are used to evaluate quality, and what are those standards?
Should degree of participation be an indicator of quality? If so, what does it
improve? If not, why encourage participation? Is the degree of impact an indicator of quality, or should traditional criteria be used to assess the quality of
research?

In some circles, only research that uses random assignment is considered
to be of high quality. Although it may be difficult to do this kind of research
in community settings, several chapters (see chapters 1 and 6) indicated that
community groups sometimes welcome these designs to help validate their
innovations.

Conclusion

Bettencourt reminded us that "psychologists have long advocated the use of
participatory action-oriented research methods" (1996, p. 215). But quoting
Chavis, Stucky, and Wanderman (1983), she reminded us that "the science of
psychology has yet to fulfill its potential in accomplishing this goal" (Bettencourt, 1996, p. 215). Our comments are offered as points of departure for
further clarifying, elucidating, and evaluating how participatory research can
be a genuine resource in communities. This effort necessarily requires that
an analytical and self-critical attitude be invoked so that the meaning and
significance of such methods of doing research "with" instead of "on" communities can be realized.

References

Bettencourt, B. A. (1996). Grassroots organizing: Recurrent themes and research approaches.
    Journal of Social Issues, 52, 207–220.
Bond, M. (1990). Defining the research relationship: Maximizing participation in an unequal world.
    In P. Tolan, C. Keys, F. Chertok, & L. A. Jason (Eds.), *Researching community psychology:
    Issues of theory and methods* (pp. 183–185). Washington, DC: American Psychological
    Association.
Chavis, D. M., Stucky, P. E., & Wandersman, A. (1983). Between scientist and citizen. *American
    Psychologist, 38,* 424–434.
Hunter, A., & Riger, S. (1986). The meaning of community in community mental health. *Journal
    of Community Psychology, 14,* 55–71.
Mirvis, P. H., & Berg, D. N. (Eds.). (1977). *Failures in organization development and change: Cases
    and essays for learning.* New York: Wiley.
Reason, P., & Bradbury, H. (Eds.). (2001). *Handbook of action research.* London: Sage.
Riger, S. (1999). Challenges in collaborative research on violence against women. *Violence Against
    Women, 5,* 1099–1117.
Segall, M., Dasen, P., Berry, J., & Poortinga, Y. (1999). *Human behavior in global perspective: An
    introduction to cross cultural psychology* (2nd ed.). Boston: Allyn & Bacon.

Serrano-Garcia, M. (1990). Implementing research: Putting our values to work. In P. Tolan, C. Keys, F. Chertok, & L. A. Jason (Eds.), *Researching community psychology: Issues of theory and methods* (pp. 171–182). Washington, DC: American Psychological Association.

Tolan, P., Keys, C., Chertok, F., & Jason, L. A. (Eds.). (1990). *Researching community psychology: Issues of theories and methods.* Washington, DC: American Psychological Association.

Tolman, D. L., & Brydon-Miller, M. (Ed.). (2001). *From subjects to subjectivities: A handbook of interpretative and participatory methods.* New York: New York University Press.

Part VI ⎯⎯⎯⎯⎯⎯⎯⎯⎯⎯⎯⎯⎯

Concluding Thoughts

Conclusion

Leonard A. Jason, Margaret I. Davis,
Yolanda Suarez-Balcazar, Christopher B. Keys,
Renée R. Taylor, Daryl Holtz Isenberg,
and Joseph A. Durlak

The editors and contributors of this book hold the premise that to better understand communities, researchers need to venture out of their traditional university settings and interact with individuals within the social framework of their community (Dalton, Elias, & Wandersman, 2001; Kingry-Westergaard & Kelly, 1990). In a sense, this book reaffirms the notion that in addition to becoming more familiar with the complex contexts and processes that make up community functioning, there are many benefits when investigators seek community collaboration, effort, and ownership in these participatory research endeavors (Jason & Glenwick, 2002). Our purpose in assembling this book was to present a series of participatory research approaches and related case studies that illustrate how researchers at urban universities have been working with grassroots organizations to promote constructive university–community collaborations.

By working collaboratively, the researchers have been able to develop and maintain a relationship that not only promotes respect for community members but also supports their growth, their knowledge of their community, and their ownership of the research. Through the collaborative enterprises, we have seen many examples of community members who have gained self-awareness, established important network connections, and achieved social change. These are changes that will remain within the community and neighborhood groups long after the researchers depart (see chapter 3). Similarly, the community groups provided the research teams with many resources, the most precious of which is a unique form of access to community members and innovations occurring in the community. Researchers also gain invaluable information when communities share their experiential knowledge—bringing their experiences to the collaborative process and sharing solutions to local problems. The work profiled in this volume also indicates the important opportunity for professionals to ally with community-based organizations and community leaders to effect change and promote health and independence (see chapter 2).

One principle adopted by many of the authors in this volume is the need to work in partnership with community-based organizations, within their fabric and structure, shifting from the role of detached observer and expert to collaborator and facilitator (see chapter 1). The chapters in this volume demonstrate that many of the most complex and intransigent social and community problems can be synergistically transformed by the recognition, appreciation, and use of the assets and inner resources that already exist within those social settings (see chapter 5).Working in collaboration provides an opportunity to identify and build on these resources. It allows for an accurate and sensitive evaluation of the community-based organization and its programs, which in turn may be used to improve the delivery and efficacy of services (Gomez & Goldstein, 1996; Ostrom, Lerner, & Freel, 1995; see chapter 6).

Another manifest principle is that the researchers in this volume exerted a conscious effort to maintain "dynamic objectivity" (Keller, 1985) to avoid being engulfed by intimate engagement with community members. This is in contrast to "objectivity" achieved through detachment and control. Conventional researchers are likely to pursue traditional objectivity by excluding research participants from knowledge of and participation in the research project and by excluding her- or himself from direct efforts to alter the field of inquiry (Keller, 1985).

Self- and mutual-help groups emphasize members' participation in the design and operation of activities and freedom from professional control. These groups also offer opportunities to learn new skills, participate in new social processes, attain a higher level of consciousness raising, and gain empowerment (Chesler, 1991; see chapter 7). The principles underlying collaborative and participatory action research agendas parallel and support the goals of such groups. The distinct opportunities (e.g., multiple voices and perspectives) and constraints (e.g., limited resources, power differentials) in research with such organizations require the development and use of nonconventional methods of inquiry and action. Adopting the assumptions of an ecological contextualist approach creates multiple opportunities for valid research endeavors that diverge from traditional positivistic models (Kingry-Westergaard & Kelly, 1990).

Evaluations of the effectiveness of service delivery systems and the goal of determining whether or not community-based programs work are the types of questions that are most often addressed via the conventional research paradigm. For example, such investigations typically consider whether members have better mental or physical outcomes as a result of participation or whether the methods used work better than professional service systems. Notwithstanding this norm, the authors of this volume demonstrate the utility of adopting a less conventional paradigm. This collection of experiences demonstrates that when working with community organizations and groups, the adoption of alternative paradigms in general, and a collaborative action research agenda in particular, is not only appropriate but a valid and effective means of generating knowledge.

At the first Chicago conference, titled Researching Community Psychology: Integrating Theories and Methodologies, in 1988, James Kelly challenged our field to engage in "adventuresome research" (Tolan, Keys, Chertok, & Jason, 1990). Kelly used this term to refer to research that is risk-taking and imaginative. Adventuresome research uses innovative methods to explore the ecological processes of change and invites multiple voices of those within the collaborative relationships to engage in the research process. It is willing to look at issues of power within the research relationship. Various types of adventuresome research are profiled in this volume within each of the 11 topics. This book is a testament to the maturation of the field of community psychology and the adoption of adventuresome research within the field. All of the case examples selected for this book were located in the Chicago metropolitan area. The fact that there are so many adventuresome research projects occurring in this one geographic area suggests that there are similar types of creative, innovative, imaginative, and vital collaborations among academic researchers and community groups occurring in communities throughout the world.

As mentioned in the introductory chapter of this book, the editors originally framed five questions to be answered, and these questions were to be addressed to varying degrees in each of the 11 important topic areas relevant to participatory research in community psychology. The questions were written to address keys issues and provide a framework for advancing and refining the methodologies that make up participatory research. First, there is the need for more evidence to support the efficacy of participatory collaborations between researchers and community members in addressing social problems and in improving the quality of research. Second, the field faces the need for an honest and public examination of the unique challenges and obstacles that community members and researchers confront in participatory research and the lessons learned from such interactions. Third, there is a need to identify specific research designs, methodologies, and strategies most suited to participatory research. Fourth, it is important to provide a rationale for why these approaches work, and describe modifications to these approaches that may maximize their relevance to participatory research. Fifth, there is a need for increased dialogue between researchers, community agency representatives, students, and community members about participatory methodologies, and for more interdisciplinary exchange to gain from each other's perspectives and advance the dissemination of these innovative approaches.

The authors of the three consensus chapters (12, 13, 14) used these five key issues to facilitate a structured intellectual discussion concerning matters pertinent to the methodology of participatory research. Clearly, it was not possible to provide concrete answers to each of the original questions. Nevertheless, each of the consensus chapters provides a different perspective on these important issues. Each highlights the point that despite the great benefits to be gained from cultivating and maintaining collaborative research partnerships, initiating and preserving such efforts create unique challenges (e.g., issues of power, control and distribution of resources) that must be addressed to sustain a mutually beneficial alliance throughout the research enterprise.

The authors of chapter 12 also discuss how in the past many community members have been excluded from preventive and community investigations. The challenge to the field of community psychology and related disciplines is to find creative ways to involve community members as active partners and collaborators in our work and recognize more fully the wealth of knowledge that is possessed within the community. There are numerous creative methodological ways to capture the process of community change that are presented in this volume (see chapter 8). By bringing in new perspectives from community members and by having multiple available methodologies and designs, we become more effective in accurately and sensitively understanding the ecology that influences our work. In addition, we are better able to select appropriate lenses to view and understand the textures and fabric of the dynamic settings and communities in which we work.

Two key questions that remain are where should participatory community research go from here and how can we incorporate participatory community research into our work? Some summary guidelines and lessons learned on how to conduct participatory community research were presented by several authors in this volume (e.g., see chapters 5 and 6), but there is still a need to integrate the multiple sets of instructions and create more concise guidelines and practical ways of implementing this type of research. For example, readers may want to know about how one might "build the collaboration on sound management principles" (see chapter 5), but it will also be useful to provide more specific procedural strategies to guide these endeavors and increase awareness of some of the flesh-and-blood events that are part of any research endeavor. Although this book provides a foundation for advancing participatory methodologies, we certainly need additional elucidation and more research to address practical matters such as: if someone wants to conduct or improve their skills in participatory community research, where should they actually begin? What should they actually do?

Also, to date (and as evidenced throughout this volume), the definition of *participation* tends to vary, because participation can mean simply agreeing to take part in a study, providing staff support from a community organization, or actively collaborating in study implementation or having veto power at any time. These different definitions reflect the varying degrees of citizen participation, which should be specified in detail when discussing and disseminating information related to such projects. Participation can also occur at different phases of the research investigation, from generating the original idea, through planning the design, carrying out the data collection, and implementing the results. There is a need to better isolate these factors to know how and why any beneficial effects of participation may occur. Unfortunately, there are few instances in this book or in the literature where investigators actively manipulated participation as an independent variable, with results then measured and compared with a no- or low-participation condition. The lack of this type of data weakens claims that participatory research leads to better research or community outcomes. In addition, as was mentioned in chapter 14, it is important to discuss examples of interventions and programs that were unsuccessful to deconstruct, and learn from, failures.

Finally, it should be recognized that the goals of participatory research methods are sometimes political in nature, and voices in the field can, at times, be strident and polemical. In addition, participatory approaches are not always feasible or practical and in some cases a more attainable goal may be finding ways to increase both the participation of community members and the range of voices that are heard and heeded when developing community projects. Although chapter 12 effectively provides the points of view of the community consensus members, it is clear that future collaborative books and participatory conferences will need to build on this effort and enhance the inclusion of community members from many stakeholder groups.

This book emerged out of a desire to generate collaborative research and dissemination activity through the Chicago site of the network of Community Research and Action Centers (CA–RC). Bob Newbrough organized the CA–RC initiative to use research to increase collaborative social and community structures (See Appendix A). This book is intended to serve as an interface for intellectual activity and exchange between the Chicago site, community representatives, and consumers. The examples in the chapters provide important models for how we might involve multiple stakeholders in the research process. Each chapter attempts to integrate theory, research, and practice in participatory research, while also taking into account the voices of multiple perspectives, including those of community researchers, students, community agency representatives, and consumer groups.

Between the time the first Chicago conference was held in 1988 and the second one was held in 2002, many of the founders of the field of community psychology had retired. A new generation of community researchers have entered the field, and most of the authors of this volume are second- and third-generation community psychologists. This book suggests that the field of community psychology is in the process of adding vital new voices. The original spirit of the field, which emerged by psychologists who challenged the status quo and protested against societal injustices during the turbulent 1960s, continues to be alive as is represented by the contributors of this book. This augurs well for the field of community psychology.

References

Chesler, M. (1991). Participatory action research with self-help groups: An alternative paradigm for inquiry and action. *American Journal of Community Psychology, 19*(5), 757–768.

Dalton, J. H., Elias, M. J., & Wandersman, A. (2001). *Community psychology: Linking individuals and communities.* Belmont, CA: Wadsworth/Thomson Learning.

Gomez, C. A., & Goldstein, E. (1996). The HIV prevention evaluation initiative: A model for collaborative and empowerment evaluation. In D. M. Fetterman, S. J. Kaftarian, & A. Wandersman (Eds.), *Empowerment evaluation: Knowledge and tools for self-assessment and accountability.* Thousand Oaks, CA: Sage.

Jason, L. A., & Glenwick, D. S. (Eds.). (2002). *Innovative strategies for promoting health and mental health across the lifespan.* New York: Springer.

Keller, E. (1985). *Reflections on gender and society.* New Haven, CT: Yale University Press.

Kingry-Westergaard, C., & Kelly, J. G. (1990). A contextualist epistemology for ecological research. In P. Tolan, C. Keys, F. Chertok, & L. Jason (Eds.), *Researching community psychology: Issues of theory and methods* (pp. 23–31). Washington, DC: American Psychological Association.

Ostrom, C. W., Lerner, R. M., & Freel, M. A. (1995). Building the capacity of youth and families through university–community collaborations: The Development-in-Context Evaluation (DICE) model. *Journal of Adolescent Research, 10,* 427–448.

Tolan, P., Keys, C., Chertok, F., & Jason, L. A. (Eds.). (1990). *Researching community psychology: Issues of theories and methods.* Washington, DC: American Psychological Association.

Appendix A

The Community Action Research Project as Context for the Chicago Conference

J. R. Newbrough

The second Chicago Conference on Community Research: Participatory Methods evolved as a product of the Task Force on Community Action–Research Centers (CA–RC) Project of the Society for Community Research and Action.[1] The CA–RC Project was developed to have a small research network of sites that would carry out coordinated and collaborative research and action projects. Such longitudinal work was believed to be necessary so that the contextual or locality-specific aspects of the community could be studied. This conference was the first planning project for the Chicago site of the CA–RC network.

The task force was formed in 1994 to pursue the idea of a Woods Hole in Community Psychology, an idea put forward in 1969 by James G. Kelly (1970) when he was president of the Division of Community Psychology of the American Psychological Association. In his address, Kelly proposed that the field of community psychology would benefit from the model of the Woods Hole Oceanographic Institution, which is a private nonprofit research facility that has been dedicated to the study of marine life and to the education of marine scientists and has created an environment for the informal exchange of ideas. I developed the idea of having a task force to attempt to develop a Woods Hole for the field of community psychology in 1994 (Newbrough, 1995). My intention was to use the Woods Hole concept to transform the university and local community by creating partnerships that engage in mutually cooperative projects that apply the best of practice, theory, research and policy to improve community life or solve community problems.

The Woods Hole idea was an effort to address the problem in society created by the disconnection between the resources of the university and the functioning of the local community. In my experience, I have found that specialization and professionalization makes participation by local citizens less influential and less likely. In addition, community change is yielding an increase in

---

[1]This the name of the Division of Community Psychology, which is part of the American Psychological Association.

social problems and difficulties in governance. There is a major gap between what is known about what can work to solve social problems and what gets used. Finally, our universities train professionals as experts, not collaborators, and as a result, our citizenry has become dependent on professionals and does not possess the confidence or skills to actively work on solving problems. Clearly, we need to be able to work together in mutual relationships and collaborative projects for the community to develop its own resources and capacities.

The core vision for our CA–RC Woods Hole was to provide an activity center around research and practice that would pull the researchers and the community together and at the same time advance it. Instead of a single site like Woods Hole, it was decided to build a network. Initially that network would be composed of three sites and a support center called a hub. It was envisioned that the network would have common projects, where faculty and students would work together, often working in sites other than their own, where there would be a strong emphasis on conversation and argumentation. The intellectual side was to be pursued through extensive, long-term social interchange. That was what characterized Woods Hole for the Oceanography field.

By 2001, three sites had been identified: Puerto Rico, Kansas, and Chicago, with Vanderbilt University providing the hub support. The mission was to develop an organization of universities and local communities that would build community capacity by integrating community knowledge, practice, research, and theory through a practice–evaluation–practice cycle. We considered it as carrying out demonstration and diffusion like the agricultural extension service. The objectives were:

1. To promote the understanding of community and to facilitate community change through the creation of a network based on three-community capacity building centers where these exchanges would occur.
2. To establish a technical support center that would foster continuous, multisectoral, interdisciplinary collaboration among all actors in the network and that would support and sustain the network of sites through technical assistance, dissemination, and evaluation.
3. To facilitate and promote connections and exchanges at the community sites between local universities, other communities, and visiting national and international scholars that promote capacity building for a participatory civil community.
4. To facilitate the creation of the agenda for work that is driven by community-identified issues that would involve the local citizens at all stages and would be oriented to increasing the level of competence of the community as a social organization.
5. To create a Woods Hole-type center where local citizens, researchers, practitioners, and others could gather on a regular basis to spend a significant period of time together to move the disciplines interested in community improvement toward effective social change.

The second Chicago Conference on Community Research: Participatory Methods built on the theoretical work that occurred at the first Chicago Conference (Tolan, Keys, Chertok, & Jason 1990) and offered the opportunity to develop a project that the three centers could attempt to operationalize. As you read the chapters that were developed from the papers presented at the conference, consider what has been learned. There are a number of key issues essential to advancing and refining the methodologies that make up consumer-driven research that need to be adequately formulated and addressed. Such issues involve: (a) the search for evidence that supports the efficacy of citizen participation in designing, implementing, and evaluating community-based research; (b) the examination of the unique challenges, obstacles, or problems that citizen participation presents during the research process; and (c) the process of defining the state of the science regarding best practices and most relevant methodological approaches to consumer-based research. That these issues be fairly addressed, the conference planners arranged for conditions that would encourage honest, interactive conversations between researchers, community agency representatives, and practitioners and consumers (who were from multidisciplinary fields) about participatory methodologies.

One of my former students, David McMillan, had some interesting perspectives on my theorizing about community and how it connected with the CA–RC Project and the Chicago conference theme. He began by articulating my first principles:

> 1. The whole is more than the sum of its parts. 2. Giving away power creates more power and brings power back to you. 3. Researchers can never claim independent objectivity from what they are studying. We are like naturalists doting on our environment. Community is locale. It is a place, a time, and a set of participants. Being a community psychologist requires a committed involvement with the intersection of a place, a people and a time. (personal communication, March 2002)

McMillan went on to say that Kelly provided us with:

> an important notion that we must think beyond dichotomies. Theoretical thinking must move beyond the dialectic, beyond polarities. Community theorists have consistently used the polarity of the individual vs. the collective. In his article "Toward community," Newbrough (1995) proposed a third position. It is not just individual freedom (liberty) vs. the collective good (fraternity). It is more complex than that. There are three essential principles that represent the human experience. The first is autonomy (liberty); the second is "the good of the whole" (fraternity); and the third is status (equality). These are the three motivating social principles. They come together in a three-way conversation in our individual and collective minds. The questions posed are: (1) Can I do what I want? (2) How will this affect the whole of which I'm a part? (3) What will this do to my reputation or collective worth? There is an internal discourse of three voices, three important values that must be synthesized. (personal communication, March 2002)

In my 1995 paper, I had proposed that the organizing principle for the three voices of liberty, fraternity, and equality be justice. Justice is a principle and a procedure that is discovered case by case. My theoretical model is a circle defined by three points: liberty, fraternity, and equality. Justice as an integrating force brings them together. Thinking beyond dichotomies using justice to bring order from the debates among liberty, fraternity, and equality is my theoretical challenge and intellectual contribution to community psychology. These ideas gave basis to the CA–RC mission, and as you see echo through the chapters in this volume.

The Woods Hole image provides a place to go to work on community. We need a place to go where everybody knows our name, a place where we can bring our whole self; our whole life; our family, children, students, and colleagues; an informal place where we are among friends, where we can make a mistake, say it the wrong way and people will still get it; a place where we can have a bad idea and a good one and share them easily without fear. This place was Wood's Hole for the oceanographers. We needed something like it. The Chicago Conference was an important beginning in developing this type of setting.

The conference was located in Chicago because the CA–RC project needed a setting where we could closely examine a group of collaborative projects, methods, and studies that might be replicated in other local research sites. We hope to generate data that will inform and provoke more questions. This conference also provided us an opportunity to exchange ideas, have open dialogue, and develop a joint collaborative project that matters to communities and those involved.

In closing, I feel it is critically important to participate with other disciplines as we develop our ideas on the Woods Hole initiative. It is essential to bring in new voices from other disciplines as we provide direction that connects the present with the past and help prepare for the future. I appreciate the opportunity that the Task Force on Community Action–Research Centers (CA–RC) has afforded me for making a generative contribution to the Society for Community Research and Action.

References

Kelly, J. G. (1970). Antidotes for arrogance. *American Psychologist, 25,* 524–531.

Newbrough, J. R. (1995). Toward community: A third position. *American Journal of Community Psychology, 24,* 9–37.

Tolan, P., Keys, C., Chertok, F., & Jason, L. (Eds.). (1990). *Researching community psychology: Issues of theories and methods.* Washington, DC: American Psychological Association.

Appendix B _____

New Horizons for Knowledge: The Influence of Citizen Participation

Maritza Montero

After 25 years of involvement in psychosocial community research and action with a participatory approach, counting one's blessings is also accounting for the surprises and difficulties provided by a research and action practice in which two kinds of agents are responsible for carrying out tasks and producing knowledge. These active agents are the psychologists and community members acting as external and internal forces of transformation. Citizen participation in community research has been a concern since the beginning of my psychosocial community practice. Because of that, my reflections could perhaps be considered biased, because every life always tells the history of one or many biases.

In trying to give a more or less ordered account of what I have learned about people's participation in my psychosocial community research, I have classified its benefits and hurdles. These classifications include positive and negative aspects in issues regarding the construction of knowledge during community research and action (ontological, epistemological, and methodological), issues regarding the construction of the *other* in community participation (that is concerning ethics), and political issues (those related to power and economic possibilities and limitations).

Ontological and Epistemological Issues

During the 1970s, at Central University in Venezuela, some then young teachers and researchers were in a crisis. We were trying to do socially sensitive social psychology and did not know how to do it. We wanted to produce a social practice responding to the needs of the people and current psychosocial problems related to the country's circumstances. During one of those research projects, a project dealing with attitudes and behaviors toward housing and the environment, my students and I realized that by working along with the people, one could, as a psychologist and as a researcher, give some response to the problems and produce useful knowledge to introduce meaningful changes. Therefore, knowledge about what to do and actual social change should be constructed with direct exposure and consideration of the social factors involved in the situation, as well as with inclusion of those affected by it—those lacking something, needing something, and looking forward to a different kind of life. With whatever means psychology could provide, some of my colleagues, my students, and I began to work in a different manner, which later we would come to know as community psychology. Since then, the people's participation in the psychosocial research and action carried out mainly in slums, rural areas, and working-class urban zones has provided the insight and reflection leading to a conception of the research practice and of those participating in it.

This form of research practice involves having an ontological and epistemological standpoint. *Ontology* refers to the nature of what is "knowable," the nature of the object to be known, as well as the nature of the "knower" (the being who knows). *Epistemology* is about the nature and grounds of knowledge, its limits, and validity. Usually, these constructs are considered abstruse terms belonging to philosophy; however, community members' participation generates what can be considered ontological questions, and they are ever-present in participatory action research.

Usually the conception about those we work with, either as someone close and alike to oneself or as an alien who is different and strange, is accepted as something pertaining to what is considered as the natural order of things. Freire (1973) referred to this as *naturalization*—that is, as the idea that there is a natural way for things to be. However, citizen participation introduces a diversity element that changes that: It introduces new ideas, new ways to do things. It can change our research designs, our methods and techniques. It can turn upside down what we had under control, while at the same time enriching the research by providing new and meaningful outcomes. Citizen participation leads us not only to deal with our own perplexity and, sometimes, malaise, but also leads us to reflect about the people we are working with. That reflection leads us to think about the relationship we have with the people participating in the research, as well as to define them. What I have learned is that those definitions should be oriented by the inclusion of the other's diversity, not by its exclusion.

Participation and Ethics

Citizen participation means a horizontal, equal relationship. It means relating with the *other* at the same level. One understands one's usefulness as part of the solidarity produced within the relationship. Accepting the *otherness* involves admitting different modes of knowing and making possible the dialogue and the relation with the other in a plane of equality based on the acceptance of our own differences.

As ethics reside in the character and scope of the other's definition, inclusion introduces an ethical aspect. Therefore, the relationship arising from that perspective frees the one, because freedom does not resides in the isolation of others, and from others, but in the intersubjectivity that, recognizing the humanity of the other also allows the one to be human.

This also has epistemological consequences: Knowledge construction occurs within relations. In participatory research, two types of knowledge are being produced: folk knowledge and psychosocial knowledge. There are not only exchanges between them but also continuous learning processes among all those involved (Montero, 1994, 2000). As Gonçalves wrote, knowledge production in participatory psychosocial community research

> should not be understood as an unilateral process coming from the academic researcher external to the community . . . it should be considered as something much more dynamic in which [she or he] learns from community members, and they acquire knowledge from the external agent, and both of them learn from the reality researched. (1997, p. 63)

The questions elicited at this point (epistemological in nature) are: What is the nature of the relation between those who know and what is being known? Who is (or are) the knower(s)?

Methodological Issues

This approach has methodological consequences. Dussel (1974, 1998) proposed an extension of the dialectical method that he calls *analectics* (from Greek *anas*, meaning from beyond, from a higher plane, from what is exterior to a totality). That extension is needed because dialectics is considered restrictive as a result of the internal ties between its elements: thesis, antithesis, and synthesis. Those elements are enclosed in a totality whose origin resides in the thesis that sets the horizon and the limits for the antithesis. Synthesis can only happen in relation to the first two elements, and the three constitute that totality. The primary element is the thesis, because it presents the first proposition that is to be answered by the antithesis. So from that relationship, originally framed by the thesis, knowledge is supposed to stem. Analectics expands the view incorporating analogy to dialectics as a mode of knowing, of proposing a dialogue with the opposite that introduces the unimagined, and the diversity brought by the other. It includes a new possibility to the construction of knowledge: the excluded otherness constituted by those that not only are opposite or complementary but also are different, unexpected outsiders. This is translated into the inclusion of different forms of knowledge in the process of research and intervention—knowledge coming from the participants, not linked to academia or to a professional realm.

Participation and Knowledge

Citizen participation has been both the source of enlargement and enrichment of the knowledge constructed in participatory research and action and the response to the critique to narrow ways of understanding the other. But if citizen participation made community psychologists aware of the fact that they are neither the only actors in community research and action nor the only source of knowledge construction, that does not mean the relationship between external and internal agents is free of conflicts and problems. Poor participation is one of the most frustrating experiences for a community psychologist, because it can delay, impair, and even impede the external agent's activity. At the same time there are hurdles coming from that participation regarding knowledge and commitment. The following are four of those hurdles.

First, community members may have valuable cultural knowledge, but some of that knowledge may also be a source of obstacles to transformations necessary for the community. It may happen that some beliefs and practices linked to them sustain modes of relating and living that encompass dangers, exclusion, or ignorance of different and beneficial modes of carrying out certain tasks. This means a confrontation between scientific and folk knowledge regarding important issues of health, education, or of some social categories' rights.

Second, citizen participation is not exempt from the influence of political, religious, or fad movements introducing interests or needs, which could be harmful to the very same people defending them. Those influences could hurt some groups or jeopardize social or community programs, both originated in institutions or in citizen's groups.

Third, as shall be later discussed, the way leadership is exerted in some citizen participation can also be a source of problems.

Fourth, citizen participation does not mean uniform participation and commitment from all community members. Usually the people organized in groups within the community are the first to participate and the ones who participate the most. This could introduce political, religious, or extracommunity biases and tensions within the community. A possible consequence could be the establishment of alliances with external interests that end by excluding certain community sectors or prevailing over the community interests and goals. As Perdomo (1988) has pointed out, this could lead to political partisan activism and clientelism, or to institutional programs, assuming authoritarian measures, leaving aside the community and its participants. Within this context, clientelism is understood as the generation of clients in a community or group, dependent on the external agent's activities.

Political Issues

Politics refer to public life and how we relate with other people within it. But also—and this seems to be the core of politics—it refers to power and action lines; to doing and saying within society. So it is about having a voice, about speaking out, and hearing the voice of those who have been spoken of albeit left out in silence. Citizen participation, therefore, has political consequences and can be the outcome of specific policies.

The definition of *participation,* a common sense word of daily use, is far from being simple. To participate is to have part, to be part, and to take part (Hernández, 1998) in some situation or activity. It may include possession, and it means a mutual transformation between the participants and the circumstances in which they are participating. It implies rights and duties, self-accomplishment, decisions, actions, and it is a condition of freedom and power (and empowerment). Participation of community members has been redefined through practice. It is usually understood as:

1. The collective action of a group that shares goals and interests. Collaboration is labor shared by the group.
2. A process implying the exchange of advice, resources, services, and the knowledge produced within.
3. A socializing and consciousness-raising action, transmitting, sharing, and modifying behavior patterns.
4. Participation is part of *relatedness*. Participation is carried out within relationships where people share ideas, share material and spiritual resources.
5. Organizing, directing, engaging in decision making, and carrying out tasks to reach the community-established goals.
6. Participation implies democratic patterns of communication between participants.
7. Participation implies *reflexivity*. Capacity to jointly evaluate, in a critical way, the job done.
8. Through participation *solidarity* can be developed.
9. Participation implies several degrees of commitment to the community projects and engagement with community goals.
10. Participation is creating and accepting norms to function as a group.

Overall, the main feature of this ample concept is the emphasis in participation as collective phenomena in which citizens' acts produce and receive meaning.

The Complementing Relationship Between Participation and Commitment

Community participation and commitment are related and intertwined. One cannot consider participation without considering commitment. This relationship shows one as a function of the other: the more participation, the more commitment, and vice versa. Participating then requires a degree of commitment, and this in itself is responsible for the quantity and quality of participation.

Citizen participation has led community psychology to revise the notion of commitment. Commitment has been defined as "the strength of one's intention to pursue the goal or one's actual adherence to its pursuit" (Klinger, 2000, p. 188). Social sciences' literature of the last quarter of the 20th century (cf. Fals Borda, 1981) usually referred to the commitment of social researchers in relation to the communities they worked with, presenting it as something due to the people they were working for; as a benevolent disposition of the external agents; as the right attitude to have. In Latin America, it was part of the vocabulary used by social scientists linked to leftist projects for social change. Although many among them were sincerely committed, this external standpoint referred only to a one-sided commitment and that implicitly meant a patronizing concept or idea of the people as weak and fragile—a conception circumscribing commitment to the circle of experts coming to help, to teach, or to cure. In doing so, a position of superiority is maintained, because the one-sided commitment to the poor, helpless, hopeless, needed, and so on, also implicitly meant that external agents saw themselves as the source of social change, whereas communities were considered in a passive, lower position—something akin to the relationship between Sleeping Beauty and the Prince Charming.

This also leads to an interpretation of the concept according to which it was enough to claim oneself as identified with the defense of the proletariat's or the low-income population's interests, to consider that the commitment existed. Frequently, such use of the concept more likely served partisan, religious, economic, or cultural organizations regardless of the communities' needs. But citizen participation in a dialogical relation implies that citizens need to be as engaged as the external agents. As Gonçalves wrote, "Establishing the exchange and commitment codes of the people involved in the research, diminishes the risks of the external researcher being the only one obtaining profit of the information given by the community" (1997, p. 62).

Nevertheless, commitment is not a monolithic process. There are degrees of commitment as there are degrees of participation. Variation in those degrees oscillate along three axes: one that goes from individual interest to collective welfare; a second one that goes from group selectivity (commitment to certain groups, not others) to the consideration that any group and many interests could produce it; and a third one that goes from external agents to internal agents (see Figure B.1).

This teaches us that promotion of community participation has to take into account the existence of different degrees of commitment and participation that can be found in any community. I like to represent this phenomenon as a system of concentric circles (Montero, 1996, 1998a). In the first three ranges of the center of the circle one can find leaders, members of organized groups, and highly participatory people. In psychosocial community interventions it is important to promote the movement of community members toward the innermost circles and to allow rotation of leaders from circle N°1 out to the second or third circles, so they can rest from the pressure usually experienced by leaders. This does not mean that those in the outer circles are to be considered as less important. Participation assumes several ways to manifest itself, and as it has been observed, those looking at what others do with a complacent eye might later place themselves in the range of those that carry out important deeds. Those who assist with smaller but indispensable tasks such as phone calls, writing letters, delivering letters, spreading information, or baby-sitting allow other things to go on. Future leaders can arise from the outer circles (see Figure B.2).

Community Leadership and Citizen Participation
Community Leadership: The Joys

Leadership is a main issue in citizen participation in community movements regarding psychosocial community work. Contacting natural leaders in a community and facilitating the development of leadership skills among community

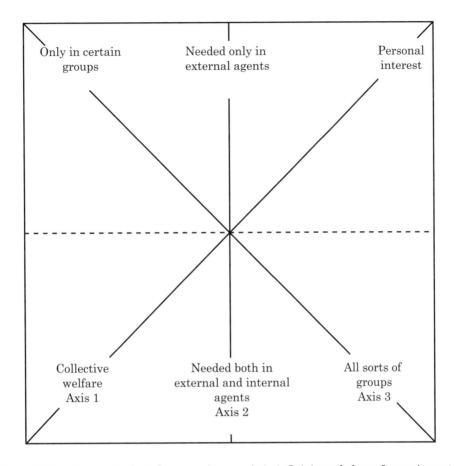

Figure B.1. Scopes attributed to commitment. Axis 1: Origin and place of commitment; Axis 2: Categories of people committed; Axis 3: Realm of commitment.

members are part of the collaborative effort of community psychologists and external agents. What have we learned about the assets and the obstacles of mobilizing community groups to achieve the goals its member have defined?

Every group has some people who will assume the direction of the group's activities. Usually they are the people who make the first suggestions, present ideas and solutions, and begin acting and proposing ways to organize the group. When a participatory approach is being implemented, the group's direction emerges through the process of discussion and reflection.

Community participation makes possible what has been called *transforming* leaders (Bass, 1985). Leadership is characterized by a strong and intense affective component reciprocated by community members. These are leaders who display energy and hard work and who generate a solid bond with community members participating in organized community groups. The actions of transforming leaders usually have a motivating effect on organized group

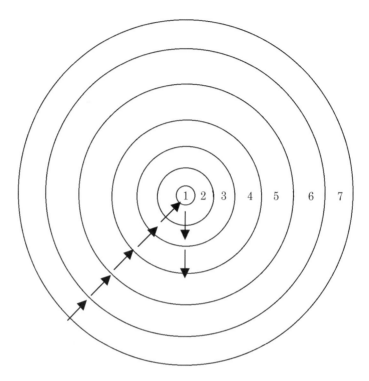

Figure B.2. Dynamics and levels of participation and commitment in the community. 1: Core of highest participation and commitment; 2: Frequent participation, high commitment; 3: Specific participation, low commitment; 4: Sporadic participation, low commitment; 5: Initial or tentative participation, low commitment (i.e., economic contributions, material support); 6: Tangential particiaption. Undefined commitment (i.e., approval, agreement); 7: Positive or amiable curiosity. No commitment; →: Direction of movement between levels.

members, as well as on other community members, by setting an example for others to follow.

Participation in community leadership makes an imprint on people. Hernández (1998) has found that leaders in many Venezuelan Andean rural communities evaluated themselves as: (a) having developed organizing skills, (b) having capacity to cope with new situations, (c) having a solid commitment to their communities, (d) as models and sources of information, (e) as significant community servants impelling activities and transformations, (f) being able to promote the participation of other community members, (g) influencing and transforming the lives of members, and (h) responding to a political engagement expressed in the achievement of collective welfare. In contrast, many members of rural communities avoid assuming leadership positions because of the extra work it implies.

Community Leadership: The Sorrows

Although leaders and the communities they belong to can obtain excellent outcomes, they can also have a negative side or *perverse effect* (Boudon, 1984). In my experience, I have observed charming community leaders who are convincing, full of promises, and ready to help and carry out community work but, at the same time, are also blocking other community members' work. I call them narcissistic–seductive leaders. These leaders can have a positive or a negative orientation.

In the first case, the *positive narcissistic–seductive* leader, although doing a great deal of activity for the community benefit, in a subtle but convincing manner blocks ideas and actions that do not arise from him or her. This is a *good* bad leader. I highlight the first adjective because it is the characteristic mark of that type of charming leader.

The *negative narcissistic–seductive leader* could be considered as a *bad* good leader. These are people with a participatory interest, as long as they are the center of the activity; admiring the leadership status and wanting to have it, enjoying popularity, admiration, and being congratulated. Their motivation then is mostly egocentric and narcissistic and not oriented toward the welfare of the community. This type of leader understands the achievement of community goals as a means to his or her own ends.

There are five negative factors affecting community leadership: First is the difficulty in breaking out from traditional ways of conducting or assuming particular roles. Second, power struggles are frequently present among community members leading different activities. Hernández (1998) considered that in the case of rural communities that could be a remnant of the traditional practices of rural bosses (*caudillos*; Hernández, 1998). Nevertheless, this struggle is also present in urban settings and in many community organizations. Struggles among leaders should be considered as part of the leading history of any group. The problem is not the wrestling for power but the difficulty community members face in coping with and solving conflicts. Additional difficulties arise from the concealment of struggles or from the affective ties between the leaders and community members. Those ties can impede the group in correctly assessing the problem or taking necessary measures to solve it, for fear of hurting the beloved leaders. However, if the community addresses these problems in a democratic way, with its objectives and interests prevailing, the relationship between the leaders and the community can only be strengthened.

A third factor that affects community leadership is the amount and the difficulty of the tasks to be carried out by organized community groups. The amount of work required can produce both high leader rotation and a high burnout rate. This leads to reluctance in assuming leadership roles in the future. In this case, one can understand the conflict between personal and community needs, and the time consumed by the latter can take a toll on the leader. A fourth factor is the ritualizing of certain leadership practices that have been successful in the past and tend to be maintained by the leaders despite not being appropriate for new circumstances. This means that being successful can have a negative effect, making the successful leader resistant to changes. Fifth, overloaded leaders also have the problem of being so busy, tired, and worried that they seldom have the time to learn something new, to reflect about their practice or about changes happening in their communities or groups (Hernández, 1998).

Leadership can be a great burden, to which is added anxiety about not having someone to share the tasks with or to replace him or her at a certain moment. Therefore, in spite of the prestige that community leadership may bring, its costs can be very high. A solution to this problem is the distribution of tasks, delegation, and organized participation of other community members. However, it is critical for community researchers to achieve community participation, to understand the leadership composition and history of the community.

The Meaning of the Political Character of Citizen Participation: A Concluding Overview

Citizen participation is a topic of interest to community psychology that also belongs to the psychopolitical domain. Martín-Báro said that

> an action could be considered as political if it includes any one of the following three conditions: First, the actor's political quality. That is playing a political role, such as being President or a social movement leader. Second, the quality of what one does. For instance, actions might include voting, affiliation to a political party, fulfilling a civil duty, or demanding a civil right. Third, the social sense of what one does, defined by that author as the relationship between the actor and her/his action, and the social order. (1995, p. 211)

Citizen participation clearly belongs in the second and third conditions. Community development, consciousness-raising about needs and resources, acting and reflecting about that action, obtaining and spreading information about rights and duties are all expressions of alternative modes of political action. Such behavior is also the expression of citizenry. A participatory orientation in community research and action includes a reflective practice, which leads to what Freire (1964, 1970) called "conscientization." By that he meant the mobilizing of consciousness, raising it to understand the social meaning of what the community is trying to achieve.

Nevertheless, social meaning is not always explicit or understood by all members of a community. As long as an act has influence over the social structure, over power relationships, changing or subverting them, reinforcing or imposing them, it is a political act. The people's participation can turn a community movement into an active minority (Montero, 1998b, 1998c), and the social influence exerted by that consistent group can introduce innovations in the realm ruled by a majority. Of course, majorities can also convert community leaders and members. Nevertheless, beyond nonconscious forms of social influence, or in spite of them, the first political consequence of psychosocial community action is the development of the people's awareness about their civil rights and duties through their participation. Empowerment, deideologization, conscientization, denaturalizing, and problematizing (not accepting as natural and normal a situation linked to community needs and critically reflecting about it) are citizenry-generating processes that strengthen civil society. As long as participatory community researchers obtain new knowledge and transformations within the community and in its members' quality of life, they can influence power relations, social order, and disorder.

However, this should not be seen as a significant structural revolution, in spite of the possible transformation of certain conditions. What is happening at the microsocial community level could be called a "homeopathic revolution." What are being transformed are those behavior habits that, without consciously being identified as such, maintain active negative ways of living; oppressive and submissive relationships; apathy and passivity and self-deprecating perceptions, to support inequalities. All this is achieved through a process made of contradictions and positive and negative aspects: the process of citizen participation.

References

Bass, B. M. (1985). *Leadership and performance beyond expectations*. New York: Free Press.

Boudon, R. (1984). *La place du désordre* [The place of disorder]. Paris: Presse Universitarire de France.

Dussel, E. (1974). *Método para una filosofia de la liberatión* [Method for a philosophy of liberation]. Salamanca, Spain: Sigueme.

Dussel, E. (1998). *Etica de la liberación* [Ethics of liberation]. Madrid: Trotta.

Fals Borda, O. (1981). *Ciencia propia y colonialismo intelectual* [Indigenous science and intellectual colonialism; 5th ed.]. Bogotá, Colombia: Carlos Valencia Editores.

Freire, P. (1964). *La educatión como práctica de libertad* [Education as the practice of freedom]. Mexico City: Siglo XXI.

Freire, P. (1970). *Pedagoia del Oprimido* [Pedagogy of the oppressed]. Montevideo, Uruguay: Tierra Nueva.

Freire, P. (1972). *Pedagogy of the oppressed*. Harmondsworth, UK: Penguin.

Freire, P. (1973). *Education for critical consciousness*. New York: Seabury Press.

Gonçalves de Freitas, M. (1997). La desprofesionalización, la entrega sistemática del conocimiento popular y la construcción de un nuevo conocimiento [Deprofessionalizing systematic delivery of folk wisdom and the construction of new knowledge]. In E. Wiesenfeld (Ed.), *El horizonte de la transformatión: Acción y reflexión desde la psycilogia social communitaria* [The transformation horizon: Action and relfection from community social psychology; pp. 55–66]. Caracas, Venezuela: AVEPSO Fasciculo 8.

Hernández, E. (1998). Assets and obstacles in community leadership. *Journal of Community Psychology, 26*, 269–280.

Klinger, E. (2000). Commitment. In A. Kazdin (Ed.), *Encyclopedia of psychology* (pp. 188–191). Washington, DC: American Psychological Association.

Martín-Baró, I (1995). Procesos psíquicos y poder [Psychic processes and power]. In O. D'Adamo, V. García-Beaudoux, & M. Montero (Eds.), *Psicología de la acción política* [The psychology of political action; pp. 205–233]. Buenos Aires: Paidos.

Montero, M. (1994). Investigación-acción participante: La unión entre conocimiento popular y conocimiento científico [Participatory action-research: The union between folk knowledge and scientific knowledge]. *Revista de Psicología, VI*, 31–43.

Montero, M. (1996). La participación: Significado, alcances y límites [Participation: Meaning, scope and limits]. In M. Montero, E. Hernández, J. P. Wyssenbach, S. Medina, S. Hurtado, et al. (Eds.), *Participación: Ámbitos, retos y perspectivas* [Participation. Ambit, challenges and perspectives; pp. 7–20]. Caracas, Venezuela: Cesap.

Montero, M. (1998a). La comunidad como objetivo y sujeto de acción social [Community as objective and as subject of social action]. In A. Martín-González (Ed.), *Psicología Comunitaria: Funda-*

mentos y aplicaciones [Community psychology: Foundations and application; pp. 210–222]. Madrid: Visor.

Montero, M. (1998b). Psychosocial community work as an alternative mode of political action (The construction and critical transformation of society). *Community, Work & Family, 1*(1), 65–78.

Montero, M. (1998c). Social influence and the dialectivs between active minorities and majorities. *Journal of Community Psychology, 27*(1), 299–317.

Montero, M. (2000). Participation in participatory action research. *Annual Review of Critical Psychology, 2,* 131–144.

Perdomo, G. (1988). El investigador comunitario¿ Cientifico imparcial o gestor del cambio social? [The community researcher: Impartial scientiest or agent of social change?] *Boletin AVEPSO, XI,* 34–43.

Index

About the Editors

Leonard A. Jason is a professor of psychology and the director of the Center for Community Research at DePaul University. His interests are in community building, the epidemiology and treatment of chronic fatigue syndrome, and efforts to reduce youth smoking.

Christopher B. Keys is chair of the Department of Psychology at DePaul University and professor emeritus at the University of Illinois at Chicago. He uses participatory methods to study the empowerment of people of color with disabilities and their families from low-income communities.

Yolanda Suarez-Balcazar is an associate professor in the Department of Occupational Therapy at the University of Illinois at Chicago. Her interests include the participatory evaluation of community health initiatives and participatory needs assessments with Latino immigrants and individuals with disabilities.

Renée R. Taylor is an associate professor and clinical psychologist within the Department of Occupational Therapy at the University of Illinois at Chicago. Her interests include community-based approaches to health care, participatory action research, and chronic fatigue syndrome.

Margaret I. Davis serves as a project director at DePaul University's Center for Community Research. Her interests include the study of substance abuse recovery processes, the interplay of social and personal resources, and efforts to empower youth with disabilities.